Selected Journalism

Selected Journalism
from the English Reviews
by
STENDHAL
with translations of other Critical Writings

EDITED AND WITH AN INTRODUCTION BY
GEOFFREY STRICKLAND

ALMA CLASSICS

ALMA CLASSICS
an imprint of

ALMA BOOKS LTD
3 Castle Yard
Richmond
Surrey TW10 6TF
United Kingdom
www.almaclassics.com

This selection of Stendhal's articles and reviews first published by John Calder (Publishers) Ltd in 1959
First published by Calder Publications, an imprint of Alma Books Ltd in 2010
This new edition first published by Alma Classics in 2019

© Calder Publications and Alma Books Ltd 1959–2019

Cover design: Will Dady

Printed and bound by CPI Group (UK) Ltd, Croydon, CR0 4YY

ISBN: 978-1-84749-850-2

All rights reserved. No part of this publication may be reproduced, stored in or introduced into a retrieval system, or transmitted, in any form or by any means (electronic, mechanical, photocopying, recording or otherwise), without the prior written permission of the publisher. This book is sold subject to the condition that it shall not be resold, lent, hired out or otherwise circulated without the express prior consent of the publisher.

CONTENTS

	page
Introduction	1
Notes on the text of the present edition	18
Articles in the English reviews:	

I POETRY AND THE NOVEL

Scott and Mme de Flahaut-Souza★	23
Scott's appeal to the French public	24
Lamartine and Victor Hugo★	27
Adolphe	29
Vigny and the divine tear	29
Monsieur le Préfet	31
Lamartine and Béranger	33
Lamartine and Byron	43
On the present state of Italian literature	55
Adolphe and Benjamin Constant	70
Second letter on the present state of Italian literature	72
Chateaubriand	88
Scott in Paris	92

II MUSIC AND THE THEATRE

Rossini★	99
Théodore Leclercq and the Proverb★	118
Music in Italy★	124
The wit, lack of energy and monotony of Leclercq's Proverbs	131
Talma	134
Talma (continued)	142
Macready and Kean on the Parisian stage	146

III THE CURRENT OF IDEAS

Thoughts on the Philosophy of Helvétius★	151
An account of Kant's philosophy★	153

Charlatanism and the necessity of criticism	156
Victor Cousin and the interrogation of consciousness	158
The revolution in literature and the reaction in philosophy	162

IV POLITICS AND SOCIETY

Benjamin Constant and the new public morality	167
General Ségur on the campaign of 1812	181
Benjamin Constant in the Chamber of Deputies	197
A Chateaubriand of the mob: Bishop Frayssinous	202
Comments on a reply to General Ségur	204
Chateaubriand, Daru and the Duc de Montmorency in the French Academy	207
The Jesuits and the aristocracy	223
A charity concert in the Vauxhall	232
The women of Italy	239
The Frenchman's knowledge of England	267
The misfortunes of a nobleman under the Restoration	273
Censorship and the decline of satire	281

V OTHER CRITICAL WRITINGS

Notes on Corneille*	287
*The Aristarch**	292
Memories of Lord Byron*	294
Lord Byron in Italy*	300
Walter Scott and the *Princesse de Clèves**	322
Appendices	327
Index	333

* The asterisk indicates where I have translated from the French of Stendhal. Elsewhere the originals have been lost and the text is derived from the translations of the period in the English reviews. (Editor.)

ACKNOWLEDGMENTS

I wish to thank the following people for the help and advice they have given me in preparing the present edition: Mr Norman Henfrey, Mr John Holloway, Miss Rosanna Martelli, Mr H. A. Mason, Mr David Matthews and Mr Morris Shapira. I am particularly grateful to Mr Simon Gray and to my brother, Mr Edward Gale Strickland for the trouble they have taken going through the text and for the many corrections they have suggested.

Since this book went to press, the death has occurred of M. Henri Martineau, to whom I am indebted, not only for the help he gave me in the initial stages, but, like all students of French literature, for his work as editor of a reliable and comprehensive text of the writings of Stendhal.　　　　　　　　　　　　　　　　　　　　G.S.

In repudiating Mr Paton's assumption that he is a light writer, we would fain express that singular something which is fairly described neither as serious nor solemn—a kind of painful tension of feeling under the disguise of the coolest and easiest style. It is the tension, in part, of conceit—the conceit which leads him with every tenth phrase to prophesy in the most trenchant manner the pass to which 'les sots' will have brought things within such and such a period—and in part of aspiration, of deep enjoyment of some bold touch of nature or some fine stroke of art. This bespeaks the restlessness of a superior mind, and makes our total feeling for Beyle a kindly one. We recommend his books to persons of 'sensibility' whose moral convictions have somewhat solidified.

HENRY JAMES

[from a review in *The Nation*, September 19th, 1874.]

INTRODUCTION

In 1821, when he was thirty-eight years of age, Henri Beyle was living in Paris, after seven years of voluntary exile in Milan, on a small private income of 1,600 or 1,800 francs a year and an even smaller military pension. His contacts in the world of letters were few, and it was only gradually, over a number of years, that he was able to build up a connection with such publications as *Le Journal de Paris* and *Le Mercure de France* which enabled him to supplement his resources and lead the kind of independent, respectable existence to which he had become accustomed in Italy. Meanwhile, however, through the intermediary of an Irish lawyer and journalist named Stritch, he became the French correspondent of the *New Monthly Magazine*, whose editor was the poet Thomas Campbell, and two years later of the *London Magazine*. Already, in January 1822, a number of his essays, among them the first two chapters of *Racine et Shakespeare*, had begun to appear, either in French or in an English translation, in the *Paris Monthly Review*. The *New Monthly*, however, was to remain the principal source of his income, which was thus increased by as much as two hundred pounds a year. In return Beyle contributed, on one occasion, as much as fifty-five pages to a single issue of the *London Magazine*, and in the same month, ten columns to the *New Monthly*. Délécluze, in his *Souvenirs de Soixante Années*, has recalled how Beyle would listen to the argument and gossip among the eminent politicians and thinkers in the salon of Mme d'Aubernon, and how, on leaving, he had been known to exclaim, 'Mon article est fait!' The arrangement with London was kept up for five years, until, in 1827, Henry

Colburn, the proprietor of the *New Monthly*, began to withhold payment—at the very moment, furthermore, when Beyle's military pension was about to be cut by half. Like Charles Lamb before him ('May Coal-burn him!') Beyle realised that Colburn's magazine was the most dubious of business enterprises. He continued, after the intervention of his friend, the barrister Sutton Sharpe, to contribute his *Sketches of Parisian Society, Politics and Literature*, though we have no evidence that he was ever paid for them. At the same time, the *Athenaeum* published a number of his other articles. His situation was now, however, almost desperate and he was unable to continue the life of a free-lance journalist. His last article in the English reviews was probably that which appeared in the *New Monthly Magazine* in August 1829, two months before he began the first chapters of *Le Rouge et le Noir*. The Revolution of July brought power and influence to his liberal friends, and in September 1830 he was appointed French Consul in Trieste.

Beyle's articles in the English reviews appeared regularly from 1822 until 1829 and were published in translation under a variety of pseudonyms. No one, until the beginning of the present century, seems to have associated them with the author of *Le Rouge et le Noir*, and it was only in 1909 that an attempt was begun to establish their authenticity. There are still, probably, many English admirers of 'Stendhal' who do not know that his book reviews and chronicles of French and Italian life were appearing under the same covers as the essays and poems of Charles Lamb, Hazlitt, de Quincey, Landor and John Clare, or that a large portion of his work exists only in a slipshod early nineteenth-century English translation.

In France, the investigations begun in 1909 by Miss Doris Gunnell in her doctorate thesis, *Stendhal et l'Angleterre*, led, twenty-seven years later, to the publication by M. Henri

Martineau of *Le Courrier Anglais*, a translation back into French of all the articles known for certain to be by Stendhal, together with the few French originals that have survived in his correspondence. This edition, which has never been reprinted and which it is now almost impossible to find anywhere but in M. Martineau's bookshop in the Rue Bonaparte, is the only available text of some of the most remarkable literary criticism ever to have been written in France and a rarely surpassed account of a crucial phase in the development of European civilisation.

There is much that might be said to qualify this assertion. The analysis in these articles of social conventions and political intrigue is certainly penetrating, but seems insufficiently developed in its more serious implications when we think of *Le Rouge et le Noir*, *La Chartreuse de Parme* or the second half of *Lucien Leuwen*. Similarly, the criticism, though unmistakably Beyle's in its 'intelligence, integrity, frankness and courage'[1] suffers, on the whole, from having been thrown off too hastily. It is inferior to the essay on *Sir Walter Scott et la Princesse de Clèves*, and the early *Notes sur Corneille*, which, though they are unaccountably little known, are surely among the great classics of French criticism. In reading the latter particularly, we seem to witness the growth and development of the intelligence itself; it is as if we can see the critic achieving, through a sustained effort of understanding, a firmer and freer general awareness.

When all this and a great deal more has been said, however, the way in which Beyle's journalism has been allowed to remain almost completely neglected is difficult to understand. It would be less so, possibly, if his critics had dismissed it as of secondary importance in order to insist all the more strongly on the achievement of his finest work—an achievement in

[1] See *The Aristarch*, page 292 of the present edition.

which historical insight and critical intelligence are inseparably combined. Yet it is rare to hear of his profound insight into the changes that were coming over French civilisation during his lifetime—for an account of these, we are generally told to read Balzac and Flaubert. It is even rarer to be told that Stendhal was a great critic, perhaps the greatest modern critic that France has produced.

The penalty that he paid for what he wrote and uttered concerning the literature of his time is best described by quoting from the late M. Julien Benda's essay *Qu'est-ce que la critique?*, written at the end of his life and published in *La Nouvelle Revue Française* for May 1954:

> Un adage enseigné dans toutes les écoles de droit déclare que la justice est le rempart du droit contre les entraînements populaires. Pareillement, dirai-je, la critique doit être le rempart de la vraie valeur des oeuvres contre les engouements des foules. Or nous voyons qu' aujourd'hui elle suit ces engouements, bien plutôt qu'elle ne leur tient tête. Il y a à cela d'ailleurs une raison; c'est que ne point marcher avec les passions du jour se paie cher (oserai-je dire que j'en sais quelque chose?) et que la fermeté du caractère, qui devrait être la loi du critique n'est pas toujours son propre.[1]

To talk today of the 'puerility' of what is offered in the way of 'thought' in Lamartine's poetry would not be regarded as narrow or eccentric; any more than to talk of the empty verbosity of Victor Hugo's *Odes et Poésies Sacrées* and *Han d'Islande*. Yet this, together with his adverse comments on Vigny and Chateaubriand, has been enough to secure his

---

[1] A proverb taught in every school of law tells us that justice is the bulwark of law itself and is there to protect it against the misled enthusiasms of the people. In the same way, I maintain, criticism must be a bulwark to defend the true value of the work of art from the infatuations of the crowd. Yet today it gives in to such infatuations far more than it controls them, and for this there is a reason; for the man who does not give in to the passions of the day does so at his own cost (dare I say that I speak from experience?) and firmness of character, which should be the law of the critic, is not always one of his characteristics.

condemnation. Opinion regarding the Romantics has changed. Baudelaire brought into French poetry the sights and sounds of the modern world and the idiom and preoccupations of a restless and vigorous intelligence. Far more than Lamartine, Vigny or Hugo, his poetry exhibits the sort of *romanticisme* which Beyle defines in *Racine et Shakespeare* and sought to encourage in this and all his other critical writings:[1]

> Le romanticisme est l'art de présenter aux peuples les oeuvres littéraires qui, dans l'état actuel de leurs habitudes et de leurs croyances sont susceptibles de leur donner le plus grand plaisir possible.... Il faut du courage pour être romantique, car il faut *hasarder*.[2]

There is little point in trying to imagine what Beyle would have thought of *Les Fleurs du Mal*. What we do know is that, through his integrity and perception, through his insistence on *la vraie valeur*, he anticipated what have now become conventional judgments concerning the *Ecole de* 1820. Despite this, however, nearly all those who have written on his criticism—including the scholars and editors who have rescued it from total obscurity—have used their influence to perpetuate the conventional verdict of Beyle's contemporaries.

The conventional verdict is best exemplified by the two essays which Sainte Beuve devoted to Beyle after his death:

> Il est à remarquer qu'en fait de style, à force de le vouloir limpide et naturel, Beyle semblait en exclure la poésie, la couleur, les images et ces expressions de génie qui revêtent la passion et qui relèvent le langage des personnes dramatiques

---

[1] Emile Faguet, in *Politiques et Moralistes du XIXe siècle*, finds it 'paradoxical' that Beyle should have preached Romanticism and yet disliked the Romantic school of 1820. He explains the paradox by saying that Beyle 'defended the name precisely because he detested what it stood for'.

[2] Romanticism is the art of giving to a people the works of art which in the present state of its habits and beliefs are capable of giving it the greatest possible pleasure.... It takes courage to be a Romantic, for one has to take risks. (*Racine et Shakespeare*, chapter 3.)

même dans Shakespeare—et je dirai surtout dans Shakespeare.[1]

Sainte Beuve does not exaggerate when he says that Beyle was uninterested in 'style' and 'poetry' for their own sake. Beyle's alert, demanding intelligence could not remain satisfied with inexplicable beauties of form and manner, and when he does talk of an author's style, it is in order to reveal all the more completely what is conveyed—or given away—by his use of words. There is no better instance of what I mean than the early *Notes sur Corneille*, sketched out in 1811 and rescued years later by his editors. Here the strong feeling for style which we find in *Cinna* is seen as genuinely impressive in its terseness and dignity. It goes, however, with a misleading simplicity and a sacrifice of what the verse is able to convey:

> In general, in what we have seen of the play, we do not acquire an *intimate knowledge* of the characters. Basing our judgment merely on what they say, we are able to form three or four totally distinct impressions of their character.[2]

In talking of *intimate knowledge*, Beyle is not thinking of an unaccountable verisimilitude of character. He shows, for instance, how the eloquence of Emilie's speeches, for all its apparent clarity, prevents one from understanding what the play is really about:

> Is Emilie moved by the sheer love of liberty, by filial piety or by the proud desire not to remain unavenged?[3]

In talking of *intimate knowledge*, Beyle is thinking in fact of the expressiveness and precision of mature Shakespearean verse, that of *Macbeth*:

---

[1] It is to be noticed that, as far as style is concerned, through wishing it to be limpid and natural, Beyle seemed to exclude from it the poetry, the colour, the images and those expressions of genius which clothe the passion and which elevate the language of dramatic personages even in Shakespeare—and I would say, above all in Shakespeare. (*Portraits Contemporains*, volume 3. Paris, 1905.)
[2] See page 291 of the present edition.
[3] Ibid., page 291.

After ten lines, we know one of Shakespeare's characters through and through, a talent that Corneille either did not possess or else, seeking to appear noble, was unable to exhibit. It is more probable, however, that he did not possess these gifts, for it was he who reigned over the theatre and established its rules.[1]

To admire the poetry of *Macbeth* for the way in which it defines and creates the dramatic themes is an astonishing proof of genius, when we think of the conventional approach to Shakespeare in 1811, not only in France but in England. Johnson, whose *Preface to Shakespeare* Beyle read for the first time three years before he sketched out his commentary on Corneille, struck him as 'the only commentator who has possessed the gift of thought'. Yet whatever else he got from the *Preface*—and this was a great deal; some of Johnson's finest criticism reappears, unacknowledged, in the *Racine et Shakespeare*—it would not have encouraged him to look for expressiveness in Shakespeare's use of language, least of all in the poetry of *Macbeth*.[2]

The intelligence that we find in the *Notes sur Corneille* would be no less remarkable if the insights had been achieved only to be forgotten later on, as the young self-educated genius turned his talents to some other field of activity or became a successful man of letters, acutely aware of the prevailing literary fashions and increasingly insensitive to anything else. Beyle, however, did neither and the *Notes sur Corneille* are evidence of what was a decisive phase in his development. It is for this reason that, twelve years later, when he was writing for the English reviews, the grand manner cultivated by the Romantic

---

[1] Ibid., page 291.
[2] cf. from the *Preface*: In tragedy his performance seems constantly to be worse, as his labour is more. The effusions of passion which exigence forces out are for the most part striking and energetic; but whenever he solicits his invention, or strains his faculties, the offspring of his throes is tumour, meanness, tediousness and obscurity.

poets and in the prose of Chateaubriand was to seem to him so drastic in its limitations—far more drastic, in fact, than in Racine:

> Style seems to be the constant and earnest object of his [Chateaubriand's] attention and there is no doubt that his latest novel will fully satisfy every admirer of the emphatic phrase. The author has described, in the most dignified language, petty circumstances such as would have shocked Racine. . . . M. de Chateaubriand has failed to observe, however, that extreme elevation of tone can be achieved in French only by the rejection of the words that have been degraded by common use. This discrimination, moreover, casts an immediate veil of obscurity over all that is said, which, in a novel, is the most deadly of faults.[1]

To say, as Sainte Beuve does, that Beyle wished to limit the possibilities of expression is in fact the opposite of true. What he condemned was a literary idiom which sought to limit itself and to exclude a whole range of meaning and experience. Beyle is one of those critics of whom it is often said that they are insensitive to poetry for the paradoxical reason that they make the most exacting demands on the poet and are prepared to regard the poet's vision as of the utmost conceivable importance. It is in this way that the limitations of Lamartine's *Méditations*, for instance, are seen as the limitations of an experience which, through a failure of 'thought', is never truly related to human experience as a whole:

> He has found touching accents; but, as soon as he attempts to express anything other than love, he is puerile. He is incapable of the elevated thought of the philosopher or the observer of men; he is always and only a tender heart in despair at the death of his mistress.[2]

The failure is seen in another review as a consoling remoteness from the life of his time:

---

[1] See page 90 of the present edition.   [2] Ibid., page 28.

I am perfectly aware of the fact that a poet is permitted to be ignorant of the realities of life. I will even go further and say that it is necessary to his success that he *should* be so. If a man of honour and sensibility like M. de Lamartine knew as much about mankind as a Robert Walpole or a Villèle, his imagination and his sensibility would go sterile. I have always thought that this was the meaning of the reply made to Hamlet by his father's ghost.

If Lord Byron had not enjoyed the advantage of being an Englishman; if he had not been compelled by his pride, as an aristocrat, to assume at least something of the prevailing good sense of his countrymen; if he had not associated with Douglas Kinnaird, the Hobhouses and others well versed in the realities of political life; if he had not seen a little of the world as it really is, which he could not fail to do as a member of the Literary Committee of Covent Garden, he would never have written *Don Juan*; his genius would never, in my opinion, have risen above that of M. de Lamartine.

Beyle's insistence that it was in *Don Juan* ('that filthy, impious poem', as Jeffrey called it[1]), that Byron found his true nature and his true strength, is in striking contrast with the pious denigration that the poem received at the hands of the English reviewers of the day.

Beyle insists, in the review quoted above, that the creative artist should 'represent his age', to use a phrase that has now unfortunately become a cliché. This does not mean to say, however, that he should exercise a mere passive curiosity or even, necessarily, that he should use his influence to further the progressive causes of the day. It is true that when Beyle's judgment *is* biassed, it is often so out of indignant sympathy for the liberal writer persecuted by Church or State. Would he, for instance, have placed Béranger's *Nouvelles Chansons* on the same level as the poetry of Lafontaine, Boileau and Racine, if

[1] In an article in *Blackwood's Magazine*, August 1819.

it had not been seized by the police? In Beyle's finest criticism, however, the relation of the writer to his age and to the society in which he lives is seen as something about which it is impossible to form any rigid preconceptions. We are reminded continually that the importance of the truly creative writer lies in the fact that it is he more than anyone else who makes us aware of the nature of our society, by revealing some aspect of our own nature as individuals; even the minor artist, if he is genuine, will give expression to some need or aspiration which the vast majority normally deny within themselves, through habit and conformity. The 'general purport' of Monti's *Bassvilliana* is 'atrocious', for instance. It is an apology for officially sanctioned murder, reactionary in the worst conceivable way. Yet its publication, Beyle maintains, contributed to the spiritual awakening of Italy:

> *La Bassvilliana*, though its general purport is atrocious, being a sustained apology for murder, supremely catholic and servile in its devotion to the ferocious religion of Saint Dominic, has nevertheless revived the taste for Dante.
>
> This great poet, the only modern who has anything in common with Shakespeare, has gone through more editions within the last thirty years than in five centuries before. He has turned the minds of the Italian people towards Protestantism, that is towards self-examination in matters of religion.[1]

The achievement of *Beppo* and *Don Juan* was that they gave full expression to the life of the age. Beyle's admiration for this achievement, however, was far from unreserved, and although he could feel nothing but anger for the persecution which the poem suffered in England, he was himself aware of a recurrent effect of Byron's humour:

> Lord Byron's humour is bitter in *Childe Harold*; it is the anger of youth; it is scarcely more than ironical in *Beppo* and *Don Juan*. But this humour does not bear too close an

[1] Page 65 of the present edition.

examination; instead of gaiety and light-heartedness, hatred and unhappiness lie beneath. Lord Byron has only been able to depict one man: himself.¹

Beyle's imaginative insight, in this passage, into the motives and attitudes that underlie the poetry is clearly the means to a deeper understanding of strong impulses and needs within himself. The enjoyment he sought in literature was of the deepest kind and he was unusually aware of the temptations to bitterness and despair which can make the close frequentation of a work of art intolerable. Yet this does not mean to say that he advocated a deliberate consolation in illusion or that he could remain satisfied with the innocence to be found in the poetry of Lamartine. The enjoyment which he sought can best be defined, perhaps, by saying that it was the enjoyment which he himself communicates in his own creative art.²

There is much danger of crude simplification when one talks of Beyle's two great masterpieces, *Le Rouge et le Noir* and *La Chartreuse de Parme*. Yet we are not surely misrepresenting either novel if we say that they constitute an 'affirmation of life'. I say this with Beyle's creative intentions very much in mind. It is common, for instance, for critics to talk of *Le Rouge et le Noir* as if the 'philosophy' behind it were that of Julien Sorel's 'indictment' of human society as he waits for death in the condemned cell.³ Such critics ignore, among other things, the author's own comment in the same chapter: 'Cette philosophie pouvait être vraie, mais elle était de nature à faire désirer la mort.'⁴ This despair, we are not only told but made

¹ Ibid., page 297.
² cf. Sainte Beuve (*Portraits Contemporains*): 'Beyle's failing as a novelist is that he came to this form of composition only by way of criticism and according to certain preconceived ideas. . . . In writing, he did not possess the same moral measure as ourselves; he saw hypocrisy where there is only a sentiment of legitimate conventionality and a reasonable and honest observation of nature, such as we wish to find even in the midst of passion.'
³ See, for instance, Paul Bourget in *Essais de la Psychologie Contemporaine*.
⁴ 'This philosophy may have been true, but it was such as to make one long for death.' (*Le Rouge et le Noir*, chapter XLIV, book 2.)

poignantly to feel, is unendurable, how unendurable in fact we are made to realise by Julien's own effort to understand and reconcile himself to its cause. If the novel ends then on so positive a note, it is because such reconciliation *is* finally achieved—achieved in Julien's clear-sighted awareness of what has made his life worth living and of the true nature, therefore, of what he has to endure.

Beyle's insistence that a work of art should be enjoyed is consistent with the most serious conception of the role that art can play in leading us to a deeper and finer self-awareness. It is not enough that the novelist should provide us with information or opinions, however topical:

> La politique, reprend l'auteur, est une pierre attachée au cou de la littérature et qui, en moins de six mois, la submerge. La politique au milieu des intérêts de l'imagination, c'est un coup de pistolet au milieu d'un concert. Ce bruit est déchirant sans être énergique. Il n'accorde avec le son d'aucun instrument.[1]

An essential quality of enjoyment is 'energy', that is something irreconcilable with timidity or inner frustration. Consider, for instance, these comments in the *London Magazine* on the 'social realism' of *M. le Préfet*, a political satire published in 1825:

> It is true that we cannot deny the author the merit of faithful depiction; only what he depicts is hideous. On reading *M. le Préfet*, I experienced the disagreeable feeling of a profound but impotent hatred. Now impotent hatred destroys in an instant all literary pleasure. . . . If the author of this novel, which I beg you to read, had possessed the least dramatic genius, he would have perceived the necessity of alleviating the abject servility of his characters.[2]

---

[1] Politics, the author resumes, is a stone round the neck of literature, which drowns it in less than six months. Politics, amidst the interests of the imagination, are a pistol shot in the middle of a concert. This noise is ear-rending, without being forceful. It clashes with every instrument. (*Le Rouge et le Noir*, chapter XXIII, book 2.)

[2] See page 32 of the present edition.

Beyle's awareness of the motives that prompted him to write —and thus of the way in which he wanted to write—led him to foresee the future development of the novel.[1] *M. le Préfet* has nothing like the powerful and subtle plausibility of *l'Education Sentimentale*. Yet the feelings inspired both by Flaubert's 'faithful depiction' and by the 'abjectness' of the central character are aptly described as feelings of 'impotent hatred'. The hatred underlies Flaubert's feelings towards life and towards his art, the art which he looked on as a form of martyrdom. His *Correspondence*, which is still read as one of the classical documents on the art of the novel, is remarkable for the violence of feeling it betrays and also for the lack of critical self-awareness—the obtuseness which can lead the author to idealise 'form' and 'style', for instance, to the complete exclusion of anything he might have to say.[2]

It is because Beyle's critical writings and journalism are so much—when we think of Flaubert—the work of a man intelligently aware of himself and of the life around him, and because they have been so consistently dismissed and neglected that I have felt it necessary to insist on what is of lasting value in them and on what emerges over and over again, far more than I have suggested, as outstandingly fine. No one, however, can read through even a careful selection of the articles, without being struck by their unevenness. Beyle's tendency to offer information and opinions at second hand in order to force an argument or fill out an article is an unaccountable breach of integrity in a writer who, in what was of real importance to

---

[1] cf. *Sir Walter Scott et la Princesse de Clèves* (Ibid., pages 322–5). It is significant that Balzac should have admired so much what he calls 'the historical intelligence' of the author of *Ivanhoe*, and, in seeking to adapt its technique to the contemporary Parisian world, should have aspired to be the 'French Walter Scott'.

[2] cf. the letter to Louise Collet (January 16th, 1852), in which Flaubert talks of a novel which will be 'about nothing, depending on nothing external, which would be held together by the strength of its style, just as the earth suspended in the void depends on nothing external for its support'.

him, was capable of the most courageous and lucid honesty. We are no less disconcerted when we find Beyle reviewing his own books under another name—despite his insistent condemnation of the practice in other writers; reviewing them, furthermore, judiciously, but with a warm feeling for their true merits. Something in Beyle's character was unable to resist the temptations offered by the pseudonym; it enabled him to describe, on what purports to be reliable personal testimony, events which he could never possibly have witnessed and it offered a licence to his all too ready willingness to sacrifice truth to an ingenious theory or a good story. The psychological disorder of which this is an outward mark was one of which Beyle was acutely conscious; to remain unaffectedly himself required an effort of which he was not always capable, though the effort is continually evident in his quickness to discern the temptations to insincerity in himself and others; it is evident above all in the transcendent intelligence of his creative art. For the tendencies in Beyle to self-deception are evident in something more than eccentric minor insincerities, something which it required formidable self-knowledge and energy to overcome; they are evident in the kind of obsession which, in talking of Byron or of *M. le Préfet*, he describes as 'impotent hatred'.

The disappointment and bitterness of Beyle's life—not only the unbearably poignant failures with women, but the knowledge that there was no one to recognise his exceptional abilities and his genius—account for much of the oddness and eccentricity of his writings and much of the violent, helpless exasperation:

> What we find, after a little examination, is that, without any exception, this is the most *stupid* Chamber that has been seen anywhere for the last thirty-five years.[1]

[1] See page 198 of the present edition.

It is as if his government [Louis XVIII's] had said to each class of society in turn: 'Turn out the greatest fools among you'; and when the order had been obeyed, appointed them to the leading positions in the state. This seems to have occurred, not only in political departments, but in the army, in science, in law and in medicine.[1]

Beyle's instinctive tendency to look for a single cause of all the evils in the established order is evident in his continual references to the Jesuits.

There is no doubt, nevertheless, that the Bourbon régime of the Restoration was, as Beyle points out, one which drove the best men into the opposition, and sought ineffectually to maintain its authority by compromise and tyranny. The highly centralised administrative system, moreover, with its extensive rights and powers, made the threat of a *coup d'état* on the part of a single, intolerant group seem a very real one and the careers, not only of Beyle, but of such men as Constant, de Tocqueville and Léon Blum, show how difficult it has always been for thinking men in France to ignore the danger. Despite the monotonous, hard, jeering note that obtrudes so often, Beyle reveals himself continually in his journalism as a subtle political thinker with a wholly serious concern for justice and the betterment of human existence. Nothing could be less like the fear and loathing of *le peuple* that we find in the letters and novels of Flaubert or in Baudelaire's *Mon Coeur mis à nu*. It is still common, nevertheless, to talk of Beyle's 'aristocratic' concern for what is valuable and unique in the life of the individual as if it were the same thing as Baudelaire's contemptuous 'dandyism'.[2] The same sort of error makes it seem

[1] Ibid., page 173.
[2] cf. Martin Turnell, *The Novel in France*: 'He [the nineteenth-century artist] was socially and intellectually out of place. The only course for him was to found a new intellectual aristocracy, a minority which lived inside society but was at odds with every section of it. This explains Stendhal's interest in the "happy few" and Baudelaire's "dandyism". Stendhal's attitude bears a certain resemblance to Baudelaire's, but in reality it was much more extreme.'

as if Beyle admired unreservedly the Napoleonic despotism, the opportunities it offered to genius and heroism and the protection it gave to a small, privileged class. When we read the articles in the English reviews on the Moscow campaign, however, we should have little difficulty in agreeing with the Stendhalian scholars that the man who wrote this also created Count Mosca and wrote the chapters on Waterloo in the *Chartreuse de Parme*. The writer is speaking, not only from personal experience of what responsibility is like and of the qualities of character it demands, but also from the point of view of a fine humanity, incapable of idealising war for its own sake and sanely clairvoyant as far as any *mystique* of the leader is concerned:

> This army [Napoleon's] was mowed down by the cannon as rapidly as the English armies which you send to Ava or the Cape are wiped out by tropical diseases. The French army submitted to this horrible lottery, and, in return, Napoleon promised them not only the advantages of pillage (that would have been a peccadillo) but licence to murder the citizens on whom they were billetted (the baker in Cassel is one example), to murder the maires des communes in France; and to pillage their own wagon train, as they did in Spain in 1809, thus causing the defeat of the French army. M. de Ségur has committed a crime which the army will never forgive him: he has directed the attention of the French to the military leprosy introduced into France by Napoleon.[1]

The forthrightness, bold independence and irreverent humour that we find in Beyle's critical writings and in what he says of the politics and society of his age rise from an instinctive generosity and humanity of feeling of the kind that is evident here. It is a sinister comment on modern French criticism that so many of the writers who have been impressed by the free-

[1] See page 204 of the present edition.

dom and energy with which Beyle expresses his convictions should have seen in him a prophet of modern 'realistic' totalitarianism, and at the same time, agreed with Sainte Beuve that he was incapable of any true delicacy of feeling, perceptive but immoral in his judgment of human relations and intolerant of poetry and the expression given to the finer shades of human feeling. How could anyone have sensibility of this kind, it is assumed, and still have anything of practical use to tell us of politics and public affairs? These prejudices and assumptions are to be found not only in literary criticism. M. Lacoste, the socialist resident minister in Algiers, for example, is able to appeal to them when he condemns the 'moral exhibitionism' of the 'intellectuals' who protest against military atrocities. In perpetuating them and in perpetuating the view of Beyle which goes with them, one is, unwittingly perhaps, increasing the chances of a despotism as tyrannical as any which Beyle himself exposed and condemned.

Clermont-Ferrand,
March 1958   G.S.

Notes on the Text of the Present Edition

FEW of the manuscripts which Beyle sent off to the English reviews to be translated have survived, and the only texts we possess today are those which are to be found in the files of the *New Monthly Magazine*, the *London Magazine*, the *Athenaeum* and the *Paris Monthly Review*. It was only in the *Paris Monthly Review* that a number of articles, among them those on Rossini, Kant and Helvétius, appeared in the original French and the few other original versions to have survived are those which can be read in Beyle's correspondence with Stritch, who is assumed to have translated them. All the articles which I have translated myself in the present edition are taken from M. Henri Martineau's edition of *Le Courrier Anglais* (Paris 1935).

I hesitated for some time before deciding not to reproduce the translations of the 1820s as they stand. They are written in a stilted Regency idiom which manages to give the effect at the same time of slang and pedantry. The innumerable gallicisms, furthermore, make them a bad guide to Beyle's original meaning for anyone who doesn't know French. The most carefully written of the translations is the *Women of Italy* and here it is evident that the translator has used the original text as a pretext for long diversions and stylistic exercises of his own.[1] I have kept these in, but at the same time I find it impossible to believe that the arch, literary manner employed here is Beyle's:

> The most girlish fancy no longer pictures him [Cupid] as a wicked urchin laughing in his heart as he affects to weep....

[1] See pages 245 of the present edition.

Nor let it be imagined that he runs about naked, as he used to do. He is clad from head to foot in the dress of a lawyer. His quiver is turned into a blue bag, and his arrows into deeds and settlements—the most powerful weapons both with men and women, etc.

Despite such intrusions, Beyle's voice comes through unmistakably throughout most of the article in a directness of observation and judgment and an unequivocal denunciation of certain well-defined abuses.

The title, the *Women of Italy*, is taken from the *London Magazine*, and though I have re-written sentences which seem to me unnecessarily difficult to read, I have tried to remain true to the sense of the whole article from beginning to end. The titles of the other articles are my own and the articles themselves are nearly all extracts from Beyle's long monthly newsletters. Beyle's own practice was to put book reviews, reports on proceedings in the Assembly, and comments on social life in a single letter with no other indication that he was changing the subject than a new paragraph. I will not, therefore, be found guilty, I hope, of having mutilated articles which were never, in any case, intended to form a coherent whole.

For the texts of the *Notes on Corneille*, the *Aristarch*, the two short memoirs on Byron and *Sir Walter Scott and La Princess de Clèves*, I am once again entirely indebted to M. Henri Martineau. All these writings, with the exception of the prospectus to the *Aristarch*, which can be found in volume one of *Le Courrier Anglais*, have been published in volume three of *Mélanges de Littérature* (Editions du Divan, Paris 1933). The *Notes sur Corneille* were discovered by M. Martineau in the archives of the library of Grenoble, written partly in Beyle's handwriting and partly in that of his friend Louis Crozet. The *Aristarch* and *Souvenirs sur Lord Byron* were found among Beyle's manuscripts by Romain Colomb and published in his edition of Beyle's *Correspondance*; *Sir Walter Scott et la Princesse de Clèves* appeared in Thier's *National* and *Lord Byron en Italie* in *La Revue de Paris*.

I
POETRY AND THE NOVEL

SCOTT AND
Mme DE FLAHAUT-SOUZA
La Comtesse de Fargy, par Mme de Flahaut-Souza. 4 vol. in-12.

This novel could be translated into English. You have already given a favourable reception to *Charles et Marie* by the same author. The *Comtesse de Fargy* exhibits an extreme delicacy in the presentation of human feelings, a merit which is made up for, however, by the absence of any *trait* of profundity or strength.

Mme de Flahaut is always what Scott never is. A hundred pages of delicate love depicted by Mme de Flahaut would have brought to life all three volumes of *Nigel*, for instance. She would have introduced grace and charm into the romance of the cold Margaret and her young Scottish lover. Walter Scott is unjust towards love; there is no force or colour in his account of it, no energy. One can see that he has studied it in books and not in his own heart. Mme de Flahaut, who was brought up at the court of Louis XVI, describes continually and also rather lengthily the effeminate mode of love which was the fashion at Versailles in 1780. The first volume of one of her novels is always extremely entertaining, the fourth is always wearisome. This is because of the unwholesome sensibility of her principal characters. Morality was so lighthearted an affair in 1780 that, in order to portray it at all, one is compelled to ascribe to it a robustness and vigour that was in fact no longer to be found among the upper classes of the period. It is this vigour, however, that Mme de Flahaut is unable to present in a natural-seeming way; although this novel is written with much more *finesse*, delicacy, seriousness, nobility, etc., than *Marguerite*

Aymon, I prefer Mme de Cubière's first novel to Mme de Flahaut's last. M. de Souza's grandchildren are half-Scottish.

New Monthly Magazine, December 1822

SCOTT'S APPEAL TO THE FRENCH PUBLIC

A volume entitled *Manuscrits de l'Ancienne Abbaye de Saint Julien à Brioude* has been published by M. Auguste Trognon. The only writer since the restoration of the Bourbons who has enjoyed a really popular success is Sir Walter Scott. Jenny Deans, Flora M'Ivor, or the sublime Rebecca are better known in Toulouse, Dunkirk and Besançon than either the queens of France, Clotilde and Marie de Médicis, or the principal characters in Voltaire and Pigault le Brun. The novels of Walter Scott have been translated in an infamous manner, and published by a catchpenny bookseller named Ladvocat. You will have some idea of the excellence of these translations if I tell you that where, instead of the name of an author beneath an epigraph at the head of a chapter, Scott himself has written 'Old Play', his translator has presumed this to be the name of a poet and printed in his own version, *Traduit de Monsieur Old Play*. You can imagine from this how delicately the translator has handled the finer points of expression. In spite of this enormous disadvantage, Walter Scott has stirred every heart. As he has depicted *love*, which is the bugbear of every mama, in a cold and uninteresting manner, nearly every mother has given her daughter permission to read him. The circulation of his works has extended, as a result, throughout every province, while Lord Byron is only appreciated in Paris and Dijon.

This unprecedented success has proved to be an asset to English literature and even to the English themselves as individuals.

An Englishman who has made his tour in Scotland, and can talk of the places described by Walter Scott, is sure of being listened to in any French drawing-room. The popularity of this kind of romance which depicts ancient customs rather than passions has drawn the attention of all the writers who have their contacts in the French newspapers and who are therefore sure of having their novels flatteringly reviewed. Already, nevertheless, MM. Kératry, Félix Bodin, Salvandy and le comte Pastoret[1] have had the satisfaction of being publicly derided for their productions. Next comes M. Trognon, whose novel is generally dull, though, like the *Julia Severa* of poor M. Sismondi, who writes in the French of Geneva, it contains, if not literary talent, at least a certain erudition. The first of M. Trognon's tales, for there are two in this volume, is entitled *Histoire admirable du Franc Harderad et de la Vierge Romaine Aurélia*. The king Théodebert has just conquered Auvergne and distributes the territories of the conquered among his generals or *Leudes*. Harderad, the Achilles of Théodebert's army, young, valiant and handsome, takes possession with his soldiers of the domain which the king has assigned to him. He finds here Papianus, a wealthy Gaul, who, at the approach of the barbarians, has fled into the mountains of Auvergne with his daughter Aurélia. Harderad is struck by the beauty of his young slave and attempts to seduce her. He finds her to be a girl of magnanimity, courage and genius. He learns that from her earliest youth Aurélia has made a vow of chastity and consecrated her life to God. The barbarian is

---

[1] Here are the titles of these unfortunate novels: Kératry, *Le dernier des Beaumanoirs*; Félix Bodin, *Le Père et la Fille*; le comte Amédée de Pastoret, *le duc de Guise ou la Révolution de Naples en 1642*; Salvandy, *Islaor ou le barde chrétien* and *Alonzo ou l'Espagne*. (Note in the *New Monthly Magazine*.)

astonished; the resistance which she offers to him, in the name of heaven, makes a profound impression on his soul, and, after a fashion, civilises him. He thinks no more of battles and the mere exertion of physical strength. He meditates upon the feelings of the heart. The savage, now tamed, submissive and respectful, spends all his time in spiritual conversation with Aurélia. In the end the maiden enters a convent and is assured of the protection of King Théodebert. Harderad is in despair and finishes by turning priest. The king, considering that it might be useful to him to have a man of loyalty and courage in holy orders, brings the story to an end by translating him to a bishopric.

If M. Trognon had possessed one hundredth of the genius of Fielding or of our own Abbé Prévost, you will have perceived by now that his story might have been given a certain interest. Such a *dénouement* was common enough in France in the seventh century. Unfortunately M. Trognon depicts all the passions as Walter Scott does love, that is to say by hearsay. M. Trognon has had the folly to impose upon himself a very singular restraint. Sir Walter Scott pretends, rightly or wrongly, to paint the past as it was. He sees it nevertheless from his own times, and, whatever his love for archaic institutions may be, he always writes like a man of genius living in Edinburgh in 1825. M. Trognon, on the other hand, has adopted the extraordinary idea of writing the history of Harderad and Aurélia in the character of their contemporary Optatus, a monk of Saint Julien à Brioude. The coarseness of the monk's language, which is historically authentic and indispensable according to his plan, prevents his book from being read by women. It so happens, furthermore, that women are the only readers of books in France. In the leading circles of society two hours a day are set aside for reading, and then only the newspapers and political pamphlets are consulted, since these alone take up all the time. In Paris no man can utter a word in a drawing-room if he has not read or looked through eight newspapers during the morning. M. de Pradt and Walter Scott run away with the rest of the time which most people can give to reading. M. Kératry's novel is of so gloomy and horrifying a cast, and those written by MM. Pastoret, Bodin and Salvandy are so affected and dull, that they have confirmed us in our former habit of reading only novels written by women. At least they contain a certain delicate observation of the human heart. I take this opportunity of recommending you to read *Marguerite Aymon*, a romance published about two years ago by Mme de Cubières, the wife of a young colonel, who has since followed her husband to Cadiz. *Marguerite Aymon* describes Parisian society as it was in 1820.

New Monthly Magazine, December 1822

LAMARTINE AND VICTOR HUGO

Odes et Poésies sacrées, par M. Hugo. 1 vol.

Writing correct verse has now become an occupation in itself in French literature. If he works hard and spends four years studying Racine and Delille and learning them by heart, a young man will succeed in writing verse which is both correct and passably good at the first reading; unfortunately, however, after barely fifteen or twenty lines, the reader will be overcome by a strong desire to yawn.

This is the point that was omitted in the excellent article on French poetry in number 74 of the *Edinburgh Review*. We have in Paris four thousand young men of letters who compose good French verse; three or four perhaps among them have succeeded in putting their own thoughts into their verse. This is no small achievement. Among these four thousand poets many have thoughts of their own; but how are they to express them in the language of Racine? As soon as they can no longer talk of *Muses, Apollon, Hélicon, inspiration, mélancolie* or *souvenirs*, they are lost.

M. de Lamartine has led the life of a poet, a romantic life, a life disturbed by grand passions and heroic feelings. He lost, when he was in Naples, a wife whom he adored. After four years of grief he has induced his heart to give utterance in verse. He has found touching accents; but, as soon as he attempts to express anything other than love, he is puerile. He is incapable of the elevated thought of the philosopher or the observer of men; he is always and only a tender heart in despair at the death of his mistress.

Furthermore, the *Edinburgh Review* is completely mistaken in supposing M. de Lamartine to be the poet of the *ultra* party. This party, which is so skilfully directed by MM. de Vitrolles and Frayssinous is trying to annex all the glories. It has procured for M. de Lamartine nine editions of his poems; but the true poet of the party is M. Hugo.

This M. Hugo has the kind of talent that is to be found in the *Night Thoughts* of Young. He is always coldly exaggerated; his party procures him a considerable success. There is no denying, moreover, that he knows how to write very good French verse. Unfortunately he is soporific.

New Monthly Magazine, March 1823

ADOLPHE

Adolphe, a novel by M. Benjamin Constant. Third edition.

M. Constant's book on religion, which is a kind of *Capucinade Protestante*[1] and an attempt to keep in with every party, has failed to meet with the success that its author expected. He has therefore sought to console himself by publishing a new edition of *Adolphe*, a novel which has far more singularity than excellence. Adolphe seduces a woman whom he does not love; but his victim becomes so passionately fond of him that her ever-increasing tenderness renders him miserable, all the more so because he lacks the necessary firmness to confess to her his repugnance. It is a novel that might be described as a tragic *marivaudage*, in which the difficulty lies, not, as in Marivaux, in making a declaration of love, but in making a declaration of hatred. Once this has been made, the story is at an end. This production of M. Constant's youth contains a number of maxims and phrases evidently borrowed from Mme de Staël, with whom M. Constant was on the most intimate terms for a number of years.

New Monthly Magazine, December 1824

VIGNY AND THE DIVINE TEAR

Eloa, a Poem by the Count de Vigny, Member of the Society of Bonnes Lettres.

It would puzzle the most acute diviner of enigmas to discover

[1] A *capucinade* is a dull sermon of the kind for which the Capuchin friars apparently were notorious. The humour of the phrase, which is untranslatable, lies in the fact that Constant's *capucinade* was a Protestant one. (*Editor*.)

what the subject of this poem actually is; but, in order not to keep our readers' imagination in needless suspense, we shall inform them at once that *Eloa* is the story of a tear shed by Christ. This tear, shed by the Son of God on seeing some example of human wretchedness, becomes, according to the testimony of M. de Vigny's extraordinary verses, an angel, and what is more, an angel unlike any that theologians have ever heard of, that is, a female angel. What does the reader suppose is the fate reserved for this female angel and former tear? She is seduced, and by whom? By no less a personage than Satan himself. This tear, which we are meant to believe has fallen from the Godhead, makes love with the Devil, is led down by her lover to the nether regions, and there becomes queen. What I am going to say will hardly be believed, and yet the fact is true: this incredible combination of absurdity and profanity is actually admired by a large city containing eighty thousand inhabitants and called the Faubourg St Germain in Paris. All the ancient nobility and all those who look forward, however remotely, to the blessings promised by the Church, maintain that this delirious rhapsody is a masterpiece and that M. de Vigny is Lord Byron's most gifted imitator. There is perhaps one thing more wonderfully absurd than the actual writing of the poem, and that is that the description of the incarnation and *amours* of a tear should be taken for an imitation, and a successful one at that, of the author of *Don Juan* and the *Corsair*. Strange to say, the author of the poem is not in fact insane; for a great many of his lines are well turned and most elaborately polished, so much so as to make it clear how much art and labour he has spent over them. These pains, however, are thrown away, at least on his more mundane and unmystical readers. These find it impossible to read a hundred lines of the poem without yawning and two hundred without falling into the most profound slumber.

This wholesome effect was probably never contemplated by Count Alfred de Vigny, *bon homme de lettres*, when he sat down to write the touching story of the love between Satan and the incarnation of a divine tear. At the risk of being profane, it might be reasonable to suggest that the author drew his inspiration from rather too deep a potation of that famous Italian wine, *Lacryma Christi*.

New Monthly Magazine, December 1824

MONSIEUR LE PRÉFET[1]

Monsieur le Préfet, a novel in four volumes, is an admirable theme spoiled by an author incapable of doing it justice. There are eighty-six prefects in France, little despots who reign almost as absolutely in their departments as, eight years ago, the Aga of Athens over the birthplace of Socrates. Each prefect has his court, and, if he is under seventy years of age, this court has its Madame de Pompadour. Usually it is the wife of the *receveur général* or else of the mayor who has this honour. The necessary go-between in *M. le Préfet*'s love affairs is *Monsieur le capitaine de gendarmerie*. The author of this novel has painted with remarkable accuracy all the shades of servility which surround the prefect of the day. Every morning the prefect opens the *Moniteur* with trembling hand, dreading lest he should read news of his own resignation. As soon as he is assured on this great point, he writes an affectionate word or two to Madame de Pompadour. *Monsieur le secrétaire intime*, who is also one of the important figures of the court, carries his

[1] This novel was published anonymously by Baron E. L. de Lamothe-Langon (1786-1864), Prefect of Toulouse under Napoleon, and after the Restoration novelist, playwright and historian. (*Editor*.)

master's letter himself, and scarcely is it dispatched before
M. le Préfet gives an audience to the chief of police, M. le
capitaine de gendarmerie. 'What's that rogue of a bishop up to?'
is the first question addressed to his captain of gendarmerie by
every prefect who has the misfortune to have a bishop in his
town. Under Napoleon the general was the bugbear of the
prefect; at present it is my Lord Bishop who makes them both
tremble. After the bishop, the principle fear of the prefect,
who dreads the loss of his pashalik, is caused by the committee
of Jesuits who meet at the *petit seminaire*, as they call the school
or college.

On the appearance of this novel, the town was highly amused
by eight or ten dismissed prefects who happened to be in Paris
at the time, and who all went to complain to M. de Villèle,
the effective king of France, about the insolent author who had
just published a personal libel against them. It is true that we
cannot deny the author the merit of faithful depiction; only
what he depicts is hideous. On reading *M. de Préfet* I experienced
the disagreeable feeling of a profound but impotent hatred.
Now impotent hatred destroys in an instant all literary
pleasure. It is for this reason, I suppose, that to introduce
politics into any work of literature in France is fatal. If the
author of this novel, which I beg you to read, had possessed
the least dramatic genius, he would have perceived the necessity of alleviating the abject servility of his characters. The
author excuses himself by saying that he took for his model
M. Trouvé, the natural son of La Revellière-Lépeaux, one of
the five Directors. M. Trouvé was formerly a prefect and is
now a violent *ultra*, and the printer of his party.

London Magazine, February 1825

LAMARTINE AND BERANGER

Letters from Paris by Grimm's grandson no. v

Paris, April 18th, 1825

My dear friend,

We critics are, on the whole, kindly and condescending people, bestowing our attention, as we do, on the great majority of books which are every day sent out into the world. It is tacitly understood that those which we praise as being less tedious or affected than the rest will be utterly forgotten in twenty years time. Only during these twenty years, the period of their natural lives, there is a chance that they will provide some pleasant reading, especially to a foreigner who has no intimate knowledge of our national character and social life, and is therefore less likely to be struck by insipid commonplaces.

This month, however, is a particularly fortunate one. It has seen the appearance of a literary masterpiece, which, as is to be expected, has already been seized by the police. This work may soon perhaps take its place as one of the imperishable models of our literature and the name of its author repeated in the regions inhabited by the ghosts of Lafontaine, Boileau and Racine.

M. de Béranger's *Nouvelles Chansons*, even though fear of prison has prevented the author from publishing the best of them, can be compared with the work of the greatest poet France has ever produced; I mean Jean de Lafontaine, a poet whose merits are probably very little understood outside France. Molière and Corneille need the aid of an actor; their greatness lies in such things as their moral philosophy and their profound insight into human passions. A Frenchman can feel all the captivation of Lafontaine, without all this trouble being taken. Half a sheet of paper and a little ink were all that he needed in order to give the most intense pleasure that any human being can receive by such simple means, to any reader who was a perfect master of the language. His most exquisite productions rarely exceed a page. In this they are like de Béranger's song *Le vieux sergent*, of which I shall quote the first two stanzas:

> Près du rouet de sa fille chérie,
> Le vieux sergent se distrait de ses maux,
> Et d'une main que la balle a meurtrie,
> Berce en riant deux petits-fils jumeaux.
> Assis tranquille au seuil du toit champêtre
> Son seul refuge après tant de combats,
> Il dit parfois: 'Ce n'est pas tout de naître;
> Dieu, mes enfants, vous donne un beau trépas!'
>
> Mais, qu'entend-il? le tambour qui résonne;
> Il voit au loin passer un bataillon,
> Le sang remonte à son front qui grisonne;
> Le vieux coursier a senti l'aiguillon,
> Hélas! soudain, tristement il s'écrie:
> 'C'est un drapeau que je ne connais pas.
> 'Ah! si jamais vous vengez la patrie,
> 'Dieu, mes enfants, vous donne un beau trépas!'[1]

It might very well have been thought that every dress that satire can adopt had already been worn threadbare in France. Read the song entitled *Octavie*, however. It is aimed at the Comtesse de Cayla, a lady who, while still young and beautiful,

---

[1] Next to the spinning-wheel of his beloved daughter, the old sergeant is trying to forget his troubles, and laughs as he rocks his two twin grandsons with a bullet-scarred hand. Sometimes, as he sits peacefully at the door of his cottage, his only refuge after his many battles, he will repeat, 'It isn't enough merely to be born. God grant you a good death, children.' But what is this that he hears? A beating drum; in the distance he sees a battalion passing. The blood returns to his greying temples; the old charger has felt the spur. But suddenly he cries in despair, 'Alas! It is a flag I do not know. Ah! If ever you avenge your country, my children, may God grant you a good death!'

submitted to the embraces of the most disgusting man in France and in return received a pension of a million francs a year.

There are two men of considerable merit who will suffer greatly from the publication of this little volume. The old amateurs of poetry have not failed to perceive what is lacking in M. de Lamartine and Casimir Delavigne and what it is that makes it impossible to class them with Lafontaine, Voltaire and Boileau. Many, however, only went by the facts. Two years ago, the works of MM. de Lamartine and Delavigne gave the public as much pleasure as the first collection of Béranger's songs. Needless to say, the public was perfectly willing to believe that France could actually boast three great poets.

Do you recall, my dear friend, that in *Tom Jones*, one of the greatest works that modern literature has produced, Partridge, after the play, is asked which of the actors he preferred? He is somewhat indignant at the question, which strikes him as being an insult to his powers of judgment. 'The King for my money', he replies. 'He speaks all his words distinctly, half as loud again as the other. Anybody may see he is an actor.'

In a similar way, the French public set out vehemently to admire MM. de Lamartine and Delavigne, because they talked about *melancholy*, *glory*, *liberty* and *death* in the best tragical manner, and the fashion lasted for two years. Like Partridge, they admired the man who spoke loudly and dressed splendidly. Under these circumstances, what sort of popularity was to be expected for a poet who does not deal in exaggerations and who lets his pen follow the unaffected promptings of his heart and imagination? This extraordinary man was so little indebted to formal education, that numerous faults of spelling are to be found in his earliest poems. This is not surprising when we consider that he is the grandson of a poor tailor, and that he began life as a waiter at an inn.

Even today, if you talk to certain pedants about Béranger, they ask you *what he has done*. A song which is only a page long seems to them a most insignificant production when compared with a fine, long poem, printed in quarto, with a wide margin, beautiful vignettes, and, for subject matter, *life, death, melancholy, glory*, etc., all of them spoken of with that pompous emphasis without which a stupid man thinks that nothing is serious or impressive.

M. Delavigne and M. de Lamartine, the former ever since he began to write and the latter ever since he acquired a reputation, are men of talent, who deliberately sit down at their desks and say, 'Lord Byron and Greece are all the rage. Now, therefore, I shall write about Greece and liberty, making certain not to overlook the shade of Leonidas. We cannot be too emphatic and grandiloquent on such subjects.'

M. de Béranger, unlike his noble rivals, has been exposed, ever since he was a child, to the most painful anxieties and suffering. As a young man, he was extremely poor. As soon as the manual labour by which he earned his living was over, he would sit down and write a song; this was his way of fixing things in his memory, and of writing his journal. His life, and also his genius, bear a considerable resemblance to those of the sublime Robert Burns, whom your Edinburgh pedants allowed to die in poverty. The Parisian public, which is rather more civilised, did not wait for *influential people* and *good judges* to point out de Béranger's merits. Under Napoleon, he obtained a sinecure which brought him in an income of roughly seventy pounds a year, a sum which, for him, was affluence, and enabled him to leave off working as a journeyman in a printing office. The Bourbons, who are the natural enemies of all true merit, dismissed him, on which his friends encouraged him to publish the first two volumes of his songs. This brought him in upwards of eleven hundred pounds, an enormous sum for our philosopher. The third volume, which has just been published and which the Bourbons instantly seized, has made nine hundred. De Béranger will probably be condemned to four or five months confinement in Ste Pélagie and in any case his bookseller, M. Plassan, will be ruined. De Béranger suffers terribly from the tedium of confinement, and this tedium leaves its mark on everything which he writes in prison.

The third volume contains several songs composed in Ste Pélagie during the poet's first imprisonment; they are noticeable for their lack of wit and vigour. The sight of the countryside and cheerful sunshine are necessary to the health of a man who suffers from a severe complaint of the chest.

The volume which has just been seized had been greatly reduced in bulk before going to press for reasons of prudence. M. de Béranger, it would seem, however, was not prudent enough. He has written more than two hundred songs which he calls his *Chansonnier Noir* and which will not appear until after either his death or that of the régime. Several of the songs in this latter collection are very much in the style of Horace's *Intiger vitae scelerisque puris*. The prudence, which ought to have been more prudent than it was, prevented M. de Béranger from giving us more than fifty-three songs, and of these only ten are worthy of the famous *Du bon Dieu*.

I have already pointed out that, when de Béranger's poor little Muse made her first appearance in the world, it occurred to nobody, apart from two or three old dreamers, that there could be any comparison between these rather frivolous little songs and the noble *Messéniennes* of Casimir Delavigne or the sublime *Méditations* of Alphonse de Lamartine. The latter, at the time, was being puffed by the *ultra* party as worthy to touch the harp of David, and as the inspired successor of J. B. Rousseau. I have no small gratification in telling you that I myself was one of those two or three dreamers and wrote an article on Béranger's songs for a journal whose editors were induced to insert it merely out of civility to me. M. de Béranger's style was something entirely new and novelty is always unfavourably received in France. People are afraid of exposing themselves by admiring it.

What has happened to our poets in the last two years is as follows: the liberal party has been consistent in its approval of M. Delavigne, and he, in his turn, has not been inattentive to the interests of his own reputation. Whenever any event, such as the death of Lord Byron, has held the public attention, he has celebrated it without fail within a fortnight. M. de Lamartine's works have enjoyed a better sale, however, for the *ultras* who support him are at least twice as rich as their opponents. The *ultras* are generally landowners and buy a great many books in order to help them to kill time when they are living in their country houses. The wealthy liberals are manufacturers or bankers and are by no means at such an advantage as far as the time available to them for reading is concerned. The reputation of both of these poets, however, despite their apparent success, is undoubtedly on the decline. Repeated experience is teaching the public to appreciate the enormous difference between the man of genius and the man of talent, however great the latter may be. But, even before my pen reaches the end of the last sentence, I feel how unjust I am being towards M. de Lamartine. The reputation of this young poet would be more untarnished than it is, if he had published nothing since the first volume of *Méditations*. Like the best of Byron's songs, they are the voice of his soul. Ever since, elated by the sort of reputation conferred upon him by the *ultra* party, M. de Lamartine has *chosen* to write. He has, in so doing, revealed the fact that, together with great sensibility and a talent for describing natural objects in harmonious verse, he has an empty and sterile brain. This incredible absence of the faculty of thought is evident if one reads his poem on the death of Socrates, four thousand copies of which were sold in two days. There is not a single salon in the whole Faubourg St Germain, which is like a large town in itself, in which M. de Lamartine's poems are not a necessary item of furniture. He is patronised by M. de Genoude, the editor of *L'Etoile*, a paper which is at the same time ministerial and Jesuitical. This, you will agree, is not bad management.

Our young men of fortune, who do nothing, who are dying of *ennui*, and who describe their consequent spleen as 'sensibility', discovered that the first volume of the *Méditations* provided a faithful account of the languor and tedium of which they are themselves the victims. They were scandalised by the gay, voluptuous spirit which breathes through M. de Béranger's early songs, and are now even more so after reading *Octavie*, a song which certainly does rather exceed the limits of decorum. De Béranger has this misfortune in common with Lafontaine, with whom I insist on comparing him—he offends the prudish.

The first volume of M. de Lamartine's *Méditations* was composed when he too was suffering from poverty and ill-health. He was being nursed at the time by friends in a furnished hotel, the Hotel de Richelieu, in Paris. M. Delavigne's career, however, has been marked by unbroken success, or so at least I have been told. He first distinguished himself by carrying off the prizes in every college in Paris and by gaining the favour and esteem of the professors. He has been the object of constant admiration and applause, and his labours, if we are to judge by their results, have all been directed to his own personal advantage. He has always worked regular counting-house hours; four hours a day, which produce a net profit of eighty pounds a month.

I trust that you will not conclude from this long exposition of what I think of our three greatest living poets that I am insensitive to the great merits of Lamartine and Delavigne. All that I wish to contend is that de Béranger is the foremost of the three, the one whose work has the greatest chance of being read in the twentieth century. After *Le bon dieu*, *Le vieux sergent*, and a few other songs, I would place, in order of preference, the first volume of M. de Lamartine's *Méditations*; and only after this, M. Delavigne. In 1820, most poetry readers would have considered this judgment as preposterous blasphemy; at the moment, they condescend to discuss it, and, in two or three years time, I have little doubt that it will be the general opinion of the public.

I should add, however, that I am prepared to alter my opinion in an eventuality which is as unlikely as it is desirable, that is to say, should MM. Delavigne and de Lamartine publish works in a style unlike that which they have till now adopted in the poetry by which they are best known. M. Delavigne is at the moment preparing a tragedy based on the life of Louis XI, and suggested by Scott's *Quentin Durward*. The first scene shows us Philippe de Commines writing his memoirs and is thus reminiscent of the absurd conventions of the *vaudeville anecdotique*; we are reminded inevitably of *Guillaume Helvétius*, *La Maison de Molière*, and other plays in which illustrious Frenchmen are made to appear on the stage, nearly always, when they are writers, with their manuscripts in their hands. M. Delavigne will almost certainly manage to produce some good lines in the manner of Delille and Dryden. Will he ever prove to be capable of the sublime energy of tragedy, however? This is a question to which I should be very happy to reply in the affirmative.

I have recently heard a few pages of a new poem by M. de Lamartine, called *The last canto of Childe Harold*. Your English vanity must certainly be flattered at seeing that two of the most eminent of French poets are avowedly inspired by Walter Scott and Lord Byron. The truth of the matter is, that the influence of our present form of government is perceptible everyday in our growing affinity to the English ways of thinking and feeling. Frivolity is on the decline and gravity and melancholy are gaining ground. Canals are finding their way through our fields and melancholy into our drawing-rooms. However true this may be, M. de Lamartine is the poet of a rich and powerful party; a bookseller has therefore ventured to give him four hundred pounds for his latest poem, which contains two thousand lines. This is an enormous sum in France. The speculation was very successful, for, having bought the poem, he sold the rights for the second and third editions for four hundred and eighty pounds. The first edition will therefore be clear profit.

Many of the lines of M. de Lamartine's poem which I heard read out struck me as carelessly written. The same word is frequently repeated in two consecutive lines, or even sometimes in the same line. Faults such as this, however, never seem faults to me. The construction of French verse has become such a mechanical affair that M. de Lamartine has probably left these marks of negligence in order to stand out from among the two or three hundred poets who fill the Parisian *salons*, all of them perfectly correct and all of them perfectly dull. There is probably not one poet from out of the whole melodious company who has not learned ten thousand lines of French verse by heart, or who cannot command, for instant use, thirty or forty different turns of phrase to express the most trifling and ordinary sentiment. With all their accomplishment, however, they are incapable of producing a single thought or feeling which is truly original.

The last canto of Childe Harold is the story of the last years of Byron's life. In France, we tend to consider that, because of his aristocratic pride and his lack of dramatic genius, Lord Byron was never able to describe anyone but himself.

It is my own opinion, however, that M. de Lamartine chose the title of his poem with one predominant idea in mind. The sentiments expressed in the opening lines are more or less as follows: 'There are only two things in the world worthy of occupying a great mind; these are Love and Liberty. I have felt the power of Love, I have tried to sing this power. But now, divine Liberty, it is to thee that I turn.'

M. de Genoude, who is responsible for two thirds of M. de Lamartine's reputation and who obtained for him the patronage of the rich *ultra* party, will have to delete this invocation to Liberty. Otherwise his poet will begin to profit from the huge stock of ideas which are there for him to use in innumerable political pamphlets. This will be an inestimable advantage to a writer whose main defect is a painful sterility of ideas. M. de Béranger, on the other hand, would be distinguished as a profound thinker, if he were not a great poet. It is said that there is scarcely anyone in Paris who can give proof of such depth and originality of thought in his discussion of politics and literature, in short, of everything which occupies the minds of the French people today—that is, if you will condescend to describe such a collection of timid, sprightly egotists as a people.

If there are any Englishmen capable of understanding Lafontaine's hundred exquisite fables, you would do well to insert one or two of de Béranger's songs every month in the *London Magazine*. All the English reviews, however, print such extraordinary blunders, whenever they pretend to quote French, that we are forced to conclude that the refinements of our language are entirely wasted on you. Harriet Wilson's *Memoirs*, which, in France, are considered to be extremely witty and intelligent, become ridiculous as soon as they make any pretensions to an understanding of French, as soon as they say, *à la distance*, for example, instead of *à distance*. These expressions have an entirely different meaning. What will be your astonishment, and even your virtuous indignation, when I say that we find love more delicately evoked in Harriet's memoirs than in Sir Walter Scott's novels? After such a proof of contrariness in our tastes and sentiments, I have every reason to tremble for the fate of my own letters. We Parisians live on subtle shades of meaning. You Londoners seem to despise them.

London Magazine, May 1825

LAMARTINE AND BYRON

Letters from Paris by Grimm's grandson, no. vii

Paris, June 18th, 1825

My dear friend,

Allow me to congratulate your printer on the obstinate and successful war which he wages, not only against all proper names, but against any word which has the misfortune to be left in French, when it appears in one of my letters.[1] He has made it seem as though I wrote *Chaget* and *la charlatanisme*, whereas I myself wrote *Chazet* and *le charlatanisme*: two words, I assure you, which go very well together. M. Chazet is an

[1] Our excellent correspondent forgets that his handwriting is very unlike anything that has been seen in England before, and that a great many of the names of modern French writers are entirely unknown on this side of the Channel. We have long accused the French of mangling our proper names in a most barbarous manner; the fact is that the offence is mutual and very difficult to avoid. In the absence of familiarity with the name, there is no guide of analogy, or at least but little to lead a foreigner right. *Chaget* is just as good French as *Chazet* to our printer; and there are many gentlemen in Yorkshire or Devonshire, who think it of very little consequence whether that illustrious writer spells his name with a z or a g. The other error pointed out is indeed unpardonable, and we quite agree with M. Grimm *le jeune* that Mr Parker should look to his genders. (Note in the *London Magazine*.)

author whose success disturbs the sleep of every underling writer in France.

After being a Southey to Bonaparte, he has now become Southey to the Bourbons and a favourite of the Sosthènes. He enjoys thirteen sinecures and seven pensions. The nation gives him 1,200 pounds sterling a year, in spite of which he is never able to pay for a cab. The privileges which he enjoys are a cause of extreme irritation to a number of eminent Frenchmen, among whom are Messieurs Ancelot, Desaugiers, de Bonald, Soumet and le chevalier Jacquelin.

Now that I have found fault with your printer I must find fault with myself. My last letter strikes me as having been too political. What I had undertaken to give you was a general picture of the moral and literary life of Paris. In order to carry this out faithfully, I should have confined myself this month to the absurdities that were committed on the occasion of the Coronation and which have occupied the entire attention of the public. They have been all the more striking because of the contrasts between the 'beautiful' ceremonials devised by Messieurs Corbière and Sosthène and the perfect cordiality and graciousness of Charles X, and the dignified loyalty of the Dauphin.[1]

The past month, however, has produced four outstanding works of literature, and it is about these that I prefer to speak. They are *Le Dernier Chant de Childe Harold* and *Le Chant du Sacre* by M. de Lamartine, the Spanish plays of Clara Gazul,[2] and the *Prisonniers du Caucase* by le Comte Xavier de Maistre. The last two of these will almost certainly be translated into English. As for M. de Lamartine's poetry, I find it almost

---

[1] We cannot help thinking that these expressions are dictated by prudence and by fear of the inspectors of the Post Office. A king of any understanding would not allow a Corbière to retain a place in his councils. The Bourbons play a desperate game in giving themselves up to the guidance of the Jesuits. (Note in the *London Magazine*.)

[2] The pseudonym adopted by Stendhal's friend, Prosper Mérimée.

impossible to imagine how a foreigner can appreciate its merits. He is, in my opinion, the second greatest of living French poets; but he is totally lacking in common sense. This is true to the letter.

In *Le Dernier Chant de Childe Harold*, he makes a vessel set sail, without weighing anchor:

> La voile, qui s'entr'ouvre au vent qui l'arrondit,
> Monte de vergue en vergue, et s'enfle et s'agrandit;
> Et couvrant ses flancs noirs de l'ombre de son aile,
> Fait pencher sur les flots le vaisseau qui chancelle;
> On lève l'ancre, il fuit. . . .[1]

What is most amusing perhaps is that M. de Lamartine has often been to sea. Instead of wondering what was going on in the ship, however, or watching the seamen at work, he was absorbed in some waking dream. If M. de Lamartine is incapable of grasping a truth as simple as the necessity of weighing anchor before setting sail, what on earth will he make of all the moral and political truths which are, as it were, the currency of everyday conversation, and the basic constituent of our national fund of good sense?

M. de Lamartine has not so much as a suspicion of their existence and the thoughts which form the basis of the two poems mentioned above have an air of perfect childishness. You probably know that M. de Lamartine, or so at least it is commonly said, was educated in an *ultra* family, no less remarkable for its nobility than for the narrowness of its ideas. The mind of the young poet was never able to expand beyond the limited range of the petty and obsolete ideas in which it had been trained; and now, ever since the publication of the *Méditations Poétiques*, which have been ranked as a masterpiece, he has been under the powerful and terrible

[1] The sail, half opening, as it curves out in the wind, climbs from one yardarm to the next and swells and grows immense. The tottering vessel leans over under it, as the shadow of her wing covers her black sides. The anchor is raised. She flies. . . .

protection of the Jesuits. A certain M. de Genoude, editor of *L'Etoile*, the French *Blackwood's*, is also a patron of M. de Lamartine. Everything thus conspires to keep this unfortunate young man in perpetual ignorance of the elementary realities of life. It can be said with truth that he is deficient in understanding, though a man of genius; that he is of an upright character, and yet lends himself to actions which, in another man, would be considered mean. If I were to quote for your benefit his poem on the Coronation, you would blush with indignation at eight or ten different passages, and I should be compelled to explain to you that M. de Lamartine is perhaps the only man who fails to comprehend the drift of what he has written. I am perfectly aware of the fact that a poet is permitted to be ignorant of the realities of life. I will go even further and say that it is necessary to his success that he *should* be so. If a man of honour and sensibility like M. de Lamartine knew as much about mankind as a Robert Walpole or a Villèle, his imagination and his sensibility would go sterile. I have always thought that this was the meaning of the reply made to Hamlet by his father's ghost.

If Lord Byron had not enjoyed the advantage of being born an Englishman; if he had not been compelled by his pride, as an aristocrat, to assume at least something of the prevailing good sense of his countrymen; if he had not associated with Douglas Kinnaird, the Hobhouses and others well versed in the realities of political life; if he had not seen a little of the world as it really is, which he could not fail to do as a member of the Literary Committee of Covent Garden, he would never have written *Don Juan*; his genius would never, in my opinion, have risen above that of M. de Lamartine. The French poet, on the other hand, has always lived in the country, buried in a château and surrounded by narrow, *ultra* prejudices. No stupidity at present to be found in France can be compared with the stupidity of the provincial noble, living, as he has done for the last thirty-five years, in a state of perpetual anger against everything happening around him, and in reality knowing nothing. You have a specimen of what I mean in the present Chamber of Deputies. 'At no time in the last century has such a collection of fools been seen', one of our most profound orators, M. Royer-Collard, has said. It has been M. de Lamartine's misfortune to spend his life among people of this kind. He has never seen society; its heartlessness disgusts and repels him.

From what then does he derive his genius? From his heart alone. He never rises to the height of the best poetry of our time, unless it is when he expresses in simple language a sentiment which comes from the soul. After any such passage, you will find it impossible to read twenty lines without coming upon some puerility or other so astonishing that it utterly destroys your pleasure. This is never the case when one reads Béranger's songs; and it is one of the reasons for which I consider Béranger our greatest living poet. M. Baour-Lormian is no more than an unintelligent manufacturer of harmonious verses, equally devoid of sentiment and wit. M. Casimir Delavigne has all the sense and awareness of reality which M. de Lamartine lacks; but he lacks in his turn the soul of a poet; he is never, that is, happy or unhappy from purely imaginary causes. M. de Talleyrand has suggested that, if we could make one poet swallow the other whole, we should have a perfect man of genius.

No French poet, not even Racine, Voltaire or Lafontaine, has produced anything to equal the Dedication to *Le Dernier Chant de Childe Harold*. There are, it is true, three or four signs of carelessness in the two pages of which it consists, for the exaggerated praises of the *ultra* party seem to have turned the poet's head and harmfully affected his genius. Lafontaine, despite this, is the only man who could have surpassed M. de Lamartine's achievement.

At the time of Lafontaine, no one would have dared express such ideas, or rather such feelings with any boldness. In spite of the immense superiority of his genius, Lafontaine's manner, or his brushwork (to use an expression from painting) seems distorted by its minuteness, when we compare it with Lamartine's. Our modern poet owes his own breadth of touch to his singular good fortune: he comes after both the talent of the Abbé Delille and the genius of Byron. I do not know whether you, as a foreigner, will be able to sense the charm of the following lines, lines which depend so little for their effect on any thought and so much on their wording.

DEDICACE
Te souviens-tu du jour où, gravissant la cime
Du Salève aux flancs azurés
Dans un étroit sentier qui pend sur un abîme,
Nous posions en tremblant nos pas mal assurés?
Tu marchais devant moi. Balancés par l'orage,
Les rameaux ondoyants du mélèze et du pin,
S'écartant à regret pour t'ouvrir un passage,
Secouaient sur ton front les larmes du matin;
Un torrent sous tes pieds s'écroulant en poussière,
Traçait sur les rochers de verdâtres sillons.

. . . . .

Un nuage grondait encore
Sur les confins des airs, à l'occident obscur,
Tandis qu' à l'orient le souffle de l'aurore
Découvrait la moitié d'un ciel limpide et pur,
Et dorait de ses feux la voile qui colore
Des vagues du Léman l'éblouissant azur!
Tout à coup, sur un roc, dont tu foulais la cime,
Tu t'arrêtas: tes yeux s'abaissèrent sur moi;

Tu me montras du doigt les flots, les monts, l'abîme,
La nature et le ciel . . . et je ne vis que toi ! . . .

. . . . .

Des cascades l'écume errante
Faisait autour de toi, sur un tapis de fleurs,
De son prisme liquide ondoyer les couleurs,
Et d'une robe transparente
Semblait t'envelopper dans ses plis de vapeurs !
Tu ressemblais. . . . Mais non, toute image est glacée,
Rien d'humain ne saurait te retracer aux yeux ![1]

The magic of these lines makes every object described by the poet seem present to the thoughts and soul of a fellow-countryman. What more have Dante, Shakespeare or Tasso done, or, in his occasional moments of genius, Lord Byron?

M. de Lamartine describes the last years in the life of the poet. However, his narrative lacks clarity. It is sometimes impossible to know who is speaking, and whether the poet is assuming the role of Byron himself or not. This is unlikely, since Byron is the poet described. It is plain, nevertheless, that M. de Lamartine has not condescended to go over his own poem; he has even left a number of defective lines. What foreign readers will find most striking, unfortunately, is the incoherence, and often the absurdity of its general argument.

---

[1] DEDICATION: Do you remember the day when, as we climbed up to reach the crest of the blue-flanked Salève, we stepped, trembling and uncertain of our foothold, along a narrow path that hung over an abyss below? You were in front of me. Rocked by the storm, the swaying branches of larch and pine bent back reluctantly to let you pass, and shook the tears of morning on to your brow; beneath your feet, a torrent dissolved into spray and drew greenish furrows down the rocks. . . . A cloud still muttered in the outer limits of the sky, in the dark west, while, in the east, the dawn wind opened out one half of a pure, limpid sky. Its fires gilded the sail which tints the dazzling blue waves of the Lake of Geneva! Suddenly, from a rock, onto the top of which you had stepped, your eyes looked down towards me. You pointed to the waves, the mountains and the sheer drop beneath, to Nature and the heavens . . . and I could only see you ! . . . The wandering foam of the cascades glittered its refracted colours around where you stood on a carpet of flowers, while it was as if you were wrapped in their rising folds of steam, as in a transparent gown. You looked like . . . but no, every image is frozen. Nothing human can recall you to my eyes.

They will have to do as we do, therefore, and content themselves with extracts. Here is a description of Genoa. It is blurred and misty and nothing is sharply defined:

> Il est nuit; mais la nuit sous ce ciel n'a point d'ombre.
> Son astre, suspendu dans un dôme moins sombre,
> Blanchit de ses lueurs des bords silencieux
> Où la vague se teint du bleu pâle des cieux;
> Où la côte des mers de cent golfes coupée,
> Tantôt humble et rampante et tantôt escarpée,
> Sur un sable argenté vient mourir mollement,
> Ou gronde sous le choc de son flot écumant.
> De leurs vagues remparts les Alpes l'environnent;
> Leurs sommets colorés que les neiges couronnent,
> De colline en colline abaissés par degrés,
> Montrent, près de l'hiver, des climats tempérés
> Où l'aquilon, fuyant de son âpre royaume,
> De leurs tièdes parfums s'attiédit et s'embaume.
> A travers des cyprès, dont l'immobilité,
> Symbole de tristesse et d'immortalité,
> Projette sur les murs ses ombres sépulcrales
> Que les reflets du ciel percent par intervalles,
> S'étend sur la colline un champêtre séjour:
> Un long buisson de myrte en trace le contour;
> Sur des gazons naissants, de flexibles allées,
> D'un rideau de verdure à peine encore voilées,
> Egarant au hasard leurs cours capricieux,
> Conduisant en tournant, ou les pas, ou les yeux,
> Jusqu'au seuil où, formant de vertes colonnades,
> La clématite en fleur se suspend aux arcades;
> Sur les toits aplatis, des jardins d'oranger
> Ornent de leurs fruits d'or leur feuillage étranger;
> L'eau fuit dans les bassins, et, quand le jour expire,
> Imite en murmurant les frissons de zéphire.
> De là, l'oeil enchanté voit, au pied des coteaux
> Gênes, fille des mers, sortir du sein des eaux,

Les dômes élancés de ses saintes demeures
D'où l'airain frémissant fait résonner les heures,
Et les mâts des vaisseaux qui, dormant dans ses ports,
S'élèvent au niveau des palais de ses bords;
Et quand le flot captif les presse et les soulève,
D'un lourd gémissement font retentir la grève.
Quel silence!... Avançons... tout dort-il en ces lieux?[1]

The description of Byron leaving his sleeping mistress is of great beauty. There is one passage which is equal to the sublimest things in Lafontaine:

Mais non, tout ne dort pas; de fenêtre en fenêtre
Voyez ce seul flambeau briller et disparaître;

. . . . .

La porte s'ouvre; un homme, à pas comptés, s'avance.
Une lampe à la main il s'arrête en silence.

. . . . .

Dors! murmurait Harold d'une voix comprimée;
Toi que je vais quitter! toi que j'ai tant aimée!
Toi qui m'aimas peut-être, ou dont l'art séducteur,

---

[1] It is night; but night under this sky has no shadow. Its star, hung in a dome less dark than the silent shores, whitens them with its gleam, where the wave is tinted with the pale blue of heaven and where the sea-shore is cut out by a hundred bays. Sometimes the shore will creep humbly down to die softly in the silvered sand; elsewhere, it is a sheer drop and booms under the shock of the foaming waves. The hazy ramparts of the Alps surround them; their coloured peaks crowned with snow gradually slope down and reveal, near the region of winter, temperate climes where the north wind, fleeing its harsh kingdom, grows warm and fragrant. On the hillside stretches a rustic dwelling, standing among the cypresses, those symbols of sadness and immortality, which throw sepulchral shadows on to the walls, picked out here and there by patches of sunlight. A long thicket of myrtle follows its contours. On the fresh growing lawns, bending paths, scarcely yet veiled in a curtain of green, wind their capricious paths and, turning, guide the footsteps or the gaze as far as the threshold. Here flowering clematis, hung from the arcades, forms green colonnades, while, against the flat roofs, orange gardens adorn with golden fruit their strange, foreign-seeming leafage. Water runs into stone basins, and, when the day is dying, its murmur imitates the quiver of the south wind. From here the enchanted eye can see, at the foot of the hills, Genoa, daughter of the seas, rising from the bosom of the waters, the soaring domes of her holy dwellings whose trembling bronze vibrates the hours, and the masts of vessels lying asleep in their docks, their masts as tall as the palaces round her quays. Whenever the captive sea presses and raises them, their heavy groan resounds along the waterfront. What a silence!... Come.... Is everything here asleep?

Par l'ombre de l'amour trompa du moins mon coeur!
Qu'importe que le tien ne fut qu'un doux mensonge?
Je fus heureux par toi; tout bonheur est un songe![1]

At the end of this admirable description, there were four lines which the Jesuits made the author suppress, on the grounds that they were too voluptuous, and even that they were open to the charge of indecency. The party made his compliance the price of their protection, and the poet, who is fully aware of its value, obeyed with alacrity.

The doubts of Harold concerning the existence and attributes of a Deity which permits so many horrors, which brings Byron's career to an end at the age of thirty-seven and prolongs that of Ferdinand VII, has been considered sublime. At the end of the poem, in order to conciliate the most rigorous of his patrons, the author gives us to understand that Lord Byron is damned:

Harold! dit une voix, voici l'affreux moment![2]

The absurdity of this conclusion has shocked everyone. Is Lord Byron, who devotes himself to the liberty of Greece, damned? What fate then remains for those members of the Holy Alliance who send artillery officers to Ibrahim Pasha?[3] The author, who shares the illusions of the *ultra* party, fails to realise how much good sense has been diffused among the French as a result of forty years of revolution.

The damnation of Lord Byron has had a very unfavourable effect on the popularity of the poem. So far, it has gone into only four editions. This may be called a bad sale for anything

---

[1] But no, everything is not asleep. Look at that solitary flame which in one window after another glows and disappears. . . . The door opens and with measured tread a man steps forward. A lamp is in his hand, he stops in silence. . . . Sleep! murmured Harold with a stifled voice, thou who I am about to leave and whom I have loved so dearly, thou who loved *me* perhaps or whose seductive art deceived *my* heart at least with the shadow of love. What does it matter if yours was only a sweet lie? Through you I was happy; all happiness is a dream.

[2] 'Harold!' said a voice, 'now is the fearful moment.'

[3] At the siege of Navarino, a historical fact. (Note in the *London Magazine*.)

by Lamartine, vigorously as it is sure to be pushed by all the papers which are read by the richer classes of society. If M. de Lamartine goes on like this, he will be obliged in two or three years time, to rely on his merit for his success. So much the better both for him and for us.

If, like my illustrious grandfather, I could write letters of forty pages, and, moreover, write them once a fortnight, I should quote the whole description of the departure of Childe Harold. I strongly recommend you to publish it, for your readers' benefit, in some other part of your magazine, even if you have to use small type to get it in. You might begin at:

Mais où donc est Harold, ce pélerin du monde?[1]

and finish with:

Retarde un désespoir qui l'attend au reveil![2]

I also advise you to quote Harold's doubts:

Du sceptique Harold le doute est la doctrine;
Le croisant ni la croix ne couvrent sa poitrine;
Jupiter, Mahomet, héros, grands hommes, Dieux
(O Christ, pardonne-lui) ne sont rien à ses yeux.[3]

The limited space at my disposal does not allow me to undertake an analysis of *Le Chant du Sacre*. It is a poem in which creatures are praised who are the object of such general contempt, that part of it will be reflected on the poet. The excuse for him which public opinion makes is his utter ignorance of the world for which he is notorious.

In a dialogue between M. Latil, Archbishop of Paris and Charles X, the poet betrays a total ignorance of the accepted social forms. He also makes the King utter the strangest things imaginable. Notice too that the King here plays a secondary

---

[1] But where then is Harold, that pilgrim through the world?
[2] ... delays that despair which awaits him when he wakes.
[3] The doctrine of the sceptic Harold is doubt; neither Crescent nor Cross cover his chest. Jupiter, Mahomet, heroes, great men, gods (O Christ, forgive him) are as nothing in his eyes.

role; the Archbishop, who plays the part of an interrogator, has a clear advantage. The poem is dedicated to the King. The author, however, did not deign to ask whether the language which he attributed to him was such as he would wish to acknowledge, even though, in France, this is a formality which is observed with respect to the humblest citizen. You may gather, from this, to what extent the prestige of the monarchy has declined. M. Delavigne refuses a pension from the King, and M. de Lamartine, an *ultra* poet, puts him into a poem and makes him speak without even consulting him.

One of the best lines in *Le Chant du Sacre* is that in which the poet, speaking of the King, says:

... Que son coeur aime mieux
Un grand nom qui surgit, qu'un vieux nom qui s'éteint.[1]

The reference to the Faubourg St Germain is unfortunately only too evident, and it has excited the indignation of all the great names in that quarter of Paris, which, it must be admitted, *s'éteignent un peu*.[2] The king has reproached M. de Sosthène for having persuaded him to decorate M. de Lamartine with the Cross of St Louis. 'As I admire the poet', the King is reported as saying, 'I shall try and forget his latest work.'

While describing, if one can call it describing, the marshals who surrounded the King during the ceremony, M. de Lamartine found a great deal to say. The only difficulty arose from the immense number of great military actions which he had to recount. When he came to the ancient nobility, however, he was at a complete loss. He could find nothing to praise but their piety, nothing to talk of but their ancestors. To crown his blunders, he ended the poem with four lines so offensive to the Duke of Orleans that the Duke, though not usually given to taking offence, considered that he owed it to

---
[1] ... that his heart prefers a great name which is being made to an old one which is dying.
[2] ... are growing somewhat dim.

himself to complain to the King. This attack on the Duke of Orleans, who, because of the excellent education he is giving his six sons, is an object of aversion to the entire Faubourg St Germain, will perhaps make up for the poet's other misdemeanours; but the last line I have quoted is engraved on every memory.

London Magazine, July 1825

ON THE PRESENT STATE OF ITALIAN LITERATURE

Rome, August 1825

My dear friend,

I comply with your request, though with a certain trepidation; I will try and give you some idea of the present state of Italian poetry. If there is one country which enjoys a peculiar advantage in judging the poetry of other nations, it is unquestionably England. In dramatic poetry she possesses a genius who not only sets her above the reach of all competition, but whose distinctive trait is extreme variety. The nation which is happy enough to enjoy in its native tongue the poetry of the creator of Richard III, Ariel, Imogen and Lady Macbeth may have an equal relish for the energy of Dante and for the humorous and perhaps over-licentious graces of Buratti.

Who is this Buratti, you may wish to ask. He is a very great poet of whom you know nothing, but who suggested to Lord Byron the theme of his *Don Juan*. My principal motive in undertaking to write at some length on the subject of Italian poetry is the following: the Italians are the only people whose poetry has not been utterly spoiled or at the best vitiated for a certain period by its imitation of the philosophical and artificial style of Parisian verse. In 1793, Italy was the scene of a great literary phenomenon. Vincenzo Monti, in publishing *La Bassvilliana*, a poem which is atrocious as far as its subject is concerned, rescued Italian poetry from becoming a mere imitation of Pope, Boileau and Voltaire. You in England can appreciate the extent of the danger and the value of the service; for, at the Restoration of Charles II, you did not escape the contagion. Thanks to Monti, Italian poetry has preserved its character of originality and energy. More than a century ago, a ridiculous Jesuit called Saverio Bettinelli undertook to turn Dante into an object of ridicule. Bettinelli had the merit of serving two conflicting interests at the same time. In the first place he was rendering a service to the Jesuit order which has consistently persecuted Dante's memory. The works of that great poet tend to encourage the self-examination which is looked upon with horror by the Court of Rome and its most enlightened defenders, the Jesuits, in so far as it can lead to Protestantism and the use of reason. By abusing Dante, however, Bettinelli also became a partisan of the poetical school of which Voltaire was the originator. The merely courtly energy of the latter, destined to charm the frivolous *habitués* of the salons of Paris and Versailles in 1750, could not tolerate the strength and awful vigour of Dante which could inspire the men, truly worthy of the name, who peopled Italy in the fourteenth century. Dante is inferior to Shakespeare, only because, in general, he is less interesting. He has always been an object of aversion to the school of Voltaire, and to the admirers of that effeminate style of poetry to which l'abbé Delille, de Collardeau, de Dorat, de Bertin and so many other insipid writers, now forgotten, have in turn owed their reputation.

All that was critical and ironical in Voltaire's works gave the most exquisite pleasure to the Italians of the year 1750. Never did any nation enjoy the delights of novelty as much as poor Italy, doubly cursed as she had been, since 1530, under the yoke of Spanish despotism and the stifling influence of the Papacy. The immense popularity of Voltaire's little prose satires[1] nearly brought the writing of Italian poetry to an end. While the Abbé Saverio Bettinelli was publishing his witty blasphemies against Dante,[2] Pignotti, whose posthumous fame rests upon the best history of Italy that has yet been written,[3] acquired the reputation of the first fabulist of Italy, a reputation which has fortunately not survived him, and for which he was wholly indebted to his imitation of Pope. Bettinelli, Pignotti, and a dozen inferior poets, such as Ugoni and Algarotti, who are no longer read, even in Italy (this despite the efforts of the French pedant Ginguené to restore them to life in his commonplace history of Italian literature), were busy digging the grave of Italian poetry, reducing it to a mere imitation of the poetry of France and England, when Monti appeared.

This great poet, born at Fusignano near Urbino in 1758, is still living in Milan on the pension granted to him by Napoleon and reduced to one half by the Austrian Government. I intend to write you a letter devoted entirely to Monti's works. My only purpose at the moment is to call your attention to a remarkable and probably unique instance of the way in which the decline of the poetry of a whole nation was arrested by the genius of a single man. His versatile character, susceptible as

[1] *La Revue Britannique*, in its translation of the article (January 1826) prints, for 'little prose satires', 'ses vers satiriques' ('his satiric verses'). See too *Le Courrier Anglais*, vol. IV, page 235. (*Editor*.)
[2] *Lettere Virgiliane*, 1757. The author pronounces that, out of the fifteen thousand lines in Dante, three hundred approximately are competently written. (Note in the *London Magazine*.)
[3] This is a history of Tuscany as far as the age of the Medici, that is as far as the institution of a form of tyranny modelled on that of Philip II. It has been translated into English. (Note in the *London Magazine*.)

it was to inspiration from varied and contrasting sentiments, the obsequious court he paid to the nephew of Pius VI, and his extreme poverty, all conspired to ensure his success as the renovator of Italian verse. Monti had already published a few short poems, which immediately placed him in the foremost rank of modern poets. These, however, were not sufficient to alter the situation in Italian poetry, and it could be said that it owes its salvation to one particular incident.

On the 13th of January, 1793, Cardinal Albano caused the assassination of Hugues Bassville, a diplomatic envoy from France to Italy, who dealt rather more openly in espionage and in conspiracy against the established government than was consistent with the usual laws and practices of diplomacy. This same Cardinal Albano has recently been sent as plenipotentiary legate from Padua to Bologna by Leo XII. He stands pre-eminent, I may almost say alone, in atrocious wickedness among the members of the Sacred College. Poor Monti, who was fundamentally very humane, considered that, by writing an apology for this murder, committed in the light of day by Roman citizens in the pay of Albano, he would secure the favour of the Cardinal and his party and succeed in making his fortune. The apology for the murder of the French agent produced the immortal poem entitled *La Bassvilliana*. I am compelled to hesitate before I decide whether to place *La Bassvilliana* above all the poems written by Lord Byron. After mature deliberation, it seems to me that it is at least the equal of the *Corsair* and the finest passages of *Childe Harold*, and that *Don Juan* alone is superior to it.

La Bassvilliana was published in Rome in 1793, and all that Pignotti, Bettinelli and their followers had been doing for thirty years to turn Italian poetry into the imitation of something else was annihilated, as it were, in the twinkling of an eye. The appeal of Monti's poetry was to the individual and deep-seated feelings of every Italian. In Italy, a country totally devoid of the vanity of France and England, every man laughs at his neighbour and even despises and detests him. His judgment of the arts is founded solely upon his own feelings. The unfortunate Italians, parcelled out as they are under six petty tyrants, form a total contrast, it is clear, with the inhabitants of France and England, who are better off politically, but who have been deprived of all individual character by their ambition to become, in every sense of the term, a fashionable and wellbred copy of a certain conventional pattern. Unlike the Englishman or Frenchman, the Italian listens only to the promptings of his own heart, employing all the energy of his character to give strength and predominance to his own peculiar mode of feeling. With more of the qualities of a philosopher and with some traces even of the savage, he believes and maintains that his own way of thinking and feeling is the only way, and that any other is detestable and absurd.

This peculiarity of the Italian character is precisely what ought to enhance its prestige in matters of literature in the eyes of every worthy judge in Europe or America. The French, I am compelled to add, whose poetry consists of copies of some prevailing fashion, are less deserving of serious consideration.

Monti's *Bassvilliana* was read by every literate Italian in a nation of eighteen millions, except for the *literati* whose vanity and interest led them to support the school of Bettinelli and Pignotti. The decision was favourable and unanimous. 'For centuries', was the general cry, 'we have had nothing to equal this.' The *Bassvilliana* proved Monti to be, first the disciple of Virgil and secondly the disciple of Dante.

In an edition of the *Bassvilliana* printed at Mantua which lies on the table before me, Monti, in a spirit very different from that of most poets, takes the credit for his own plagiarisms, provided, that is, that the author from whom he borrows is ancient. Because, for instance, Lucan says:

Nec polus adversi calidus qua mergitur austri[1]

and Bernardo Tasso, the father of Torquato:

Or sorto il caldo, or sorto il freddo polo,[2]

Monti, who is, however, by no means ignorant of physical science, has included the following lines, in the second canto of his poem, on the moment of Louis XVI's death:

Tremonne il mondo; e per la maraviglia
E pel terror dal freddo al caldo polo
Palpitando i potenti alzar la ciglia.[3]

The ludicrous part of the story is that a blockhead of the name of Pessuti wrote a dissertation, at Monti's request, to prove that a hot pole actually exists. Among the authorities to whom he refers are Newton and Halley (see page 124 of the 1798 Mantua edition). In spite of this absurdity to which Monti should have pleaded guilty, he is in general a true disciple of Dante. His adoration of the ancients, that is to say, is confined to an adoration of their style, to their way of presenting their thoughts. As for these thoughts themselves, they are entirely his own; they are those of a Roman of the year 1793, before Napoleon had enlightened Italy. They have all the ferocity of Roman Catholicism, inspired continually by an abject fear of God, the God whom the Church invariably presents as an oriental despot, easily irritated and implacable in his vengeance. The lesson which Monti has given to the poets of Italy is twofold in its implications; firstly, express the feelings by which you are genuinely moved; secondly, express them in the style of Dante, and, as the Italian language is still closely modelled

[1] Nor the hot pole of the hostile winds of the south in which it is mingled. . . .
[2] Sometimes when the hot pole has come out, sometimes when the cold pole has emerged. . . .
[3] At this the world trembled and the mighty raised their eyes trembling, from the cold pole to the hot.

on Latin, do not hesitate to use Latin terms of expression or to give to words their original meaning in the Latin of Virgil.

This decisive step once taken, there is little room left for the affectations to which the spirit of chivalry has given rise, while it prescribes irrevocably the elegant conceits, so tiresome in their pettiness, which distinguish French poetry. To find the style of poetry which least resembles that of the *Bassvilliana*, you have only to take up a canto of the *Henriade* or a poem by the cold and elegant Abbé Delille.

You may therefore have some idea of the immense service that Monti has rendered to the poetry of his country. Camillus, after the defeat of Brutus, was called the second founder of Rome; Monti, though inferior to Dante, Ariosto and Tasso, the three founders of Italian poetry, has nevertheless been more *useful* than any one of them. There are two men who have contributed to produce the same results; their merit, however, is by no means equal. Whatever M. Ginguené, from his own limited and above all French point of view, may say to the contrary, Alfieri is not the true descendant of Dante. He has, it is true, adopted Dante's style, exaggerating its defects and rendering it more dry and hard, but he has not expressed Italian thoughts, he has not given voice to the Italian soul. The Italian soul is more susceptible to gentle passion and to the 'milk of human kindness'. Alfieri's sentiments are those of an aristocrat irritated and discontented at being only a count; he renders them in that peculiar form of the tragic spirit which was established by Racine and Voltaire. Just as he exaggerates the style of Dante, however, so does he exaggerate the already sufficiently tedious severity of French tragedy. If I seem unjust towards Alfieri, I should like it to be considered that I have frequently seen his plays performed and that, for a whole year, I saw them acted in Naples by Marini, the greatest tragic actor in Italy. Although Alfieri's character and temperament were in general those of a tyrant, his Filipo should be compared with Schiller's Don Carlos. The two poets have taken the same subject and wrote at the same time.

It seems to me therefore that Alfieri cannot share with Monti the honour of having awoken the Italian spirit and of having inspired it with a proper contempt for the tawdry, French style of poetry to which Algarotti, Pignotti and Bettinelli[1] had prostituted their divine language.

Parini, a native of Milan, had succeeded, it is true, in imitating Pope and Boileau while giving his poetry an essentially Italian character. Maria Theresa was wise enough to make Parini Professor of Literature at Milan, and here his exhortations stimulated his pupils to study the beauties of Dante, while his own poems revealed to them the absurdity of all the admiration which had been lavished on the French school of writers. Parini, however, was a satirist and satire in Italy can never assume any more than minor importance. Italy lacks entirely the monarchical spirit; she experienced an immediate transition from the liberty which she was unique in enjoying for the six hundred years from 900 to 1530, to Terror, the mainspring of the despotism under which she has groaned for the last three centuries. In countries where monarchy has taken deep root, the kings have courted the affections of the people, they have tried to gain popularity by means of the influence of their nobles and by fictitious notions of honour.[2] It is thus that great nations like France have come to see in the imitation of a certain model the highest form of happiness. This model has been adapted for every class by the King or his ministers, and, in seeking to follow it, a nation exhibits that *esprit monarchique* of which so many French writers have spoken.

[1] See Bettinelli's Epistle on Vesuvius. (Note in the *London Magazine*.)
[2] This was the spirit of the entire reign of Louis XIV. cf. Saint Simon. (Note in the *London Magazine*.)

A Frenchman who is bold enough to ignore the monarchical spirit, that is the imitation of the models laid down for the class of society in which chance has placed him, immediately becomes ludicrous. Hence the pre-eminence of comedy and satire in France; hence too the remarkable pre-eminence in Italian poetry of a simple expression of profound passion, passion whose every shade and fluctuation an Italian will find in his own heart. It is from this that the distinctive character of Italian poetry is derived and to this that *La Bassvilliana*, a poem entirely made up of profound passion in all its shades and varieties, owes its immense popularity. As a faithful historian of Italian poetry, I should have added that, long ago, Alfonso Varano, a poet of nobility, imitated Dante nearly as closely as Monti has since.

I need only give you a brief outline of *La Bassvilliana* to show both how Roman and how Italian the poem is in its conception.

Lucifer abandons the body of Bassville as soon as he loses all hope of carrying it off to hell. The guardian angel of Bassville, specially entrusted to do so by the Deity, has repelled all his attacks. The astonished soul of Bassville then turns to look at the body from which it has just been driven:

> E la mortal prigione, ond 'era uscita
> Subito indietro a riguardar si volse,
> Tutta ancor sospettosa e sbigottita.[1]

What is strange and revolting in the fable is forgotten in the beauty of lines such as these, admirable as they are for their naturalness and simplicity. The guardian angel speaks to the soul of Bassville: 'Fear not, you will not be damned; but you will not enjoy the immediate presence of God, until the crimes of France have been punished. Until then, your torment will be to witness the deeds of your infamous country and the

---

[1] Suddenly she turned and looked at the mortal prison from which she had emerged, still uncertain and bewildered.

innumerable crimes to which you, during your own lifetime, have contributed.' After this speech, the angel leads the soul to France where it is obliged to look on at all the enormities of 1793.

You will agree that it is impossible to imagine a poem more deeply imbued, in its general design, with the spirit of Papacy, that evil genius which has extracted from the Gospels a religion of its own and whose ambition has been throughout the centuries to convert the Italian people into a nation of scoundrels. The proof of this is before our eyes. The poet confesses that Bassville was assassinated by the Roman populace and the following words are used by Bassville himself as he addresses his own body before leaving Rome and witnessing the atrocities in Paris:

> Oltre il rogo non vive ira nemica,
> E nell 'ospite suolo, ove io ti lasso,
> Giuste son l'alme, e la pietade è antica.[1]
> Canto I

There is no need for me to point out to you the base flattery to which Monti descends in thus attributing to Bassville an eulogy of the populace by which he has just been murdered. Monti, when he was writing this, was in love, and, having very undeservedly acquired the reputation of a *philosophe*, he was afraid lest he should be exiled from Rome. All his life he has been on opposite sides. Some time after the publication of the *Bassvilliana*, he wrote a magnificent ode to celebrate the execution of Louis XVI. Nevertheless, strange though it may appear, he has never been the object of the contempt which Southey has known in England or Baour and Chazet in France. The public has realised that Monti always writes

---

[1] The enemy's anger does not live beyond the scaffold and in the hospitable soil in which I leave you the souls are just and the piety ancient.

under the influence of passion, whether it be love or fear, and never from the dictates of calculation, never from a mere desire to make money or to have his poems read by a rich aristocracy; Monti's poetry gives so genuine and heartfelt a delight to Italian readers that they cannot bring themselves to despise, or class with the renegades of London and Paris, the man to whom they are indebted for such enjoyment.

I am obliged to leave out a great deal that I feel I ought to say about the *Bassvilliana*, a poem which, in any case, I imagine, is well known in London. I shall confine myself at present to one remark. It is regrettable that, having chosen to found his poem on the religion of Saint Dominic, Monti should not have adhered to his original plan and made the soul of Bassville a spectator of all that took place in France from 1793 to 1816. This surely is a truly magnificent subject for poetry and, in his *Mascheroniana*, Monti has in fact narrated the events of one year in the life of Bonaparte, from his return from Egypt to the Battle of Marengo.

As I wish to give you an accurate idea of the present state of Italian poetry and in so doing, imitate however humbly, the descendant of Grimm,[1] I should stress one particular fact which I have already mentioned in passing. The Jesuits have for centuries persecuted the works of Dante. This persecution, though never open, has been so bitter and inveterate, that thirty years ago Lombardi, one of Dante's most able commentators, dared not acknowledge his own commentary in print. The Jesuit, Bettinelli, together with a number of talented but soulless writers, such as Pignotti, Algarotti and many others, tried to inoculate Italy with the poetry of Pope and Voltaire. *La Bassvilliana*, though its general purport is atrocious, being a sustained apology for murder, supremely catholic and

---

[1] A reference to the 'Letters from Paris by Grimm's grandson' published in the *London Magazine* and written by Stendhal himself. (*Editor.*)

servile in its devotion to the ferocious religion of Saint Dominic, has nevertheless revived the taste for Dante.

This great poet, the only modern who has anything in common with Shakespeare, has gone through more editions within the last thirty years than in five centuries before. He has turned the minds of the Italian people towards Protestantism, that is to say towards self-examination in matters of religion. It is a singular fact that this impulse should have been encouraged by the Austrian Government which seems to be still inspired by the principles of Joseph II. It maintains schools of theology at Pavia and Padua whose tendency is to foster self-examination and it selects its bishops from among priests who, like the Bishop of Padua, Monsigneur Farina, have quarrelled with the Court of Rome. The various religious opinions taught at Pavia are known in Italy under the name of Jansenism, a doctrine which Leo XII intends to overthrow through the agency of the Society of Jesus to which he gives every encouragement. These so-called Jansenists have their great work of theology in the *Vera Idea della santa fede* written by an energetic priest and professor, Father Tamburini, and recently translated into French. I have met Father Tamburini. He is an old man of eighty, full of fire and energy. He has written forty octavo volumes criticising the pretended infallibility of the Pope. He used the following argument in my presence. 'Pope Clement XIV, who was afterwards poisoned by the Jesuits, suppressed the Jesuit order on account of their atrocious crimes. He was infallible. Pius VII has restored them; he too was infallible. Nevertheless, one of these two Popes must have been fallible. Therefore, *habemus confidentum reum*, the doctrine of infallibility is absurd. I defy the Papists to reply to this argument.'

I hope, however, to return to my main theme, that I have clearly shown how it was that the appearance of the *Bassvilliana* caused such a revolution in Italian literature; also, how the most *ultra* and sanguinary poem that was ever written, an apology for murder, could indirectly have turned men's minds towards self-examination in matters of religion and thence towards Protestantism and humanity. The more eminent Italians do not publish. It is a sure means of drawing down upon themselves the persecution of the Jesuits and that of five out of the six despotic governments whose sole object seems to be to degrade the noble souls with whom Providence has chosen to people that beautiful country. If you publish, you are sure to be persecuted by the government of the King of Sardinia, by the Austrian government, by the petty tyranny of the Duke of Modena and by the Papal government under its senile, eighty-two-year-old guide, Cardinal Della Somaglia, who is himself the instrument of Father Fortis, the General of the Society of Jesus. Lastly there is the government of Naples. Only the Grand Duke of Tuscany has till now been kept within the bounds of good sense by his clever wife and by his minister Fossombroni, the well-known mathematician.

As thinking men who prefer tranquillity to popular applause do not publish, the field is left open to pedantry. The Florentines are the least given to thought, the least enthusiastic and the most pedantic among the peoples of Italy. They have laid it down as a general rule, first of all, that they are the only people in Italy who can write; secondly, that the long, obscure sentence which Boccaccio borrowed from Cicero is the only true Italian construction, and thirdly, that any sentence in which an effort has been made to introduce the clarity of French is not Italian. These principles have been adopted by a pedant of the name of Botta, who, in 1815, published in Paris a history of the United States of America, followed, in 1824, by a history of Italy over the last thirty years. The former is curious for the absurdity of its style and the latter for its innumerable lies, told for the base purpose of flattering Austria and discrediting Bonaparte, the regenerator of Italy.[1]

The Florentine conceptions of good Italian have found an antagonist in Monti, who, old and heart-broken at seeing the evil genius reign paramount in Italy, has ceased to write poetry. He has published five octavo volumes entitled *Proposta di Emendazioni al Vocabulario della Crusca*. Although Monti knows very little about grammar in general and scarcely understands at all the arguments of the school of Condillac, he has the soul of a great poet and judges the appropriateness of certain words in certain styles of writing with an admirable tact. I recommend everyone who understands Italian to read Monti's book. It has reminded me of the French line:

Même quand l'oiseau marche on sent qu'il a des ailes.[2]

To these dry grammatical controversies, envenomed as they are by all the fury of Italian pedantry, Monti succeeds in communicating a certain grace and charm. This is no mean achievement, for, in their discussion of literature, Italians still display the urbanity of the fourteenth century, referring to one another politely as 'ass' and 'animal'. Such incidental questions, however, as whether one should write exactly as men wrote in fifteenth-century Florence, or whether some allowance should be made for the French clarity and simplicity of construction, have frozen up the stream of Italian song.

Every true-hearted Italian, furthermore, is engrossed by politics and by Carbonarism. In many parts of the country, the magistrates, whose function is to persecute the Carbonari, their gaolers and the soldiers sent out to arrest them, are all

---

[1] In the French version of this article in the *Revue Britannique*, there is a footnote to these remarks in which the *Revue* finds 'une étrange légèreté' and 'une brutalité qui n'est pas de bon goût; les critiques français ont été moins sévères et plus justes envers les estimables ouvrages de M. Ch. Botta' ('a strange flippancy' and 'a brutality which is not in good taste; the French critics have been less severe and more just in their treatment of the estimable works of M. Charles Botta').

[2] Even when he walks, one feels the bird has wings.

Carbonari themselves. It is clear that subjects of interest such as these must necessarily throw poetry into the background. People may perhaps go on reading, but they no longer write. Literature is thus abandoned by the more generous hearted to the pedants, or to men who are mediocre enough not to excite the suspicions or alarm of established government. Everywhere the more distinguished minds are disheartened. 'Italy will one day be free', they say, 'but when? In 1880 perhaps.' With this thought in their minds, they retire to the country and cultivate their estates.

The great poetical revolution brought about by the immense success of the *Bassvilliana* has made Italians adore once more the works of Dante. It has not inspired any masterpieces, however. After 1796, Bonaparte engaged the attention of Italy, though, if other governments had acted with the moderation of the Grand Duke of Tuscany, she would probably have fallen asleep once more after 1814. The country, as it is, is kept awake by the persecution of Carbonarism, an institution which is as feeble as it is innocent. The total dearth of literary creation is a terrible portent for the various tyrannies and the Jesuits by whom a beautiful country is oppressed (every government is Jesuitical except the Austrian). It is a proof that the mind of every Italian of deep and earnest sensibility is fixed upon politics. Italy teems with men of talent, genius and intelligence. The reason for this is obvious. In France there is only Paris—every provincial writer seems ridiculous. Lyon, Nantes, Marseilles and Bordeaux, towns of a hundred thousand inhabitants, do not possess a single poet or prose writer of genius. In Italy, on the other hand, Bologna laughs at the literary fashions of her neighbour Florence, while Milan annuls the literary decrees pronounced in Turin or Venice. This situation, which dates from the time of the mediaeval republics, makes Italy a country which cannot fail to interest and intrigue every lover of literature. Another characteristic of her literature is that Italian writers, except for a few of the lowest order, are never mere imitators of the French. If anything today they are more inclined to take as their model Lord Byron. In Rome I found a number of poems by that illustrious writer translated and in great demand.

In this letter I have tried to give you some idea of the state of Italian literature during the period of the Congress of Milan in the year 1825. The length of what I have already written, however, compels me to postpone until another occasion the remarks I wish to make concerning the unfortunate Italian language, which is in reality a compound of ten different languages. Buratti and Tomasso Grossi, the two greatest Italian poets after Monti, do not, for instance, write in the Italian of Florence and Rome, the Italian, that is, of *La Bassvilliana* and *la Gerusalemme*.

Adieu and believe me. . . .

C.D.
London Magazine, December 1825

ADOLPHE AND BENJAMIN CONSTANT

Have you ever read M. Benjamin Constant's novel, *Adolphe*? He has just published another edition of it. Adolphe is a man of brilliant talents, who is totally lacking in vigour and firmness of character. He possesses therefore the precise qualities which are required to please French society. He is entangled with a woman with whom he has had the weakness to run away. The whole novel is nothing but a declaration of hatred. Adolphe tries to make this poor creature understand that he no longer loves her, and that they must part. There is a great deal of affectation in this book, but, finally, it does *say* something, well or badly, and this distinguishes it from most other modern books. It is said in society that M. Benjamin Constant has depicted himself. As a young man, he was famous for his bravery and for his talents; he possesses in fact so acute and lively a mind, that he is able to see the reasons for every line of conduct that it is possible to pursue. This sort of infirmity is very common in France. As vanity has taken the place of every other passion, the humiliation lies, not in changing one's opinion, but in being unable to defend the opinion one has adopted by means of brilliant shafts of wit which silence one's adversary and, above all, which amuse the whole circle around one in the *salon*. I cannot here refrain from adding that the conduct of M. Constant in 1815 and his attitude to Napoleon seem to me perfectly free from blame. This extremely clever man is poor, and people of the upper classes, who are rich, censured him for accepting a place and an income of twenty-five thousand francs from Napoleon. These same people crowd to the receptions given by Mme de Cayla, who agreed to accept an infamous and disgusting position; but then it was for a million a year. It is these people as well whose opinions and judgments of literature I am obliged to report for your information. Sometimes my contempt for the judges leads me to despise their sentences; but this, I realise, will never do. An attempt has recently been made to *puff* a novel called *Charles*, written in imitation of the *Nouvelle Héloïse* and of Mme de Staël's *Delphine*. The author tries to present the intense in passion, but never rises above the moderate. He has never felt deeply enough. He has never felt that all the goods and all the joys of life are as nothing to him beside his mistress. He expresses too much surprise at those tiny preferences which are a matter of course to a true lover, so deeply and so constantly has he felt them. If the author had been a man of acute sensibility, everything would have been forgiven him, even his ignorance of the language. Instead of looking up the established French terms for a given shade of sentiment in Pascal, Rousseau or Montesquieu, the author of *Charles* will invent a word or a trope. This is a constant practice among our young authors. It is true that, when they indulge their vanity in the creation of some new word, we usually guess what it is they mean. We fail, however, to perceive clearly the full implications of their thought, and, without clarity, there can no more be good French than a good description of the passions. We are unlike the Germans in this; the more difficult and obscure a subject is, the more clarity we demand in its expression. Voltaire is the representative French genius, above all on account of his clarity. This is also the reason for which his complete works, though they are twice as voluminous as Rousseau's, are sold so much more rapidly.

London Magazine, October 1825

SECOND LETTER ON THE PRESENT STATE OF ITALIAN LITERATURE[1]

Rome, November 12th, 1826

The most striking difference between Italian and French literature lies in the sincerity and singleness of purpose which characterise the former. An Italian writer, it is true, will tell

[1] A footnote appended to the version of this article which appeared in the *Revue Britannique*, while pointing out that it contains 'des particularités curieuses et fort peu connues', disclaims any responsibility for the opinions expressed.

all the lies necessary to avoid persecution as a Carbonarist; but, apart from what the punctilious tyranny of five royal courts obliges them to write, Italian writers will say nothing which they do not actually believe. Here, if a man knows anything, he knows it profoundly and thoroughly. Woe to you, therefore, if you ask him a question. You may wish for an answer that will take two or three minutes, but he will give you a discourse lasting an hour and a half. It never occurs to him that a reply which you have yourself provoked can appear to you too long or too minute. The principal characteristic of his writings is earnestness and sincerity. He is in no way a charlatan—he lacks the talents and also perhaps the predilections which qualify a man for that sort of trade. In Paris, it may be reliably affirmed that there are not more than four men, if as many as that, among those who seek a reputation in literature or science, who are not charlatans at heart. Whenever you see the name of a French author mentioned in a journal, you may safely assume, if he is extolled to the skies, that the article is his own. Such a situation is unknown in Italy. Severio Bettinelli, the enemy of Dante, whom I mentioned in my last letter, and the poet Foscolo, author of *I Sepolcri*, are the only writers mentioned as having made use of such doubtful methods.

The virtue of Italian writers has one very strong defence. In London or Paris an author writes to make money; your illustrious Johnson and your charming Goldsmith lived on the money they received from their booksellers. The case is very different in Italy. I have heard the great Monti declare that the printing of his works has never brought him anything but expense; a fortnight after his book was printed in Milan, it would be reprinted at Lugano, Bassano and Florence. Very often, the bookseller who published the original edition was the very one to sell the least number of copies. One of the

Italian delegates at the Congress of Vienna asked the assembled kings if they would insert an article in their treaty prohibiting these piracies. The Emperor Francis, however, refused to afford any such encouragement to the progress of letters. This was perfectly consistent with what he said to the Professors of the College of Laybach: 'Ich brauche keine Gelehrten' ('I need no scholars'). The Emperor Francis, like all the princes of the House of Austria, is remarkably well informed on statistical subjects; but, as far as politics in their association with morals are concerned, he seems incapable of understanding a thing. By thus withholding from literary merits or labours any hope of pecuniary reward, he has rendered, however, one peculiar service to Italian literature. He has excluded from it the *canaille* of scribblers who pollute and debase the literature of France and England. The five despotic governments of Italy, those of Turin, Milan, Modena, Rome and Naples, are supported only by the writers whom they enrich by entrusting them with the publication of the Gazette.

As political curiosity is intense, and as all newspapers which are not sold to the Jesuits are prohibited, the Government Journal is in great demand. Its stupidity, however, surpasses anything you can imagine in England. In Venice, such is the fear inspired by the government, that people carefully avoid seeming to read the Milan gazette with any interest, even though it is written by a man who has sold himself more completely to Austria than the editor of the Venetian newspaper. In Paris, on the other hand, at least such was the case ten years ago, the reigning ministry could always, at twenty-four hours notice, call upon two hundred writers who live entirely by their pen. These are men, furthermore, of no mean talent; they are, it is true, completely unprincipled, but this slight defect, which they share with the diplomatic servants of the public, only makes them the more dexterous in guarding and weighing their thoughts. As they know that, in a year's time, the minister will probably order them to prove the exact opposite of what they are now demonstrating, they become admirably skilled in the art of leaving loop-holes. Thus we find that some of the most distinguished French writers, Fiévée, Chateaubriand and Martainville, for example, have said and unsaid the same thing ten times over in the course of their lives. Two years ago, M. Fiévée received a pension of eighty pounds a year on condition that he held his tongue. When I relate these facts to Italian men of letters, they laugh, exclaim, 'Sempre faceto', and refuse to believe a word I say. It would be difficult to ensure the publication of a laudatory article in any but a government newspaper; and these, among a people with the integrity of the Italians, are looked upon with the most profound contempt. In Paris, on the other hand, you would have to be without friends or connections not to have your book praised in all the newspapers.

I would not have mentioned the Italian political press, edited in general by spies in the pay of the police, were it not in order to do justice to the journal published in Rome by a printer called Cracas. It appears three times a week under two separate titles, the *Diario* and the *Notizie del Giorno*. The Court of Rome is still the most skilful politically in Italy, despite the presence at the head of the government of Cardinal Della Somaglia, whose mind is enfeebled by extreme old age. It refrains noticeably from indulging in any absurdity or falsehood which does not serve some immediate end. The obituary notices published by Cracas are necessarily, in a state governed by old men, a regular feature of his two newspapers. They are distinguished by a general air of truth, due allowance being made for his habit of using the most ridiculous superlatives. The *Cracas*, for the name of the printer has been given to the newspaper, also contains articles on archeology, this being a subject of deep general interest in Italy. They are certainly the best of their kind in Europe.

The finest journal in Italy is, beyond any doubt, the *Antologia*, published in Florence by a bookseller named Vieusseux, who is himself a man of considerable intelligence. His journal, however, is not to be thought of as a garland of flowers; it is, on the contrary, verbose, laborious and often tedious. He is always commending books which lack both merit and intelligence, for he is completely deferential to the learned pedants who abound in Italy. Notwithstanding all this, the *Antologia* is an extremely useful publication.

An Italian generally fails to understand hints and *demi-mots*. He reads little—he finds it laborious, and you can never be too clear or explicit for his taste. The pungency of the allusions and innuendoes which constitute the charm of La Bruyére, Voltaire and Montesquieu, would appear to him obscure and unintelligible. Ariosto, it is true, possessed something of this very same charm, but he was a poet and lived two hundred years ago. There is nothing in the least akin to French wit in the *Antologia*, but this defect is compensated by great good faith. I am certain that any author who were to ask M. Vieusseux to insert an article in praise of a bad or insignificant work would have an unpleasant reception, if his motives were merely personal. Many contributors to the *Antologia* are men of first-rate merit. What is needed is an editor, possessed of full discretionary powers, who, without suppressing a single idea, would be able to cut down articles to three-quarters of their present length. As it is, the thoughts are dispersed and lost among an ocean of words.

The *Raccoglitore*, a literary review, is published three times a month in Milan and enjoys a wide sale as far south as Naples. It is edited by David Bertolotti. If he had been a man of greater earnestness and resolution, his modest enterprise would probably have shared the fate of the *Conciliatore*. This journal lived for about a year, and during this period—it was round about 1819—it numbered among its supporters the most distinguished men in Milan, eminent alike for their talents, probity, knowledge and generous devotion to the cause of Italy and of mankind. It was morally very earnest and feared as a result by all those who depend for their status and existence on the ignorance and delusions of the people. The *Conciliatore* was too serious and too rigorous in its mode of reasoning to be of direct service to the cause of Lombardy. It excited interest only among the watchful speculators on public events to be found in other parts of Europe. It published articles by Italy's two most eminent philosophers, Melchiore Gioja and ll marchese Ermes Visconti. The former has suffered the fate of nearly all the writers in this journal and is now in prison. It was too patriotic not to offend against the system of moral *status quo* which Metternich has been endeavouring to establish in Italy for the past eleven years. Prince Metternich has too much sense to attempt in any way to stupefy the people, as the Jesuits seek to in Turin and Modena; but anyone who attempts to enlighten them he throws into prison. Pellico, one of the best tragic poets in Italy, who is now in the fortress of Spielburg, was among the contributors to the *Giornale Blu*, as the *Conciliatore* was called, on account of the blue paper on which it was printed.

La Biblioteca Italiana, a journal which comes out once a month from the government press, has as its principal editor Signor Acerbi, who is commonly held to be a government spy. It is looked on with great contempt throughout Italy, though it is of service to the Milanese and Venetians who can get no other. Occasionally it contains very good articles on medicine and natural history.

L'Italiano continues, I believe, to be published in Turin.[1] Its purpose is to effect a change in the *status quo* of the public mind in Italy, but in the opposite way from that in which the *Conciliatore* sought to. It seeks to stupefy and mislead the people and to revive the opinions which prevailed in Italy round about the year 1650 and which were current in the rest of Europe more than a hundred years before. There is one major fact of which we must never lose sight when we discuss the affairs of Italy: ever since the taking of Florence by the Medici in 1530, despotism has done everything in its power to enfeeble and degrade the noble minds of her people. The Jesuits are even more absolute in Turin than in Paris and if the governments of Philip II and Philip III had succeeded in what they set out to do, they would have kept the inhabitants of Milan in the same state of intellectual degradation in which Napoleon found the Spaniards in 1808. I speak here of course of the masses; nobody has a more profound and sincere respect than myself for those illustrious Spaniards who are now in London. But they themselves, if their patriotism will allow them to be sincere, will admit that the gulf between the educcated and the uneducated classes in Spain is immense. In Spain this distance is at its maximum; in France at its minimum; in Italy, thanks to all that was done to deaden the minds of the people between 1530 and 1796, when the exploits of Bonaparte awoke them from their lethargy, the distance is very considerable. Not only did Italy make no progress during these two hundred and sixty years; she would find it positively to her advantage if she could revert to what she was in 1530, before the restoration of the infamous Medici. Before this date, she possessed an energy which she has now altogether lost; she was incapable of the puerility for which most of the

[1] It seems that this journal ceased publication in fact several years ago. (Note in the *London Magazine*.)

activities of the Carbonari have been remarkable. The principal occupation of the nation before 1796 was to write sonnets in imitation of Petrarch, in imitation, that is, of his defects. The poet would adopt the Platonic philosophy by which his poetry is obscured. He would fail, however, to catch the strain of genuine and deep pathos by which it is so often pervaded. Nothing today remains of sixty literary academies, famous for the singularity of their names, among them *gli Infuocati* and *gli Oziosi*, but a literary review published in Rome called *L'Arcadico*. Its main distinction perhaps is that of being the most inane publication in Europe. Apart from those I have so far mentioned, there are three or four other journals of merit in Italy, which specialise in natural history and medicine. The Italians are said to be pre-eminent in the latter, though there is a great deal of quackery in their medical practice. In Naples, I heard a great deal about the ingenious systems of Dr Rasori of Piacenza. This very distinguished physician has been in prison in Mantua for three years on a charge of conspiring against the Austrian government. I have also heard very favourable reports of the medical annals of Dr Omodei of Venice, of the journal published by Dr Configliacchi, and of several other periodicals of the same kind.

L'Ape (*The Bee*) a little journal which still, I believe, appears in Milan is much more French than Italian in character. It is owned by a bookseller in Brescia named Bettoni, a man of some talent and great enterprise, who publishes everything, whether it be good, bad or indifferent.

I have noticed that three-quarters of the books bought by the more intelligent readers in Naples are published in Milan. This appears to me astonishing. The Austrian censorship in this city is terrible and all the more sharp-sighted for being in the hands of Italian renegades, generally priests, who have sold themselves to the Austrian police. In Florence, on the other hand, there is an almost total liberty of the press; in spite of which, apart from new editions of Dante, Petrarch, Boccaccio, Ariosto, Tasso and Alfieri, the booksellers publish nothing but puerile trash. Florence has lost all her energy. The system of espionage which was brought to perfection under the Grand Duke Leopold has effectively crushed it out of existence. The Florentines are very frugal, have few wants, and consider themselves supremely happy when they are not assailed by misfortune. Their character, taken in the mass, is that of a prudent man of fifty-five. Milan, on the other hand, during an inoculation of fifteen years, has developed a considerable degree of French civilisation.

After two hundred and sixty years of a government whose sole object seems to have been to pervert and deaden the intellect of the governed, you will not expect to hear that the moral and political sciences are in a very advanced condition. Giambattista Vico, a Neapolitan philosopher, would have been known throughout Europe if destiny had chosen Rotterdam as his birthplace or even Paris under Louis XIV. Born in Naples at the beginning of the seventeenth century,[1] he produced *La Scienza Nuova*, a book which is scarcely intelligible. The excellent historian Giannone, who was also a Neapolitan, died in 1748 in the citadel of Turin into which he had been thrown by the King of Sardinia, as a favour to his royal brother of Naples. These two examples will enable you to judge the rest. Nevertheless, it was during this period of history that Ariosto, Tasso, Metastasio, Goldoni and Alfieri made the name of Italy glorious. In painting, the school of Bologna combined the expressiveness of Raphael with the colour of Titian and the grace of Correggio. In music, an art which has almost entirely escaped the minute persecution of the Jesuits, Italy produced Leo, Durante, Pergolesi, Sacchini

---

[1] Vico was born in 1668. (*Editor's note*.)

and Cimarosa, to mention only a few.

You will have probably read the History of Italian Literature written by that most Jesuitical of all Jesuits, Tiraboschi, which has been abridged in French and interspersed with liberal, but for the most part anti-poetical, ideas by Ginguené, a philosopher of the Voltairean school. I shall therefore pass over all those works that appeared before 1770, since their merits have been discussed and defined in Ginguené's History and in the *Littérature du midi de l'Europe* by the learned Sismondi. Ginguené, out of a kind of infatuation with Italian literature, which he mistakenly thought that he understood, proclaimed as excellent a thousand poets and prose writers who are today despised by their own countrymen. Apart from a very small number of well-known works, there is almost nothing worthy of attention which appeared during the two hundred and sixty years corrupted and darkened by the Jesuits.

The most outstanding of Italy's living poets are Monti, who, like Milton, is blind; Foscolo, author of *I Sepolcri*, who lives in London; Giambattista Niccolini, a tragic poet, born about the year 1790 and now resident in Florence where he sometimes contributes to *l'Antologia*; Silvio Pellico, the author of *Francesca da Rimini* and *Eufemio da Messina*, who is a prisoner in the fortress of Spielburg and whose age is, I believe, about thirty-four; and Alessandro Manzoni, who was born in Milan round about 1780. Manzoni has written some magnificent hymns and two tragedies in which the unities are disregarded, *Il Conte di Carmagnola* and *Adelchi*.

Tomasso Grossi writes in the dialect of Milan, Buratti in the dialect of Venice. Twenty years ago Father Meli wrote in Sicilian. Your own countrymen, who at that time governed Sicily, probably made you familiar with the works of this extraordinary genius, the only modern poet, in my opinion, who can be compared with Anacreon.

In Naples I came across the latest English travel books on Italy. They all struck me as mawkish and frivolous, while a number of them seemed to me mere falsehood and cant. Pre-eminent among these was the account written by a priest named Eustace on his travels in Italy. This book poisons the minds of three-quarters of the English visitors who come to Naples and closes their eyes to the physical and moral beauties, I repeat, sir, moral beauties, of this country. These beauties are not, it is true, the same as those to be found in Portland Place or the West India Docks, but why do people travel at all if they do not wish to see anything new or strange? There is only one man of sense in England who has written about Italy. That is Joseph Forsyth. My opinion has often differed from his, but the more I know of this country, the more frequently do I abandon my own preconceptions and come round to Forsyth's point of view.

Lady Morgan, whose books, for some reason which I fail to understand, have been highly commended in England, is about as good a judge, as far as the fine arts are concerned, as a Scottish Presbyterian minister. It so happens, however, that, ever since the tyranny of Philip II, Italy has been without life, motion or voice in everything except painting, music and literature. Lady Morgan fails even to perceive one of the most conspicuous features of Italian literature today: the unfortunate writer finds himself in a new and strange predicament; his own language is failing him and dying by inches beneath him.

The Italian with which you are familiar, the Italian of Ariosto and Alfieri, is spoken in Florence, Rome and Siena. These are the only cities in Italy which have the same authority, in matters of language, as London, Paris, Dresden or Madrid. Now, however, we come to the circumstance which is so dire in its consequences for Italian literature. Let us suppose that the first city you reach, after crossing the frontier, is Turin; you find your way into society and here, to your great astonishment and mortification, you find that your perfect knowledge of Italian avails you nothing. It is only here and there that you catch a word which has some distant resemblance to the language of Goldoni and Metastasio. Everybody in Turin speaks Piedmontese. Italian, it is true, is the written language, but, at the receptions given by the beautiful Contessa R——, a man would make himself ridiculous if he attempted to speak it. It is a language that the Piedmontese only ever speak out of courtesy to some foreigner who has been recommended to them. To speak it makes them feel constrained. They are much given to irony and sarcasm and to a somewhat bitter, sardonic laughter. They find it impossible, however, to joke in Italian. Having left Turin, you go south to Genoa. Here you hear nothing but Genoese and are even worse off than in Turin, for the language is even more unintelligible than Piedmontese. It took me three months of hard work to understand it, and yet, as you will know, in the absence of better qualities, Nature has given me a great facility in the learning of languages. I will offer a single example of Genoese, or Zenese, for Genoa is called Zena in its own dialect: the three Italian words *vostra signoria sa* (you know sir) are reduced to *sha sa*, the word *sha* alone standing for *vostra signoria*. You leave Genoa, however, which is only thirty leagues from Turin and make your way to Milan, which is again thirty leagues from each of these two cities. Here you encounter the language of *Minga*, that is to say the language in which *nothing at all* is translated by *minga*. It is a language which has no resemblance with either Piedmontese or Genoese. Tomasso Grossi, a very poor young lawyer, whom I consider to be perhaps the finest living Italian poet, writes in this dialect, and his admirable poem *El Di d'Incoeu*[1] is confined, as a result, to a public of some six hundred thousand. At Brescia a dialect is spoken which is at the same time very similar to Venetian and Veronese. Venetian is altogether delightful; in spirit and vivacity, it is like French, while the Venetians themselves are perfectly aware of the advantages they enjoy. Wit to them is a faculty which enables a man to amuse or charm his listeners and, unless they are bankrupt or have the spleen or are puritans, to offer them five minutes of perfect happiness. Their city, which in 1797 counted a hundred thousand inhabitants, has an impoverished population today of only forty thousand. In spite of this, the Venetians have a supreme contempt for the pedants, incapable of either passion or ideas, who inhabit Siena and the native city of Dante, which was once, however, so fertile in great men. The dialects of Bologna, Naples and Sicily differ as widely from the Italian of Florence and Rome as do Genoese and Venetian. In the city of Naples alone, which contains 330,000 gesticulators, even I, as a foreigner, was able to distinguish and acquire three languages. The inhabitants of Pizzo-Falcone, for example, do not speak at all in the same way as those of the Ponte della Maddalena.

My own opinion is that the dialects of Genoa, Milan and Naples are anterior to Latin. That of Milan, according to my theory, goes back at least to the year 600 B.C., when the Gauls invaded the country lying between the Tessino, the Po and the Alps. It was then that Milan was converted under Bellovesus from a small town to a city. It was not completely brought under the Roman sway until 191 B.C. when it was conquered by Scipio Nasica. In 452 A.D., Milan was taken by Attila and

---

[1] The subject of this poem is the assassination of Count Prina, a minister under Napoleon, who was killed in a riot in Milan on April 21st, 1814. The riot, it is said, was provoked by Austrian agents. At least, *sic fama narrat*. (Note in the *London Magazine*.)

occupied subsequently by Odoacre, Theodoric and Uraja. It was therefore in Roman hands for only 643 years.

In the twelfth century, Florence, which carried on an enormous trade, was the virtual capital of Italy. She occupied in Europe the place which, as a result of its insular position and the wisdom of its inhabitants, England holds today. At the same time she was the metropolis of letters and of intellect, an advantage she owed to her highly developed civic freedom and the good fortune of being the birth-place of Dante, the father of the Italian language, as well as of Petrarch, Boccaccio, Poliziano, Michelangelo, Da Vinci and Lorenzo di Medici. Arthur Roscoe's recent portrayal of the latter, incidentally, I find ridiculously inappropriate, mainly because he has attempted to give everything a modern colouring. Lorenzo di Medici bore very little resemblance to the *composition* which his modern biographer has created; he was, nevertheless, one of the greatest sovereigns that the world has ever known.

In 1339, absolute monarchy was established in Milan by Lucchino Visconti, who was equally outstanding for his wit and his villainy. His successors were several times on the point of becoming masters of the entire peninsula. Had they succeeded, the Milanese dialect would, in all probability, have assumed the position now held by Florentine, this despite the genius of Dante. The latter, which it is impossible to speak quickly, would have been replaced by a language which is given to rapid utterance.

Today, in 1825, Florentine or Tuscan can be compared to a young Turkish prince who has not yet succeeded in putting all his brothers to death, and, as a result, feels insecure upon his throne. Hence its insufficient clarity. If you are speaking of the most commonplace physical object, a sieve for example, its name in Milanese, Venetian, Genoese or Neapolitan immediately comes to the mind of any inhabitant of one of these cities with whom you happen to be speaking. In the same way, he is obliged to make a slight effort in order to recall the Florentine word that he wishes to use. Consider what it must be like then with the words which convey the movements and inflections of passion, the words, for example, which are to express the first jealous uneasiness in the heart of a young husband when he sees the same partner at a ball dancing all evening with his wife.

To express feelings of this kind, and they constitute the proper material of poetry, the Venetian, the Neapolitan or the Genoese fail, three times out of four, to remember the appropriate Tuscan word. Their inspiration vanishes while they are looking it up in the dictionary. We arrive thus at the following conclusion, a depressing one as far as Italian literature is concerned: the Florentine language, the language, that is, which forms the basis of the *Dizionario della Crusca*, is a dead language in Turin, Genoa, Milan, Parma, Piacenza, Verona, Venice, Ferrara, Bologna, Naples and the whole of Sicily. It is true that, in all these cities, the newspapers and advertisements of every kind are printed in a so-called Italian. But the pedants of Tuscany are perfectly correct when they point out that this is not in fact Italian at all. It is the *patois* of the region translated into Italian, with the aid of a dictionary and, as schoolboys say, 'word for word'. The words are individually translated, but not the expressions; these retain their Piedmontese, Venetian or Neapolitan character. You may not believe the following anecdote, but, when I was in Livorno, a wealthy and cultured citizen of the city of Lucca said, in my hearing, to a Florentine of his own class, 'Our government is so bigoted that it compels us to close our boxes (*logge*) in the theatre, on the eve of certain saints' days'. The Florentine at first failed to understand the meaning of the word *logge* and took it to mean *shops*. Yet Lucca and Florence are only fifty miles apart. This is typical of the state of the language in the peninsula as a whole.

You will, I think, agree that a man can be a poet only in the language in which he talks to his mistress and to his rivals. Tuscan is necessarily a dead language to everyone who was not born in Rome, Florence or Siena.[1] Hence the sustained and unrelenting emphasis and the lengthiness of the poems written in Tuscan, in those parts of Italy where it is not spoken.

Unfortunately, the least poetical people in Italy at the moment are the inhabitants of Florence and Siena. It is in Bologna, Reggio and Venice that you will find the true poetic tone or, if you prefer, the incipient madness of the poet.

What conclusions are to be drawn from these various observations? Firstly, I think, that the greatest living poets are Tomasso Grossi, who writes in the dialect of Milan, and Pietro Buratti, whose exquisite satires are written in Venetian. Everyone admires the Tuscan verses of Niccolini (see his tragedy *Nabucco*, which is a continual allusion to Napoleon). Nobody, however, reads them. What, after all, could be more tedious and uninspired than a parallel, drawn through five mortal acts, between Napoleon and Nebuchadnezzar? Such an achievement might have been considered as admirably skilful in 1650, but not today.

A comedy has just been written, however, in Genoa, from which the letter R is throughout excluded. Hearing of such

[1] There are, nevertheless, a number of facts which contradict our ingenious correspondent's theory: Ariosto was born in Ferrara, Bernardo Tasso in Bergamo, Torquato Tasso in Sorrento, Sannazaro and Constanzo in Naples, Tassoni in Modena, Maggi in Milan, Guidi in Pavia, Guarini in Ferrara, Ugoni in Genoa, Metastasio in Assisi, Chiabrera in Savona, Alfieri in Asti in Piedmont, Parini in Milan, Pindemote in Verona, Fortiguerra in Pistoia, Monti in Fusignano, Ugo Foscolo in Venice, Silvio Pellico in Turin and Manzoni in Milan.

Assisi and Fusignano are, it is true, in the Roman states, but neither Metastasio nor Monti was educated in Rome; while Fortiguerra, the only Tuscan on the list, was brought up in Pavia. None of these therefore ought to be poets, if we are to go by the definition given above. The dialects of the regions in which they were born are more or less the same today as they were during the lifetime of the oldest among them. (Note in the *London Magazine*.)

puerilities, one wonders indeed whether the happy age of the seventeenth century is not about to return, to the greater glory of the Jesuits.

I have just heard that Tomasso Grossi, whom I had thought of as a man of authentic genius, is seriously engaged in writing a poem in the Italian of Tuscany. It will be no better than his *Ildegonde*.

Vale et me ama.

L.C.D.
London Magazine, January 1826

CHATEAUBRIAND

Yet another reputation has been lost during the last month. The first two volumes of M. de Chateaubriand's works have appeared; and, in spite of a general discharge of *puffs* from the newspapers, his new novel has been esteemed pompous and dull, while the *Itinéraire a Jérusalem* has been openly described as insignificant, full of *gasconnades* and conceit and, what is even worse, laborious and insipid. This is all the more remarkable when one considers his present disgrace and the sinister prophecies he continues to make concerning the Bourbons; this too despite the fact that they have made him a peer and given him a *cordon bleu*. The *Itinéraire* was greatly admired in 1810. There cannot therefore be better proof of the advancement of good sense among the French in the last fifteen years than the failure of this edition of M. de Chateaubriand's works.

No time, moreover, could have been more favourable than the present for the publication of some work of interest or value. High society, which has just left Paris for the country, has gone off without a thing worth reading, certainly with nothing to compare with M. de Barante's *Ducs de Bourgogne* or M. Thierry's *Histoire de Guillaume le Conquérant*, the two works which last year whiled away the tedious evenings spent in the *châteaux*.

It has been found that *Le dernier des Abencérages* is merely a copy of *Zaïde*, the novel which was so popular towards the latter end of the reign of Louis XIV, that is round about 1690. The idea of making the French people go back to the past is the favourite chimera of most of our nobility, and M. de Chateaubriand has for several years been exercising his talents with a view to converting the Frenchman of the nineteenth century into the faithful subjects of a seventeenth-century monarchy. His latest attempt at this, however, has proved to be far from successful. This is easily explained. The author has chosen for his victims the very people whose interests he intends to flatter. A young lady of noble family will admit, as much as you like, the necessity of restoring the French to what they were under Louis XIV; but, owing to that austerity of manners which is now so prevalent, novel-reading is one of the greatest pleasures that this poor young lady can enjoy. Now, if you give her dull novels to read, however much she may admire your retrograde intentions, she will have good sense enough to tell you that you have failed in your object. Such is the fate which has met *Le dernier des Abencérages*. The four principal characters have one great defect: they are all perfect. This would not perhaps render them positively insipid, if they were described in detail and by a succession of picturesque anecdotes. The noble author, however, attaches more importance to the dignity of his diction than to the exactitude of the ideas which he wishes to express. In other words, he writes in the language employed by Cathos and Madelon in

Les Précieuses Ridicules. Style seems to be the constant and earnest object of his attention and there is no doubt that his latest novel will fully satisfy every admirer of the emphatic phrase. The author has described, in the most dignified language, petty circumstances such as would have shocked Racine.

The ideas which he expresses in this way are in themselves completely vulgar. Talent such as this, in fact, would be least out of place in *Le Moniteur* in describing a royal ceremony such as the coronation of Charles X.

M. de Chateaubriand has failed to observe, however, that extreme elevation of tone can be attained in French only by the rejection of the words which have been degraded by common use. This discrimination, moreover, casts an immediate veil of obscurity over all that is said, which, in a novel, is the most deadly of faults. This is something which the admirable author of *Old Mortality* has perfectly well understood and from which he derives his perfectly easy and natural style. In *Ivanhoe*, when he describes Rebecca's greatness of soul or the pride of the Knight Templar, it is the thought itself which is noble and delicate; the language is simple, the author often repeats the same phrase in the same sentence. The conciseness and apparent lucidity of M. de Chateaubriand's style is perhaps best suited to a political pamphlet, especially a royalist one. Here the writer recalls a number of well-known ideas to the mind of his readers. But the case is altogether different in a novel; for, after perusing one page, the reader should never be able to conjecture the contents of the next.

I trust that you will excuse the time I have taken describing the causes of this recent blow sustained by the author of *Le Génie du Christianisme*. Every newspaper, and consequently every simpleton, have for the last two months been proclaiming him as the greatest genius in France. He is certainly, of all others, the man whom our aristocrats would be most glad to see endowed with eminent talent. He is of noble birth, he is a peer, and his manners are far removed from anything suggesting vulgarity. This would make a fine picture to hang up beside that of your own Lord Byron. But, despite all our boasting, the most perhaps that can be said is that, at the present moment, when talent and information are to be found everywhere, but genius nowhere, M. de Chateaubriand is the least mediocre of our prose writers.

M. de Chateaubriand's whole life has been devoted to the cultivation of that moving form of eloquence which one might call *unction*, the power, that is, of impressing on those whom he addresses the firm conviction of his own sincerity. Yet he has never succeeded. Bernardin de St Pierre, when he explains the causes of the flux and reflux of the sea in his *Etudes de la Nature*, believes what he says just as much as the author of *Le Génie du Christianisme*, when he boasts of the sacrament of confirmation. I do not know why it is, however, but, in these two similar instances, Bernardin de St Pierre frequently gives proof of unction, and M. de Chateaubriand is always without it. You feel all the time that you are dealing with a very clever fellow who is trying to take you in.

When M. de Chateaubriand hits upon a good idea and does not labour too much to express it in fine language like the Madelon of Molière, he reaches the perfection of academic style. In its most brilliant days, the French Academy never listened to more elegant and meaningless phrases than the following. He is speaking of the Spaniards:

'Il (l'Espagnol) a peu de ce qu'on appelle *esprit*, mais les passions exaltées lui tiennent lieu de cette lumière qui vient de la finesse et de l'abondance des idées. Un espagnol qui passe le jour sans parler, qui n'a rien vu, qui ne se soucie de rien voir, qui n'a rien lu, rien étudié, rien comparé, trouvera dans la grandeur de ses résolutions les ressources nécessaires au moment de l'adversité.'[1]

For magnificence of style the celebrated Buffon has nothing superior to the passage quoted above.

New Monthly Magazine, September 1826

SCOTT IN PARIS

No sooner had Mr Canning left Paris than Sir Walter Scott arrived, as if on purpose to keep the attention of high society fixed on England. Sir Walter has not been by any means as popular as Mr Canning. He did not come recommended by the striking ability which Mr Canning had displayed in placing Portugal out of the reach both of France and the Holy Alliance, this too without a gun being fired or a penny spent. It would seem that the celebrated novelist is now engaged on a life of Napoleon. So much has already been written, however, on the captive of St Helena that the French public seems resolved to read nothing more on the subject until it is treated with the genius of a Machiavelli or a Montesquieu. The descriptive powers of the author of *Woodstock*, who recently offered us so singular a travesty of the character of Cromwell, strike us as inadequate if he is to portray the ambitious Napoleon who filled us with terror and admiration and whose schemes were continually changing as they grew in scope. In 1816 M. de Semonville observed that Napoleon was the most loquacious of despots. How then will Sir Walter Scott ever render his

---

[1] He (the Spaniard) has little of what is known as wit or intelligence but the higher passions compensate for the absence of that light which comes from the delicacy and abundance of ideas. A Spaniard who spends the day without speaking and who has neither seen anything nor cared to see anything, who has read nothing, studied nothing, compared nothing; that man will find in the grandeur of his resolution the necessary resource in the hour of adversity.

spirited and eloquent powers of conversation? It was Napoleon's custom to pass part of the night in the company of a number of those distinguished figures of the Revolution whom he had called to his Council of State and, when he was with them, to discuss and mature his plans. Judging from the dialogues which Scott has introduced into his novels, however, he seems to be better at describing his characters *while* they speak than at making them speak well. He excels in the depiction of the outlines of his characters and the external circumstances of their lives; but, as to the language put into their mouths, it would often be found insipid if it were not for the interest aroused by his vivid descriptions. This would be a fatal defect in reporting the conversation of Napoleon, which, even if it was extravagant and even mystical, was never insipid. This would be confirmed by hundreds of witnesses who are to be found today in the *salons* of Paris and who, because of this, can be taken as competent judges.

The King has shown Sir Walter Scott the most marked attention. When he appeared at court on the 5th of November, his Majesty addressed a few words to him in English, while Miss Anne Scott, his daughter, was much admired by the ladies of the Tuileries. She is said to have a Spanish countenance, with a fine intelligent expression and beautiful black hair. It is fortunate for Sir Walter that he should belong to the High Tory party; otherwise he might have been terribly bored by the troublesome attentions of the old marchionesses who learned to speak broken English during their emigration. He himself speaks French so indifferently that he is unable to sustain conversation in it. The old ladies of the Faubourg St Germain took advantage of this circumstance therefore to overwhelm him with their compliments in bad English. Sir Walter Scott is much more formal in manner than Mr Canning. He has all the politeness of a country gentleman who is constantly afraid of seeming impolite. His conversation was described as almost official.

During his stay he visited the *Théâtre du Gymnase* in order to see M. Scribe's popular comedy, *le Mariage de Raison*, and gave proof on this occasion of an extraordinary memory. Several of the incidents in *le Mariage de Raison* are borrowed from various novels, some of which are not very well known. The scene, for example, in which Suzette gives her husband the key of the chamber door, is borrowed from Mme de Montolieu's *Caroline de Litchfield*. Sir Walter immediately recognised this incident as well as several others. In the box which the Prefect had lent him for the evening were the Duc de Fitz-James, Mme de Mirbel and many others. All of them were amazed at his literary knowledge. In the opinion of Frenchmen, however, a knowledge of literature is not to be compared with wit and the talent for eloquent and animated conversation. Mr Canning, unlike Sir Walter Scott, gave signs, whenever prudence permitted him to, of a considerable endowment of wit. He made several unexpected sallies.

Miss Anne Scott has something of the polite formal manner of her father. She is on the whole reserved and speaks with a slight Scottish accent. Apart from the difference of age, she has been compared to Miss Fox, the daughter of Lord Holland who was much admired in Paris last winter. During his stay here Sir Walter has seen only diplomatic personalities, men whose conversation has a constantly official tone, owing to their professional habits and contracted views. He did not seem to gain the intimacy of such men as Méneval, de Bassano, Fain, Daru, Molé or Béliard who were themselves on terms of close intimacy with Napoleon over a period of years.

M. Gosselin, a Parisian bookseller, has realised ten or twelve thousand pounds by publishing bad translations of Sir Walter Scott's novels. He is now bringing out a splendid edition of the complete novels in seventy-two volumes, and has presented copies to Sir Walter, apologising for having printed the baronet's name on the title page. 'These works are mine', was Sir Walter's reply. 'Pecuniary misfortunes compel me to admit it.' This is the story which is going round Paris, and it is said to be the first time that Sir Walter has confessed to being the author of these popular works.

New Monthly Magazine, January 1827

II
MUSIC AND THE THEATRE

ROSSINI

Gioacchino Rossini, one of the greatest composers of modern times, was born about the year 1791 in Pesaro, a picturesque little town belonging to the Pontifical States, on the Gulf of Venice. The Papal government barely makes any demand on its subjects, other than that they should pay their taxes and attend Mass; as a consequence, it puts fewer obstacles in the way of a free development of energy and the passions than the governments of France and England.

The arts owe their existence and their progress to the perfection of sensibility and the rousing of the passions. The painter and the musician will look for such qualities in vain in France. He will find nothing in their stead but vanity and egoism, while in England they have been repressed by religious sentiment or else annihilated by the more imperious necessities of everyday practical life. As the short space at my disposal does not allow me to develop these ideas more fully, I will content myself by affirming that they provide me with a fully satisfying explanation of why it is that Italy is the home of the arts, and more particularly, the home of music.

The names of the most celebrated composers are associated with a number of different musical styles. We say that Cimarosa's style is comic, because the artist, by means of certain combinations of sound, has succeeded in awakening in the minds of his listeners impressions of mischievous banter, drollery and laughable absurdity. We say of Paisiello that his style is gracious and sentimental; of Mozart that it is pathetic and melancholy. Rossini might therefore be considered as the inventor of the amusing style. To put it briefly, his music is never boring, and this is the most striking characteristic of his work. But let us go back to what we were saying of his life.

His father, who was a poor inhabitant of Pesaro, lacked the means to teach him anything but music, a little religion and a taste for Ariosto.

Rossini, who at the time was a handsome young man, had concluded his education, as is often the case in Italy, in the company of women. It is also said, though I do not know if this is true, that he appeared on the stage as an amateur. In Italy, the theatre is not a definite profession, as in France and England. Here an amateur can sing for a season or two and afterwards become an unknown dilettante, without in the least compromising the respectability of his private life. It would seem that Rossini, who is now famous for his tasteful and witty rendering of the opening aria of Figaro in the *Barber of Seville*, was a failure as a singer.

Already, however, men and women were humming to themselves a number of little melodies of which he was the composer, and which, although written according to the fashions of the day, were proof of vivacity and an incontestable originality. Two or three rich amateurs in Venice commissioned him to write an opera. The manager of the theatre in which it was to be performed had anything but a high opinion of the composer, as much on account of his extreme youth as of his excessive gaiety, which resembled nothing more than the carefree mischievousness of a schoolboy. However, Rossini's protectors threatened to withdraw their patronage from the theatre itself, and finally the manager agreed to stage this first endeavour by 'the young man from Pesaro', as he was then called. The opera in question was, I believe, *l'Inganno Felice*. In it there are two or three flashes of genius (the duet for example); the rest of the work scarcely stands out at all from the musical style of the day and might be compared to the work of the young Italian composers who today imitate Rossini himself, or the acting of the young French actors who merely ape Talma. *L'Inganno Felice* was hailed as a success, and soon afterwards Rossini composed *Il Tancredi*, *l'Italiana in Algeri* and *La Pietra di Paragone*, which are considered to be among his masterpieces. In order to share this opinion oneself, it is necessary to have seen them performed in Milan. In *L'Italiana* particularly, a *prima donna* and a clown like Marcolini and Pacini, together with Galli, brought out and developed the entire spirit of this beautiful composition, of which the Parisian public is still only able to form an imperfect idea. This is not Galli's fault, it is true.

Tancredi travelled across Italy with unbelievable speed. The melody *Ti rivedrò, mi rivedrai* was taken from a Greek litany that Rossini had heard sung in one of the small islands in the lagoons near Venice. In order to be properly understood, it should be sung if possible as Mme Pasta sings it. Singing it as I have heard others do is like writing the history of France in the form of madrigals.

Either through indolence or for some other reason, Rossini shows a considerable aversion to the overture, and in fact, has failed to write one at all for *Tancredi*; it is therefore customary in Italy to introduce the opera with the overture from *La Pietra di Paragone* or *L'Italiana*.

As a man of the world, Rossini has had no less success than as a composer. Marcolini, the charming singer of comedy, became passionately attached to him. It was for her, for her gorgeous contralto voice and her admirable comic talent, that he composed the rôle of l'Italiana, a rôle whose fresh Italian vivacity and reckless gaiety have been all too often transformed in other theatres into an affected correctness and a purely Nordic prudery.

Rossini came to Milan and it was here that he won the

undisputed place which he now holds among Italian composers. For his new public he wrote *La Pietra di Paragone*, and since then, this extraordinary young man has been placed on a level with the Cimarosas and Paisiellos. It was in Milan that he took over and adopted as his own the *crescendo* effects for which Mosca, till then, had been famous. The latter was the composer of a hundred operas, among which there is one good one, *I Pretendi Delusi*.

It was in Milan too that perhaps the most beautiful of the beautiful women of Lombardy fell helplessly in love with him and abandoned her noble *cavaliere servente* for the young *maestro*. He turned her into what was probably the most accomplished female musician in Italy, for it was while she sat beside him at the piano that he composed most of the melodies which he has subsequently introduced into his operas. On leaving Milan, Rossini revisited Pesaro and his family, to which he remains passionately devoted. It is said that the only person to whom he has ever written in his life is his mother. The letters he sends her are always addressed in the following curious way: *All'illustrissima Signora Rossini, madre del celebre Maestro in Pesaro* (To the most illustrious Signora Rossini, mother of the celebrated composer, Pesaro).

This story, if it is true, is typical of Rossini. Half mocking and half serious, he talks openly of his own genius and refuses to affect a modesty which would be as hypocritical as it would be academic. Deriving his entire happiness from the creations of his genius, living among the most sensitive people in the world and surrounded with the public's homage since the age of eighteen, he is fully conscious of his celebrity, and fails to understand why a man of *his* merits should not be the equal of the greatest of the great.

It was about the time of his journey to Pesaro that Rossini obtained exemption from the military service which at that time subjected almost every citizen to its inexorable laws. The Minister of the Interior was bold enough to ask the Prince Viceroy of the Kingdom of Italy to permit an exception in the case of the young composer. The Prince hesitated at first, fearing a reprimand from military headquarters in Paris. Finally, however, he gave in to the declared opinion of the public.

After receiving his exemption, Rossini went to Bologna, where the same successes and triumphs that he had known in Milan were awaiting him: the enthusiasm of the public and the passionate admiration of the most beautiful women.

The purists of Bologna, who exert over music the same dictatorship as the French Academy exerts over the French language, reproached him (not without justification) for having sometimes neglected in his composition the grammatical rules of harmony. Rossini acknowledged the justice of the reproach, but added that he would have taken care to correct all these mistakes, if only he had had time to read his manuscript over twice. 'However', he would say, 'I have only six weeks in which to write an opera; the first month is given over to amusement and pleasure, and it is only during the last fortnight that I sit down and write a duet or an aria every morning in order that it can be rehearsed the same evening. How do you expect me to notice the trifling errors which are left in the orchestral parts?'

In spite of the candour of this excuse, the puritans of music raised a loud cry throughout Bologna over these venial sins against harmony, even though they are barely perceptible when one is actually listening to an opera. However, twenty or so composers, completely annihilated by the success of a good-looking harum-scarum of twenty, were glad of this opportunity to relieve their jealousy. Every town in Italy contains a dozen of these organ-grinders all of whom, for a sequin, would cheerfully undertake to correct the various faults in any of Rossini's operas.

Rossini was destined, however, to be attacked more overwhelmingly than by the pedantic outcry of the purists. His mistress in Milan gave up her splendid palace, her husband, her children and her fortune, and one morning descended on him in the modest little hotel bedroom that was his home. 'The first moments were superb'; but the door opened suddenly, and one of the richest and most beautiful women in Bologna burst in. There followed a scene considerably resembling something in *The Beggar's Opera*; and Rossini, like Macheath, laughing at his two beautiful rivals, sang them a comic air whose meaning was approximately: *How happy could I be with either!* After this, he fled.

After his success in Bologna, Rossini received offers from every town in Italy. Generally he was given a thousand francs for each opera, and it was common knowledge that he wrote four or five a year.

At this point, a brief glimpse at the internal organisation of an Italian theatre would not be out of place. The manager is often the richest and most influential citizen of his town. He organises a troupe which includes a *prima donna*, a *basso cantante*, a *basso buffo*, a second female voice and a third bass. He next commissions a *maestro*, that is, a composer, to write a new opera which is adapted to the range and volume of his singers' voices. The poem, or the libretto, of the opera is bought by the manager from some unfortunate hack or other for sixty or eighty francs. Thus organised, the troupe gives the forty or fifty performances for which it has been engaged and then breaks up. These performances constitute what is generally known as a *stagione*, or season. The singers who have no engagement with any such company usually go and stay in Bologna or Milan.

From this brief description of the organisation of the theatre in Italy, it will not be difficult to imagine what kind of life Rossini led from 1810 until 1816. During this time he visited the principal towns in Italy, passing three or four months in each one. On his arrival, he would be received and fêted by the musical amateurs of the district. He would then spend the first fifteen or twenty days in the company of his friends and at various dinners cursing and jeering at the insipid text which he would have to set to music. Apart from his own instinctive good taste, he had been brought up from his childhood to read the works of Ariosto, Goldoni, Machiavelli and Molière. He was thus a reliable judge of the quality of the so-called poems on which he had to work.

After approximately three weeks residence in the town, he would begin to refuse invitations and to give serious attention to the voices of his actors. He would get them to sing at the piano, and I have seen him more than once compelled to mutilate some of his most brilliant and felicitous ideas and 'reduce their fine proportions', because the tenor would have been unable to reach a particularly high note which Rossini had found essential to the true expression of his feelings. Sometimes, too, he would have to spoil the general character of a melody because the *prima donna* always sang out of tune when modulating from one key to another.

When Rossini had acquired an exact knowledge of his singers' voices, he would finally begin to write. He would get up late and spend the rest of the day composing, while his friends conversed around him. He would rarely resist their solicitations, even though the day of the first performance was rapidly approaching, and some of his most brilliant inspirations have come to him when he has been alone in his room having returned late at night from a party. He would rapidly note down these ideas on bits of paper and arrange them the following morning, or, to use his own words, *instrument* them while chatting with his friends. Rossini has an eager and lively mind, sensitive to the least impression and capable of turning to account the most trivial as well as the most important incident. When he was composing his *Moses*, someone said to him: 'What, are you going to have Hebrews singing? What will you do, make them sing through their noses as they do in the synagogue?' The idea struck Rossini's imagination, and on returning home, he composed a magnificent chorus which opens with a sort of nasal incantation peculiar to the Jewish synagogue. The labour of composition is nothing to Rossini; it is the reheasals which try him most, for then the unfortunate *maestro* has to undergo the torture of hearing his most beautiful airs defiled and caricatured.

Nevertheless, these very rehearsals are the glory of the Italian sensibility. It was while attending a rehearsal which took place in a squalid room known as the *ridotto*, or foyer, of the theatre of a tiny Italian town, a room in which there was no instrument, apart from a badly-tuned piano, that I became convinced that Italy is the home of music; it is a country in which you may hear people who are perfectly ignorant of musical theory, sing their respective rôles as if by instinct, and with the most admirable precision and intelligence.

The foreigner who arrives in Italy and who has the honesty to rely on his own impressions, will soon realise that it is absurd to hope for good composers or good singers at any distance from Vesuvius. In this part of Italy, even the baby at his mother's breast is accustomed to the sound of music.

We left Rossini directing the rehearsal of his opera with an old piano in the *ridotto* of a tiny theatre. This dark little room re-echoes, but not only with the sounds of the most divine and original music, though these are heard as well; it is also the scene of the most grotesque pretensions and disputes. What goes on among an opera troupe off-stage is the principal, if not the sole object of the entire town's attention, and it talks of little else. The future boredom or pleasure of its inhabitants during the gayest month of the year depends on the success or failure of the new opera and therefore, to a great extent, on the good or bad relations existing among the temperamental synod which is to present it. Sografi, an Italian comic poet, has written a lively and charming play in one act in which one sees the adventures and intrigues of a troupe of wandering singers.

At last the dreadful moment of the first performance arrives. The *maestro* takes his place at the piano; the theatre is overflowing, every occupation ceases, except that of listening, and even the whispers of gallantry give way to silence.

When the overture begins, the concentration of the audience is so intense that one could hear a fly buzzing; when it is over, however, the most formidable uproar breaks out. It is feverishly applauded or else mercilessly condemned. Italy is altogether different from Paris, where the success or failure of the first performance is rarely decisive and where the vanity of each member of the audience prevents him from expressing his personal opinion, for fear of its not being that of the majority. An Italian will shout and stamp his foot as hard as he can in order to impose his own opinion of the new opera on everyone else in the audience, and prove that his own opinion is the only just and reasonable one. For, strange though this may seem, there is no intolerance as great as the intolerance of the very sensitive. Whenever you hear a man holding forth calmly and methodically on the arts, change the conversation at once and talk of something else. Such a man may become an excellent magistrate, a good doctor, an enterprising business man or a learned academician, anything you like, in fact, except a man capable of responding to the true charms of music and painting.

The taste of an Italian audience is so sure that it can always tell, when it hears a melody in a new opera, if the merit is due to the composer or to the singer. If it wishes to applaud the former, it shouts 'Bravo *maestro*!' Rossini then rises from the piano, assumes an air of great gravity and makes three bows, which are followed by veritable salvoes of applause.

Rossini conducts the first three performances from the piano, after which he receives his eight hundred or one thousand francs. He then rests for eight or ten days, is invited to a farewell dinner given by his friends—that is by the entire town—and at last makes his departure. With his suitcase more full of music sheets than of linen or valuables, he makes his way towards some other town where he begins the same life anew.

Usually he writes to his mother after the success of a new opera and sends two-thirds of what he has earned to her and his aged father. Often, when he is travelling, he has only eight or ten sequins in his pocket, and yet he is the gayest of men. If he is fortunate enough to meet a simpleton on his travels, he never fails to mystify him. One day, on his way to Reggio, he passed himself off to his travelling companions as a *maestro* who was a mortal enemy of Rossini. During the journey, he took the well-known words of his best melodies and set them to the most abominable music; he then persuaded one of his fellow-travellers to sing them, and in the most comic fashion criticised them as the work of a charlatan whose name was Rossini and who was only admired by people of the worst imaginable taste.

Rossini was at last requested to come to Rome. Here the manager of the opera had been obliged to reject several librettos which, according to the police, contained dangerous allusions; he therefore proposed to Rossini, in a moment of exasperation and disappointment, the *Barber of Seville*, which had already been set to music by Paisiello. The government made no objection. Rossini, however, who is intelligent enough to be modest when he finds himself in competition with true merit, was extremely embarrassed by the choice, and wrote at once to Paisiello to inform him of the manager's decision. The old *maestro* was a man of incontestable genius, yet at the same time not without a certain boastful vanity. He replied with the utmost courtesy that he was perfectly satisfied with the choice made by the Roman police, and that he had no doubts as to the chances of his rival's success. Rossini wrote a modest preface to the libretto, showed Paisiello's letter to all the musical dilettanti in Rome, and then set immediately to work. The opera was finished within thirteen days. He has said himself that, at the first performance of the *Barbiere*, his heart was beating violently as he sat down at the piano.

The Romans seemed to find the beginning of the opera boring and very inferior to Paisiello's. One of Rosina's arias (*Sono docile*) seemed to them to be altogether out of character. They accused Rossini of having presented, not the soft complaint of an innocent, enamoured girl, but the strident and insolent declamation of a virago. The first applause broke out at the moment when Rosina and Figaro sing their first duet. The aria *Della calumnia* was judged magnificent, though, for my part, I find it too strongly reminiscent of the aria of *La Vendetta* in Mozart's *Marriage of Figaro*.

The opera, in any case, was to have a strange career. The first night was an almost complete failure, whereas, on the second, it gave rise to the most enthusiastic applause. The Roman critics, however, considered that Rossini had been, not only by his own standards, but by those of every other famous composer, a disappointment, particularly in his treatment of passionate tenderness. Rosina, finding in Almaviva a faithful lover and not the vile seducer who has been described to her, does not give way, as one might expect, to an effusion of tender and ecstatic sentiment; instead she distracts her lover and the whole audience by launching into pointless complications, trills and cadenzas. These misplaced and meaningless embellishments, however, are always applauded in Paris, whereas in Rome they have often been nearly hissed.

Music, and dramatic music in particular, has made considerable progress since the days of Paisiello. Long, tedious recitativo has been suppressed and it is more common to hear passages for two or more voices, which, because of their vivacity and general air of musical accomplishment, are effective in warding off a feeling of boredom. The opinion in Rome was that if Cimarosa had set the *Barbiere* to music, it would have been less animated, but certainly much more comic and infinitely more tender. It seems too that Rossini was considered altogether inferior to Paisiello in the quintet, *Buona sera*, where Basilio is persuaded to go to bed.

About this time, a certain Signor Barbaia of Naples, a former waiter, who had acquired a considerable fortune and had even succeeded in getting into the good graces of the king, had the good judgment to see that Rossini was the rising composer of the day. He therefore took him to Naples and made him the most advantageous proposals. Rossini agreed to compose three new operas a year, for three thousand francs each, and became straight away musical director of the San Carlo opera house. Despite Rossini's well-known versatility of character, this arrangement has lasted for the last six or seven years. His unusual constancy, however, is mainly due to the devoted attachment he has come to feel towards a Neapolitan lady.

For San Carlo Rossini composed *Otello*, *Armida*, *Zoraïde*, *La Donna del Lago*, *Elizabetta*, *Mosè*, etc. He protested in vain against the imitation, or rather against the Italian caricature, of *Othello*. The author of the libretto was Il marchese Berio, a man who inspired liking and respect and who was intimately known in the best Neapolitan society, which was often to be seen at his home. He persisted in maintaining that Shakespeare was a barbarian and that it was absolutely necessary to correct what he had written. Rossini finally gave in, but with a sigh. He has often been heard to say that the translation of Shakespeare by Letourneur froze his blood ('mi gelava il sangue'), and that, before sitting down to work on the marchese's dull, inert rhapsody, he would first of all take care to draw his inspiration from a reading of the former. This inspiration, however, seems to have had no effect on the overture, which is very gay and in no way in keeping with the drama.

On becoming rich, Rossini became miserly and even lazy. The second of these vices has certainly done harm to his reputation: in certain of his later productions, it is impossible, in fact, to find more than one or two purely original passages; the rest is hardly anything more than a re-arrangement of old ideas. The absence of novelty is far too often in evidence in his music, despite its wit and liveliness. The public in Milan, which is the second musical capital of Italy, expressed this opinion on the occasion of Rossini's last visit, when he gave *La Gazza Ladra*. Yet no opera was ever acclaimed more triumphantly at its first performance. While recognising that Rossini had merely imitated himself, the public was far too flattered at his having come specially to Milan to write a new opera, to show any dissatisfaction. Its enthusiasm, moreover, had been aroused to a paroxysm by the sublime histrionic talent of Galli and Mme Belloc. None the less, when the first enthusiasm had abated and the public had found the leisure and the calm necessary to reflect and examine, it was found that, in many ways, this opera had too much of the noise and confusion of German music. Not a single voice was raised, however, to deny the sublime beauty of the cavatina, *Di piacer mi balza il cor*. This aria breathes a profound melancholy, worthy of Mozart and Cimarosa. The full meaning of the words has never been more faithfully translated by a melody. The same might be said of the prayer chanted by Galli, *Nume benefico*. At the same time, as the result of a strange contradiction, the cruellest of trials is made to open with a waltz, *Vuol dir lo stesso*, etc. A similar objection has been made to another waltz sung by poor Ninetta at the moment of her own condemnation and the arrest of her father.

In defence of Rossini, his admirers maintain that it is a positive achievement to have disguised the atrocity of the subject beneath the light detached elegance of his cantilena. They argue that, if Mozart had composed *La Gazza Ladra* as his genius would have compelled him to, that is, in the style of the sombre rôle of Don Giovanni, the resulting horror would have been barely endurable.

The second journey to Milan was less flattering. He was given a Venetian tale, *Bianco e Faliero*, to set to music; and the music he wrote lacked originality to such an extent (being nothing from beginning to end but old ideas re-shuffled for the occasion) that it came near to being hissed on the opening night. The public, however, was rather too severe; for the opera includes one quartet, with a part for solo clarinet, that can be ranked with the finest compositions of the greatest masters. Nothing in *Il Barbiere* or *La Gazza Ladra* can be compared with it. It is a sublime effort of creation; in its sombre colouring, this quartet has all the melancholy tenderness of Mozart, and is infinitely superior to the prayer in the last act of *Otello*. It has been introduced into Vigano's ballets, where it produces the most ravishing effect.

It was in Rome, if I am not mistaken, that Rossini composed *Torvaldo e Dorliska*. This opera too was full of reminiscences of earlier works. Ambrogi, who played the tyrant, sang with an *agitato* which was so evidently copied from a passage in *Otello* that even the least practised ear could recognise it at once. There was only one original phrase, though a very fine one, in the whole opera; this was in the rôle sung by Signora Camporesi: *Mio Torvaldo dovè sei?* Since then, Rossini has written *Il Turco in Italia* for the Scala in Milan, but the public, weary of his continual repetition of old ideas, has given it a chilly reception. Nevertheless, in the performance given in Milan, Pacini, the best comic actor in Italy, was irresistible in the rôle of the husband, particularly at the moment when he rushes into a ballroom in search of his wife. In this particular scene, furthermore, the music was undeniably both original and beautiful.

French gallantry, which is not love, but a sustained, playful and sparkling imitation of what is most delightful in genuine passion, has never been better expressed than in the duet, *Le comprate, le vendete*. Another duet, *Un bel uso di Turchia*, despite its echoes of a melody by Paisiello, is full of the most graceful comic humour.

When this opera was given in Paris, it was accompanied by a number of arias from *La Cenerentola*, a work which is altogether more commonplace. The duet between the two clowns in the latter, when the valet presents his humble respects to the lord of the manor and father of the three beauties, has often been compared to the duet *Se fiato in corpo avete*, which begins the second act of Cimarosa's *Matrimonio segreto*. The comparison has made me realise how inferior Rossini's light, lively music is to the more natural and profoundly humorous work of Cimarosa, whom one might call the Molière of music. *La Cenerentola*, nevertheless, which I have the misfortune to dislike, has been performed more than four hundred times in Italy.

After the success of his principal works, *Tancredi*, *L'Italiana*, *La Pietra di Paragone*, *Il Barbiere*, *La Gazza Ladra*, *La Donna del Lago*, etc., the Italians wished to hear no music other than that of Rossini. The principal newspaper of Bologna, which is controlled by the Church, is rarely capable of simple commonsense, unless it is dealing with music; in 1819, it enumerated seventeen theatres in Italy, in which operas by Rossini were being performed. Apart from these, there were seven outside Italy, in London, Vienna, Berlin, Lisbon, Barcelona, etc. Rossini was heard to say on this occasion, 'Sono il più giovane e il più fortunato dei maestri'. ('I am the youngest and most favoured of *maestros*.')

His extraordinary and unprecedented success, however, was an obstacle to the long continuation of his popularity. One might say, in fact, that Italy is at present saturated with his music. It is for this reason that the first composer who has the courage and the genius *not* to copy him and who abandons the various effects of *allegro* and rapid *crescendo*, in order to return to a slower measure and to the authentic, natural expression of the words of the libretto, will certainly see Rossini's glory fade to his own advantage.

Rossini's facility is not the least of his extraordinary qualities. Ricordi, who is the principal music publisher in Italy and who has made an immense fortune out of the sale of the *maestro's* works, told me, when I was in Florence, that Rossini had composed some of the finest airs in, I believe, *La Gazza Ladra*, in a single hour. He did this sitting in the back of Ricordi's shop amidst the confused shouts of twelve or fifteen copyists, half of whom were dictating to the rest the notes of the score. As for the romances or love songs, which have sufficed to make the reputation of a number of minor composers, Rossini would have no hesitation in composing ten or twelve while putting on his clothes before going out.

The illustrious Vigano is a man of whom Italy can justly boast to the whole world; together with Canova, he is living proof of the fact that she is still, even today, mistress of the fine arts. Vigano has adapted to the music of Rossini his immortal mute tragedies which are known as ballets, and the best known of which are *Otello*, *La Vestale* and *Myrrha*. As Vigano has taken care only to choose the best of Rossini's melodies, it often happens that, after seeing one of his ballets, an opera by Rossini himself will seem colourless and uninspired.

Another unfortunate circumstance for Rossini is the present vogue of the semi-serious opera. This had led him to adopt a sort of bastard style, which is neither comic nor serious. In Italy, it is generally felt that serious opera is lugubrious and boring; it is, moreover, a form of composition which calls for the greatest perfection. It has been found that one serious opera a year at the Scala or San Carlo is quite sufficient. Because of the deplorable plight of the Italian people today, it is somehow a relief to find gaiety and joy, at least in the theatre. Nevertheless, the seats for a semi-serious opera are dearer than for the *opera buffa*; the theatre managers therefore prefer to stage only the former. This is particularly unfortunate for Rossini, whose genius is essentially suited to the gay and the voluptuous. An intense voluptuousness is to be found in all his best melodies. This is so evident, particularly in the sublime duet from *Armida*, that I have seen two women in Bologna become extremely embarrassed when they found themselves enthusing over its charms. This duet, a quartet from *Bianca e Faliero*, and three passages from *Tancredi*, are Rossini's masterpieces in the expression of passion and tenderness.

We have glanced at Rossini's principal works. It would be only fair to say something about the peculiarities of his style; I am obliged however, in one way, to abandon the attempt.

To make myself understood, I should have to express my ideas on the piano and not with words on paper.

The pleasure afforded by music would seem to come from the power with which it can lead the imagination through a sequence of rare but intangible illusions. The principal characteristic of Rossini's music, however, is an extraordinary briskness which never once allows the mind to give way to those profound emotions and serene reveries which Mozart's music so rarely fails to awaken in the listener's mind. On the other hand, this briskness goes with a freshness which is always sparkling and which draws a smile of involuntary pleasure to the lips. By comparison, most other music seems heavy and lifeless.

But it is perhaps because of its general dash and its continual and disconcerting variations that Rossini's music never leaves any profound impression. One might say with Shakespeare that

> It is too rash, too unadvised, too sudden;
> Too like the lightning which doth cease to be
> Ere one can say it lightens.
>
> *Romeo and Juliet*

At the moment, even the most distinguished of Italy's musical amateurs are calling loudly for something different. What will it be like in twenty years time, when *Il Barbiere* is as well known as *Il matrimonio segreto* or *Don Giovanni*? In the opera *Otello*, whose principal theme is jealousy, is there a single air which depicts this cruellest of passions as faithfully as the aria *Vedrò mentr'io sospiro* from *Le Nozze di Figaro*?

During the performance of a work in which the composer has sought to express human passions and feelings by means of musical sounds, one must listen with the utmost attentiveness, in order to feel the emotion which the composer has sought to inspire. It is scarcely necessary to add that this attention itself is not enough, if the listener's soul is incapable of responding to profound emotion. In Rossini's music, however, many passages, generally speaking, are hardly more than brilliant concert arias; only the most casual attention is required, as a result, in order to enjoy them. Thus it is that most of the time the soul has nothing, or next to nothing, to do.

Rossini's misfortune is to have ceased thinking of the passion of love as anything but a simple question of gallantry and dissipation. He is far too bent on simple amusement.

> In the light airs and recollected terms
> Of these most brisk and giddy-paced times.
> *Twelfth Night*

To put it briefly, he is never sad, and what is music without melancholy?

> I am never merry when I hear sweet music.
> *Merchant of Venice*

I will give one further proof, however, of an opinion expressed at the beginning of this article concerning the *amusing style* which Rossini has created. Although his operas conform to the general rule in Italy and are composed with a view to performances interrupted by a ballet or an interlude, they are the only Italian operas to survive the harsh test of a Parisian performance. Here it is the absurd custom to give three hours of music without any interruption. The musical indigestion brought about by this extraordinary custom is unbearable in *Don Giovanni* and other passionately inspired operas. At the end of the performance, everyone leaves the theatre either with a headache or in a state of complete exhaustion. Rossini's music, however, offers, all too often, nothing but the light and ephemeral graces of ordinary concert music. It is consequently most admirably suited to the singular arrangements of the Parisian theatre and invariably emerges triumphant from the conflict. One might conclude by saying that it is the music best suited to the meridian of Paris; music, that is, which is light and detached, rather than passionate or humorous.

I understand that Rossini is to go to London; if this is true, I would advise the manager of the King's Theatre to arouse the illustrious *maestro* from his indolence and stimulate his genius by giving him the two excellent libretti of *Don Giovanni* and *Il matrimonio segreto* to set to music. It would be fascinating to witness the resulting epic struggle between Mozart, Cimarosa and Rossini.

ALCESTE
Paris Monthly Review, January 1822

THEODORE LECLERCQ AND THE PROVERB

An immense quantity of leisurely pastimes was introduced into French society round about the year 1770. The men and women of the period were growing weary of the constant hazards and rewards which life at court offered them; it no longer occupied all their attention, and, at the same time, the discussions concerning the general good of society which were to begin in 1785 had not yet come into fashion. Till now, the theatre had been nothing but a source of amiable distraction, in which the men and women of leading French society had confined themselves to the rôle of spectators. In 1770, however, it occurred to them to become actors. It is a generally acknowledged truth that one can play the violin or some other instrument for three or four hours and not be bored; whereas it is impossible to derive any pleasure for more than an hour from music performed by someone else.

The genial Frenchmen of the year 1770 found considerable enjoyment in amateur theatricals. Little by little, however, two disadvantages became apparent. The plays which they wished to perform were those which were generally considered to be the best and, consequently, those which were most frequently presented on the professional stage. This was a dangerous source of rivalry. Polite society, finding itself at the same time in the rôle of judge and defendant, pronounced unanimously that, as far as the *tone* of their performance was concerned, the actors it had found in its own ranks were superior to the Molés, Monvels, Brizards and other celebrated actors of the day. Only, when it came to talent and the warmth of the effect produced, it was impossible to entertain the least illusion. A genteel actor can only act really well with his voice; the habits of bodily comportment he has formed and his way of holding himself on the stage belie at every instant the words uttered by his mouth. Otherwise, if he concentrates too much on his own external appearance, he falls back into his normal way of speaking, that is to say, ceases to be an actor.

It may therefore be an entertaining pastime to perform amateur theatricals in country houses; there are nevertheless a number of disadvantages in putting on the same plays that have been performed throughout the winter in the principal theatres of the capital. The spectators are left with an impression of mediocrity and inferiority as they watch men and women of their own class of society playing the same rôles which great actors before them have marked with their seal. Furthermore, the plays produced in a *salon* are, like other drawing room diversions, intended as a relief from conversation. For this, a play in five acts is too long; three acts in one play would be preferable, for, after each one, the audience would be free to talk and the conversation would profit from the remarks made during the performance.

To resume, then, the leisure enjoyed by the upper classes during the decline of the court gave them the idea of becoming actors and actresses. Soon the inconvenient lengthiness of a comedy in five acts, together with the disheartening effect of having to compare amateur performers with Molé and the other great actors of the time, led to the composition of small plays in one act.

Collé was the acknowledged master of this new literary *genre*. Society, at the end of Louis XV's reign, did not share our own conceptions of decency. *La vérité dans le vin, Ce que Dieu garde est bien gardé* and Collé's other masterpieces are too licentious, therefore, to be performed today. His plays were given the name of Proverbs, the reason for this being that the spectator, in order that he might play as active a rôle as possible, would be called upon at the end to guess which proverb it was which had provided the theme of the play. Thus, after watching a performance of Collé's masterpiece, the men would call out, 'In vino veritas'. For the play shows us a lover who, while slightly drunk, confesses his passion to the husband of his mistress. Then, as drunkards are always tenderhearted, he feels remorse at having betrayed a husband who is at the same time his best friend and, with tears in his eyes, begs his forgiveness. Fortunately, the husband is no more sober than he is, and, when they have both recovered, is easily persuaded that the confession was nothing but a bad joke. I must apologise for not being able to give a longer analysis.

The Proverbs written by Collé were performed by members of the nobility and also in the home of the Duc d'Orléans, the father of *Egalité*. This was the same Duc d'Orléans who has been slandered in the memoirs of Mme la Comtesse de Genlis, whose aunt, Mlle de Montesson, he eventually married. Mme de Montesson saved her niece from partial destitution when she was plain Mlle Ducrest, a young lady who, till then, had been playing the harp in private houses for five louis a time. Her niece, who has since turned to the consolations of religion, now ridicules her benefactress. Many details concerning the Proverbs which the pleasure-loving Collé wrote are to be found in his curious autobiography. Collé had the misfortune to be jealous of Voltaire, but, apart from this absurdity, his autobiography provides some of the most entertaining light reading that can be found.

Collé's successor in the writing of Proverbs was Carmontelle. Carmontelle has less wit and less gaiety than Collé, but a great deal more realism. In 1811, two volumes of his Proverbs were published and there have been innumerable performances of each of these tiny plays. The reader will be left with an entirely false impression of their merits if he reads straight through the collection as if it were an ordinary volume. It is best to read only one proverb a day.

The subject matter of these short comedies is altogether trivial; their merit lies entirely in the verisimilitude of incidental details and the gracefulness of the comic touch. In this, they have all the inoffensive charm and elegance that we find in Terence. They are written in a manner which entirely precludes the *vis comica*. The reason for this is evident. A forceful situation, if it is to be rendered in any but a ridiculous way, calls for a corresponding degree of energy from the actors. Energy of this kind, however, is rarely to be found in fashionable society. A good half of Carmontelle's comedies are almost certainly unintelligible in England; those, however, which depict human passions, which are universally the same, can be enjoyed as much abroad as in France. It is certain, for instance, that *Le Voyage à Rome* or *Les amants chiens* provoke laughter wherever they are performed. *La Maison du Boulevard* is an excellent character-study of a hare-brained young widow who exploits the fondness and indulgence of an elderly and immensely rich uncle. It is also a perfectly faithful portrayal of French society as it was round about the year 1778.

The principal characteristic of the age was an extreme lightness in everything and the literary masterpieces that it produced must have been very little appreciated outside France. The Revolution, however, which was suspended rather than brought to an end by the despotism of Napoleon and the theocracy of the Bourbons, gave us the seriousness which is to be found in England, in Germany and in other foreign civilisations. I have no doubt whatever that M. Théodore Leclercq's Proverbs will be enjoyed in England far more than Carmontelle's, or even the best of Collé. M. Leclercq has only offered the public three volumes of Proverbs, and, unlike most authors, has only published those with which he is least satisfied. Strange though it may seem, there is a certain affinity between M. Leclercq and Shakespeare, between the hyssop and the cedar of Lebanon. His own creations, like Shakespeare's, cease to some extent to be his own, once they have been printed; once it is in print, anyone can stage a Proverb. M. Leclercq himself is an excellent actor and is outstanding in his interpretation of the rôles that he has created. Many society actors have a strong objection to playing the more absurd parts in a play: they are afraid lest some of the absurdity should remain attached to them after the play is over. M. Leclercq, however, has made these parts his own. I have seen him giving an inimitable impersonation of a German speaking bad French and of a lover being chaffed by his friends.

There is one distinguished author now writing who is bold enough to chastise with his pen the Jesuits and M. de Villèle. M. Fiévée has written two very good novels, *La Dot de Suzette* and *Frédéric*. It is generally believed that M. Fiévée has re-written and improved many of the Proverbs written by his friend M. Leclercq. Be this as it may, as the official censorship is pitiless towards any attempt to depict the life of contemporary society, even in the comedies it allows to be performed, M. Leclercq's own Proverbs will one day have a certain historical importance. Even today, a foreigner who wishes to have some idea of the social habits of the Parisian cannot do better than read M. Leclercq's three volumes. Remember, however, that, if you wish to appreciate the true merit of plays of this kind, you must never read more than a hundred pages a day. As the French are today more solemn in their habits than in the past, M. Leclercq's little tableaux will strike the foreigner as more interesting and seem to him more intelligible than the thumbnail sketches of Carmontelle.

The Proverb which illustrates best of all the combination of the new social ambition of the Frenchman and his traditional frivolity is a play called *Le Duel*. A Frenchman cannot tolerate any witticism in his presence at the expense of the government to which he has sold his opinion. All credit is due here to M. de Villèle, who is personally responsible for having corrupted in this way the entire nation, from the civil servant living on twelve hundred francs a year to the peer whom he pays thirty thousand francs cash down to vote for the law of sacrilege. A Frenchman, once he has been bought in this way, is constantly afraid of being despised; his habitual mood is one of defiance; and, at the first joke or sarcasm he hears, he is ready for a duel. In the same Proverb there is a character who is the embodiment of unctuous hypocrisy and who has made his fortune out of Montrouge, the headquarters of the Jesuits. In presenting the latter, M. Leclercq gives the final touch to his portrait of contemporary society.

In seeking to give you some idea of these Proverbs which are so much in fashion in Paris in the present year of grace, I have found it difficult to decide whether I should translate for your benefit *Le Duel* or *Le Plus Beau Jour de ma Vie*. I have finally decided to present the latter, for fear that the *Duel*, which is moreover the least gay of the two, should be found unintelligible outside France. *Le Plus Beau Jour de ma Vie* is thus described out of irony. In it we meet an unfortunate young man to whom everyone repeats, since it is his wedding day, 'This is the best day of your life'. It happens to be a day, however, on which he is the prey to a hundred vexations. The marriage ceremony is one of the most absurd of French social customs. It has been estimated that it involves as many as a hundred little formalities, each of which, if it is overlooked, can be a cause of reproach, or, what is worse, of ridicule. I am convinced that, just as today we have manuals of physics and pharmacy, soon we will have manuals for bridegrooms. The Proverb can be performed without any preparation. Two screens will do for the wings, and two bowls of flowers and two candles are all that are needed in the way of footlights. It is customary to act them, like M. Leclercq himself, without exaggerating a single gesture. Good tone consists in doing something with no apparent effort and in maintaining a constant ease and naturalness.

London Magazine, May 1825

MUSIC IN ITALY

Naples, September 30th, 1825

You have asked me for a brief survey of the present state of Italian music. A spring rises at the foot of a huge mountain. If we are to judge its nature, should we describe the various basins into which it flows, or should we examine the contours of the mountain-side and the various qualities of its rock and soil?

I feel that I would be telling you little about the present state of Italian music, if I were to report what I have heard in conversations in Milan or Naples, or if I were to describe to you for the hundredth time the famous opera houses of La Scala or San Carlo. A biography of Rossini, Mercadante, Pacini or Meyerbeer would tell you much more, particularly if I were to analyse at the same time the talent of Lablache, David and Zuchelli. What would still be missing, however, is an account of the very source of the taste for music among a people of widely varying character, united only by the misfortune of being oppressed by the same absurd tyranny. This tyranny can scarcely be described as bloodthirsty; nevertheless, it is extremely punctilious. In Turin and Modena, a wealthy young lady, with an income of a thousand pounds a year cannot get married without three or four reports being made up by each of the seven or eight ministers or under-secretaries of the petty princes of these states, men who are chafing at their own inactivity. One of the greatest pleasures that a Frenchman can enjoy, that of genial, animated conversation in which every conceivable subject is discussed in its turn, would be among the most dangerous of pleasures in Italy. The spies are dying of boredom at their own lack of anything to do, they are at a loss to know what to put in their reports. Furthermore, almost everyone is a spy, from the monk who takes up his position at your bedroom door with a *Deo Gratias* to the barber who comes and cuts your hair or the café proprietor who sells you an ice cream. These spies sell themselves to every successive government. Thus, because of circumstances peculiar to this ill-fated country, it is dangerous to criticise even the government which is most hostile to the one in power, even when the latter seems the more firmly established of the two. One might quote the instance of a citizen of Verona who, in 1812, when his country was governed by Napoleon, criticised the slowness and stupidity of the Austrian administration. Today, thirteen years later, he is persecuted for a remark made out of servility towards what was then the established régime.

Since the irruption in Italy of a tyranny modelled on that of Philip II, that is to say since the first half of the sixteenth century, the most dangerous thing for an Italian has been to talk.

This is the dominating *trait* of the Italian character. One of the most familiar of Italian proverbs tells us that *un bel tacer non fu mai scritto* (a meaningful silence was never written down) —never written down, that is, by a spy. An Italian who has been looking at a beautiful painting is lost to everything but the delightful sensations it has produced in him for a full two hours afterwards. If he hears a new opera, he thinks of nothing else for a week. Why should this be? It is because conversation is an impossibility and because, over a period of nearly three centuries, he has grown out of the habit. How then could he ever be subject to the vanity of the French? This vanity seeks its pleasures in conversation; it only lives in so far as it is articulate; and in Italy one must above all be silent.

As soon as they have to discuss the truth of a thought or the felicity of a turn of phrase, the Englishman and the Frenchman, who have been discussing every conceivable subject for the last three centuries, have an incontestable advantage over the the Italian, who, as far as expression is concerned, is a mere inexperienced child. Italy has thus produced, under our very eyes, Canova, Rossini and Vigano; while in fifty years she has failed to give birth to three volumes of prose which have been appreciated or even translated in other European countries. Her best books, published since 1823, are so prolix and so painstaking in their efforts to leave nothing unexplained that they seem to have been written by children and for children.

The Italian, because he is never able properly to speak, is profoundly aware of everything which is in his own interest. In this he is superior to the Frenchman or even the Englishman. Ever since 1550 he has learned to appreciate what the immortal Lafontaine was bold enough to print under Louis XIV: 'Our enemy is our own master.' For two hundred and fifty years the most deeply hated of men in Turin, Bologna, Modena and Florence has been the sovereign. One might object to this by pointing out the normal state of affairs to be found in Florence towards the year 1780, but the Florentines have lost all their energy. Their power to hate has left them, and with it their vitality.

There is nothing so absurd as to expose one's life or, what is worse, expose oneself to grievous wounds. One does this in the name of whom? In the name of the sovereign, that is to say, in the name of a man's greatest enemy.

This digression has been perhaps rather long; but you will now understand the two main sources of Italian musi and painting: the impossibility of conversation and the total discredit into which the military virtues have fallen. The greatest living general might arrive in a small Italian town. He would excite less curiosity and interest than the young Pacini, a second-rate composer who lives by pillaging Rossini. The famous general would be looked on as a barbarian, a savage who has earned his living thirty times over in the lottery of the thirty battles in which he has taken part. Even if he were to utter some particularly unintelligent remark, society would not even pay him the compliment of being scandalised. This is something I have witnessed on twenty occasions when well-known generals have been visiting Naples.

A young duke in Milan would make a complete fool of himself if ever he chose to take pride in his skill at military and gymnastic exercises, that is to say, in his riding, fencing, shooting and hunting. No doubt he will have to go in for all these exercises a little. Such irksome duties are necessary precisely to the extent to which they are likely to impress the women. If our young duke looks as though he is enjoying them too much, however, the whole town is sure to repeat before long: *E uno sciocco* ('The man's a fool').

The day when Italy acquires two houses of parliament and when *opinion* begins to influence the process of government, she will cease to be exclusively preoccupied with music, painting and architecture. These three arts, which are respectively the most dearly loved among the Italian people, will, from that day, undergo a rapid decline. In the same way, the prestige of Voltaire among the French fell noticeably between 1798 and 1812. It needed the resurrection of the Jesuits in 1820 to ensure a public for twenty new editions.

Having now indicated the sources of the general passion for music among the Italian people, let us trace the history of contemporary music.

The Italians are becoming noticeably weary of the music of Rossini. No musical idiom in Italy ever lives for longer than twenty years, if as much as that. No philosopher has yet explained why this should be; but novelty and the element of surprise are a *sine qua non* for the imagination, if music is going to give any pleasure at all. Rossini, it is true, began his career as recently as 1810, when *La Cambiale di Matrimonio* was first performed in Venice. His glory dates from the production in 1812 in Milan of *La Pietra di Paragone*. Thirteen years have scarcely gone by and yet there are already signs in Rossini's work of a certain lassitude. Cimarosa, Paisiello and Buranello never abused any single musical device as much as Rossini has abused the rapidity of his crescendo and of his brilliant accompaniment. Rossini has never succeeded in conveying passion. Love in his music is never any more than a form of voluptuousness, and his style is never more than amusing and vivacious. His libretto may set out to evoke the sombre jealousy of Othello or the disappointed ambition of Assur, the accomplice of Semiramis (see the opera of this name). His principal fear, nevertheless, is that, in remaining true to life, he will merely bore. He has infinite wit and little or no passion. He is afraid of being dull, therefore, as soon as the expression demanded by an emotion is no longer sparkling, entertaining or bizarre and, above all, as soon as it is merely simple and genuine. As soon as this happens he hastens to syncopate his music. The following criticism has been made of his *Armida*, which was performed in the theatre of San Carlo during the autumn of 1817. In this opera he makes Renaldo and Armida sing a duet which is both long and dull and which only comes to life towards the end. Why should this be so? It is because, instead of depicting true love, that of Eloisa and Abelard, the composer has degraded his genius and allowed himself to express only the voluptuous.

In those cities to which the arts are foreign, such as Paris, London and Berlin, music takes much longer to grow old than in Italy. This is because, everywhere but in Italy, something other than music provides the object of the public's most passionate attention. War, the revolutions of finance, and questions such as those of the three per cent,[1] the establishment of the Jesuits or the indemnity for the *émigrés* are the subjects which, one after the other, occupy the energies of every mind. Music is a topic of conversation which is convenient rather than interesting, particularly for casual acquaintances. In reality, music in Paris or London is all that it has to be in

[1] See footnote to page 232.

countries where the government is influenced by opinion, that is, an altogether secondary object of consideration and a simple amusement.

Now that Rossini has become a mere glutton, his genius seems to have completely abandoned him. There is no longer a spark of the celestial fire. A number of Neapolitans who have recently returned from Paris saw while they were there the only work that Rossini has written in the last two years, the *Viaggio a Reims*, a sort of comic opera, put together on the occasion of the coronation of Charles X. It is full of wit, reveals great mastery and is altogether extraordinary; as far as genius is concerned, however, there is not the least spark to be found. Rossini was able to call on a number of excellent singers, among them, Mesdames Pasta, Mombelli and Ciuti, and Messrs Zuchelli, Pellegrini, Galli, and Bordogni. He therefore conceived the idea of arranging for fourteen voices to sing together without accompaniment. Nothing more lifeless than this passage can be imagined. There is a complete absence of celestial fire. I regret to say, in fact, that Rossini can now be regarded as dead as far as his art is concerned.

What names suggest themselves after his, in a Europe eager to discuss the latest music?

First of all there is Maria Weber, of whom I will say nothing. You have heard *Der Freischütz* more often than I have. Did you know, however, that Weber, instead of writing music, is now busy writing his autobiography? In it he tells us with all the clarity of German philosophy how he came to be a man of talent.

In Italy, the names which seem to be taking the place of that of Rossini are those of Mercadante, Pacini and Meyerbeer. The first of these, the composer of *Elisa e Claudio*, has genius and the inner fire without which nothing is possible in the arts. An analysis of his talent and that of his two rivals, Pacini of

Milan and the Prussian Meyerbeer, might very well form the material for a second letter, in which I shall say something as well of the famous singers of the day.

Letter to Stritch[1]

THE WIT, LACK OF ENERGY AND MONOTONY OF LECLERCQ'S PROVERBS

Great praise is being bestowed in the literary world on four dialogues attributed to M. Leclercq, the celebrated author of *Les Proverbes*. These dialogues show us a Jesuit trying successively to convert an old *émigré* marchioness of sixty, the Countess her daughter and finally a young viscount, the son of the countess. The young man is a captain in the Royal Guard, and the Jesuit hopes to win him over by the promise of promotion. These dialogues are no less witty than Voltaire's satiric jests, but it is not yet certain whether it was Leclercq who wrote them.

At all events, there is no doubt as to M. Leclercq's being the author of a charming vaudeville which was produced a few evenings ago at the Théâtre des Variétés, under the title of *Monsieur François, ou chacun sa manie*. Three speculating poets had taken it into their heads to alter parts of M. Leclercq's proverb called *L'Esprit de Servitude*. They suppressed certain passages, introduced a new *dénouement* of half a page and, having completed this task, received a round sum of money for their pains. The public, however, owe them their gratitude, for it is thanks to them that M. Leclercq's new comedy has

[1] No translation of this letter has ever been traced in the English reviews.

been able to appear. This very clever writer has introduced into his play an elderly valet who continually reminds us of the prefects, chamberlains and generals of Napoleon, who, though loaded with riches, are continually seeking employment from those who have succeeded their former master in the Tuileries. These men, though decorated with splendid insignia, have to be in service, no matter whom they serve. M. Leclercq, however, was unable to represent them on the stage without hiding to some extent their true identity.

Fashionable society in France is like the President who disliked *Tartuffe* and of whom, in an address to the public, Molière said, 'Nous allions vous donner Tartuffe mais Monsieur le premier président ne veut pas qu'on le joue'.[1] In the same way, our men and women of fashion, who make up what is known as polite society, do not enjoy seeing their own foibles taken off on the stage. Ever since the court and the salons of the Duchesses have assumed their present influence over manners, they have tried to dub any such form of parody as 'bad taste'. Such parody, it is true, almost certainly tends to bring the manners and behaviour of the upper classes into disrepute. Hence, presumably, the desire to suppress it. It is with this view that the Duchesse de Duras is said to have obtained police intervention to prevent the melodrama entitled *L'Auberge des Adrets* from being performed. In this play, one of the bandits mimics the manners of the great.

These general considerations have induced M. Leclercq who, for tone and delicacy of manner, may, without exaggeration, be compared with La Bruyère, to depict the Spirit of Servitude only in the personality of an old footman. M. François is a footman who has retired on a good income. He ought, in a way, to be completely happy, but, like most people who,

---

[1] The equivocal turn of the apology, which depends upon the two meanings of the pronoun *le*, is not translatable. (Note in the *New Monthly Magazine*.)

without feeling the infirmity of age, abandon the employment to which they are accustomed, M. François is miserable because he is no longer in service. A count, who is his country neighbour, is about to give a grand reception, and he has promised to supply him with a lackey. The man whom he has chosen for this honourable function, however, unexpectedly inherits a large sum of money, and M. François, determined to keep his word to the count, once more puts on his beloved livery. But the count has invited Madame François, a woman of more ambitious spirit than her husband, to the same reception. Your English aristocracy must not condemn this incident as improbable. On entering the drawing-room what a spectacle presents itself to her eyes! She sees her own husband in livery. To enable you to appreciate the humorous details of this little play, it would be necessary to quote them and for this I lack the space. The ostentatious Mme François, who has married the handsome valet out of pure love, and who cannot bear to hear him called by his Christian name, and the unfortunate François regretting the happy days when he was in service, together make up a highly finished comic picture. M. Leclercq would be a great dramatic writer if he possessed more energy. *Utinam fuisset vis comica!* But he is gifted with so much wit that he is afraid of being energetic, he dare not venture to be forcible, in case he should be accused of bad taste. In our present refined state of civilisation this is the shoal on which all our men of wit are wrecked. It is impossible to read right through M. Leclercq's sketches without feeling the disagreeable effects of the monotony induced by the author's timidity.

New Monthly Magazine, June 1826

TALMA

What a singular people the French must be, when the death of a great actor has every appearance of having brought about a new clause in their ecclesiastical constitution! Talma's funeral has served the purpose of establishing an important truth, hitherto unrecognised in France. This is that there is nothing indecorous in carrying the remains of a deceased person straight from his residence to the burial place, without carrying them into a church on the way.

Many philosophers have suspected this in the past; but, only six months ago, every honest *bourgeois*, and for that matter people of much higher station in Paris, would have considered it very discreditable to have the remains of their relatives interred without the funeral service being first read in church. A year ago our young liberals thought it a point of honour for the friends of a deceased person to convey the body into a Catholic church, if necessary by force.[1] The *Globe*, which at the present moment reflects the good sense of the public, has proved convincingly that to force admittance into a church is a violation of the rights which the Catholic priests possess as ordinary French citizens. Is it fair, one might ask, that a philosopher or deist who worships God in his own way and not according to the Romish faith, and who never set foot in a Catholic church during his life, should be forced into one after his death? Can anything be less liberal than this? In acting in this way the public abuses its power in the same way that the government abuses its control over the police.

On the day of Talma's funeral, eighty thousand people were

[1] The uproar which took place at the burial of the actor Philippe is fresh in every memory. (Note in *New Monthly Magazine*.)

assembled on the boulevards discussing the questions on which I have already briefly touched. Public opinion has now decided that there is nothing improper in carrying the body straight to the place of rest. Even the words in which the decision is expressed are worthy of attention. No mention is made of the word *church*. The word *straight* implies all that has to be implied, while due respect for every opinion is observed. The priests are nevertheless furious at this point of moral doctrine which has been established before their eyes and in defiance of their authority. In France, since time immemorial, it has been considered as a disgrace to be refused admission into a church after death. In this way the priests were always able to insult the memory of any man they chose, at the very moment when the admiration of his fellow-countrymen was being most enthusiastically expressed, that is, just after his death. This is the way they chose to treat Voltaire in 1778. Now, however, by means of the one little word, *straight*, which every man can insert in his will without causing a scandal, the power of the priests has been eluded, and they can no longer pronounce judgment on the dead. The final ceremonies of religion have become merely a matter of taste, and anyone may dispense with them if he pleases. This change that has now come over public opinion is of the utmost significance. It is the most resounding defeat that the fanatics have yet sustained in France. People who before had no desire to sacrifice the respectability and interests of their family by exposing themselves to public insult after their death, often thought of embracing the Protestant faith. Today, however, anyone may overcome the difficulty by following the example of Talma and inserting in his will similar directions concerning his funeral.

A great many pamphlets made their appearance on the occasion of Talma's death. The scribes who are in the pay of the booksellers have so degraded our literature, that people of taste can scarcely help feeling disgust even with what they like best, as a result of their general exaggeration and stupidity. Last year, for example, even the warmest admirers of General Foy must have been heartily sickened by the dull, extravagant eulogies which poured out in the form of pamphlets at the time of his death. Talma has been less unfortunate. M. Moreau, a man of considerable talent, has published an entertaining and well-thought account of the life of this great actor, with whom he was intimately acquainted for twenty years.

Talma was born in Paris in 1763, and was fifteen years of age when Le Kain died. He started his career in 1787; but he did not rise to any distinction until 1789, just at the beginning of the Revolution. He then performed, with a remarkable degree of energy, the rôle of Charles IX in the tragedy of that name by Chénier. Voltaire had been accustomed to reciting Alexandrine verse in a style of declamation which would nowadays seem ridiculous, and which we would describe as incantatory. Le Kain, who was formed under Voltaire's instruction, and who excelled in his tragedies, did not chant quite as noticeably as his master, and Talma chanted even less than Le Kain; yet, at the same time, he was not altogether free from a certain degree of formality. He was at his best in the delivery of half-lines of broken verse, such as the *qu'en dis-tu* in Lafosse's tragedy *Manlius*. Nevertheless, when he had twenty lines in succession to recite, he often chanted as much as Le Kain. Talma's death will probably see this style of recitation entirely banished from the French stage. Our tragic declamation at the moment is characterised by that affectation of dignity which Macready assumes in the rôle of Virginius. In time, however, it is sure to approximate towards the style of Kean in *Othello*. All our tragedians in turn will try to perform in Talma's various rôles, yet none of them probably will rise above mediocrity. The truth of the matter is that the public taste now demands simplicity, and our present actors are even more formal than Talma. They have not the sense to perceive that the Charter which Louis XVIII was forced to grant us in 1814 has produced a marked effect on our manners. Charles X is far more natural in manner than Louis XVI ever was, and the Dauphin, when he ascends the throne as Louis XIX, will be just as natural and informal as any well-bred private gentleman. The Dauphin has never witnessed any of the affectation which at Versailles, under Louis XV, was known as *dignity of manner*. A nobleman of the court of Charles X would be laughed at if ever he assumed the haughty bearing of even the most plain and unaffected of Louis XVI's courtiers.

In France we have no establishments like your Oxford and Cambridge for the exclusive training of the sons of the aristocracy. Talma's own two sons were educated at a school kept by a M. Morion whose pupils included the children of some of the best families in France. Talma's sons were sent to this establishment until about two years ago when, at a prize-giving day, the Bishop of Hermopolis, M. Frayssinous, publicly insulted them for being the sons of an actor excommunicated by the Gallican church. This was resented even by the aristocracy of the Faubourg St Germain; and in the opinion of many prudent and pious individuals it fully justified Talma's express desire to be conveyed *straight* to the Père Lachaise cemetery after his death. The son of a duke and the son of the duke's steward receive precisely the same education in a Parisian school; furthermore, if the steward's son is cleverer than the duke's, it is he who wins the prizes. The pupils are continually chaffing one another about the titles of a number of their parents. The Duc de Chartres, son of the Duc d'Orléans, who may one day be King of France, was himself educated in a lycée, and would beat his schoolfellows whenever they called him *monseigneur*.

You will understand from this that, in France, stilted tragedy died with Talma. He mounted on tragic stilts in 1780, because he was called upon to perform to men and women brought up under the old régime. The taste of the theatrical audiences of the time can only be really understood by a man who, born in 1773, was twenty years of age when Louis XVI was beheaded. A man of this age had the opportunity of observing the manners which the *émigrés* took with them to London, and brought back with them on their return to Paris. Today, however, he would be fifty-five, and how few men of that age are to be found in the audience at any theatre. As soon as one plunges beneath the surface, the character of a nation explains everything. The same circumstances which preclude any possibility of a revival of the tragic style, the style which disappeared from the stage with the death of our great Roscius, now render the restoration of the old aristocratic feelings quite impossible. The son of a poor attorney who, when at school, perhaps thrashed the son of a peer or a duke, will not be very ready to show him respect when, after they have both left school, the attorney on his way to the *Palais de Justice* meets his former school-fellow on his way to vote in the Chamber of Peers.

Talma was the son of a dentist and himself followed his father's trade as a young man. Throughout his life he was distinguished more for his generosity and good nature than for his talent. His premature reputation he owed principally to Mme de Staël, who extolled him beyond all measure. As a result of her *puffing*, he acquired in 1804 a reputation which he only began to deserve in 1812. Talma possessed talent without wit, and a considerable haughtiness, which involved him in continual disputes with his theatrical colleagues. Le Kain had attempted a reform in theatrical costume. Before his day, it had been the custom for the Emperor Augustus to be represented in red stockings and a full-bottomed wig. Le Kain ventured to perform the part in an embroidered robe. But Talma was the first to appear with unpowdered hair and in an unembroidered toga. When the celebrated Mlle Contat saw him for the first time dressed as Brutus in Voltaire's tragedy, she exclaimed, 'He looks like a statue', a remark which the fair actress intended as a bitter sarcasm.

The compilers of anecdotes have published a number of exaggerated accounts of Talma's intimacy with Bonaparte, which began in 1795. Talma never lent anything but books to the young general who was soon destined to immortalise himself in the campaigns of Italy and who, at the time, was passionately in love with Mme de Beauharnais. Bonaparte, even after he had become emperor, still kept up his friendship with Talma. He was fond of talking intimately with men of talent, for he was conscious of his own powers and was fond of displaying them. He wished everyone with whom he conversed to speak his mind freely and not to feel restrained by respect or deference. In 1802, when he became First Consul, he would frequently spend whole nights in Talma's company discussing tragic acting. An observation which he made on one of these occasions is particularly curious, since it may be regarded as proof of the profound finesse which he practised at this moment in his career in order to conceal his ambitious projects and to avoid offending the Jacobins who were still immensely powerful. Talma had performed before the First Consul the part of Caesar in Corneille's *Mort de Pompée*, in which he had to deliver the following line:

Pour moi qui tiens le trône égal à l'infamie.[1]

After the play Bonaparte desired Talma to come and see him the following morning. Talma accordingly made his way to the Tuileries, and the First Consul, having dismissed his

[1] For me who regard the throne as infamous.

generals, addressed the following words to the great actor: 'From your performance of Caesar last night, it struck me that in one point you misunderstood the part. You had too great an air of sincerity in pronouncing the words,

> Pour moi qui tiens le trône égal à l'infamie.

Here Caesar is by no means expressing his real feelings. He says this only because he wishes the Romans to believe that he holds the throne in detestation.'

Talma profited by Bonaparte's criticism, who, when he next saw him, said: 'That was better; this time it really was Caesar.'

It will be remembered that round about the year 1808, Napoleon assembled nearly all the European sovereigns at Erfurt. Talma having asked for permission to go there himself, the Emperor replied, 'Go by all means. You shall act before a whole pit-full of kings.'

During Napoleon's stay at Erfurt, wishing to enjoy a joke at the expense of his fellow sovereigns, he desired Talma to perform in Voltaire's *Mort de César*, a tragedy which was strictly prohibited in Paris. The play is full of violent attacks against royalty; and, during the performance, Napoleon was able to enjoy the embarrassment of the various royal figure-heads, who found themselves, as it were, openly insulted. Even Talma seemed embarrassed and frequently seemed to hesitate in the delivery of some ferocious Republican sentiment.

One day in the year 1808, Napoleon was conversing with Talma at the Tuileries, while several royal personages were waiting their turn to speak with the Emperor. Talma, observing this, wished to withdraw, but the Emperor detained him saying, 'No, no, let them wait'. During this conversation, which Talma related to me himself, the Emperor recommended him, above all, to be sure that his acting was always as simple and natural as possible. 'You see in this palace', he said, 'kings who have come to solicit the restoration of their states, great generals who have come to ask me for a sovereign's crown. Ambition and other violent passions agitate all around me. Here I behold men offering to serve those whom they hate, young princesses entreating me to restore them to the lovers from whom I have separated them. Are these not tragic characters? And perhaps I am the most tragic of them all. Yet you do not find that we continually strain our voices and make violent gestures. We are calm, except at those moments when our passion carries us away, and these are always of short duration. A man's natural strength would not allow him to keep up such a state of agitation for two hours on end; what is more, when he is under the influence of violent passion, he has less strength than usual.'[1]

Talma would recount his conversations with the emperor with a simplicity which made it impossible to suspect him of misrepresentation. As a general rule, he had no more than the normal degree of pretentiousness, without which it is impossible nowadays to succeed in Paris. He was the last of our great men formed by the beneficent revolution. With what astonishing rapidity they have disappeared from the scene of life! Napoleon, Masséna, Murat, Davout, David, Régnault and Talma are all numbered with the dead; and some of them have found a premature grave.

Talma owned a beautiful country residence at Brunoy near Paris on which he expended enormous sums of money. In spite of this, he has left only ten thousand pounds to his two sons. He was very charitable to the poor; and, what is rather strange, gave a great deal to the Catholic priests who were always applying to him for money for church repairs and other similar purposes. He spoke English very well, and frequently

[1] It may be said that Napoleon's judicious advice was of material benefit to Talma in reaching the high degree of perfection which he later displayed. (Note in the *New Monthly Magazine*.)

read Shakespeare in the original. Before performing in Ducis' version of *Hamlet*, he read the original play and often remarked, 'This Shakespeare electrifies me'. Nature had endowed him with handsome features and a finely proportioned figure. When he performed the part of Oreste in *Clytemnestre*, nobody would have supposed him to be more than twenty-five years old. He never came nearer to perfection than in 1821, when he performed in *Sylla*. He presented in this rôle a striking resemblance to Napoleon.

Talma had no idea of his approaching physical deterioration. During his last long illness the only circumstance which caused him anxiety was that his extreme thinness would disable him from impersonating certain youthful characters, in which he was obliged to reveal his neck. His *forte* lay in the depiction of terror, for he was indifferent on the stage as a lover. In spite of this, it was love that dominated his entire existence. He was loved by some of the most distinguished women of his time; and even at the time of his death, he was said to be in love with and jealous over his last wife.

New Monthly Magazine, December 1826

TALMA
[continued]

Paris, November 18th, 1826

Talma was more remarkable for his talent than for his intelligence. He wrote an essay on Le Kain which was printed some years ago and which is nothing more than a commonplace dissertation scarcely even possessing the merit of unfolding the writer's views with perspicuity. He was able to tell a number of anecdotes concerning Napoleon and never varied in his manner of relating them. He would tell them in the same way, whether it was when the emperor was all-powerful in the Tuileries, when he was a prisoner at St Helena or, more recently, when the progress of liberalism and the love of the Charter had turned him in the eyes of the younger generation into a mere despot, remarkable for his talents and his misfortunes.

One day Napoleon said to Talma, 'I have just been acting in a tragic scene. The Princesse d'Eckmühl (Mme Davout) has been tormenting me for some time for a private audience. I gave her one this morning and what do you think she wanted? Nothing less than a throne for her husband. He is, as it happens, a prudent man; and if he and I escape the dangers of war for a few years longer, I may perhaps give him what he wants.'

On another occasion, he observed to Talma, 'The Austrians have only ever had one good general; and, because I did not praise him, they allowed him to perish in an inferior command'.

Speaking of heroism, he said one day, 'Your tragedies are very absurd when they attempt to portray military heroism. Battles are won by judgment and perseverance, and sometimes by chance. When two armies of a hundred thousand men begin to engage battle, the majority of the troops on each side have the strongest inclination to fight. As long as this ardour prevails, a general has nothing to do, at least not more than a coachman who drives down the Rue St Honoré. When the battle has been going on for five or six hours, however, the love of fighting begins to diminish on both sides, and it is then that the general must show the talent needed to animate his own troops and dishearten those of the enemy. This talent, or whatever one is going to call it, must be of the kind that can respond at once to an unforeseen situation. Furthermore, it calls for true judgment, if a man is going to see things as they are; not your tragic enthusiasm which is so misleading and which raises false expectations as to what men are capable of doing. Murat was a tragic hero, but a poor general, whereas Desaix was a true hero, while at the same time too simple and natural for tragedy.' He then pronounced judgment on all the distinguished men he had known.

One day towards the beginning of April 1815, just after his return from Elba, Napoleon sent for Talma. The latter on his arrival found the Emperor very much out of humour. 'It is being said', he exclaimed, 'that I took lessons from you in order to learn how to mount my throne and how to make a speech.[1] In any case, whether you gave me lessons or not, it is proof that I have played my part well. I understand', he added, 'that Louis XVIII thought very highly of you. You could be nothing if not flattered by the approval shown by a good-natured man who has also seen Le Kain.'

The harmless calumny to which Napoleon alluded was not so awkwardly contrived as some which were invented by the reactionary party. The latter did everything within its power to detract from the glory and prestige of the one extraordinary man to whom kings are indebted for the survival of monarchy in the nineteenth century. When Napoleon was angry, his gestures and countenance strongly resembled those of Talma. The likeness was particularly striking when Talma appeared in the rôles of Manlius and Cinna. Napoleon's fits of rage were sudden and violent. I was at the Tuileries one day when he suddenly turned his gaze on the Abbé d'Astros (today Bishop of Bayonne) who had been maintaining illegal correspondence with the Pope, Pius VII. The Pope had only some short time before excommunicated him. 'Do you realise, sir, what you

---

[1] The royalist pamphlets of 1814 were continually ridiculing Napoleon for having been obliged, as they alleged, to place himself under Talma's tuition. Talma was insulted by the officers of a regiment at Lille, I think, on account of the supposed lessons given to the impromptu sovereign. (Note in the *New Monthly Magazine*.)

have been doing?' were the Emperor's words. 'You will end up by bringing about civil war in your own country. I would do well to have you tried and shot within twenty-four hours.' Napoleon was like a madman; he was unable to restrain his feelings, and I was never so forcibly struck by the resemblance with Talma.

M. Tissot has just published a pamphlet on the latter, which contains a number of interesting pages, such as those in which we are told about Napoleon's advice as to the proper way of performing the rôle of Nero in Racine's *Britannicus*.

The constant object of Talma's ambition was not to shine in society but to excel in his profession. He devoted himself entirely to the advancement of dramatic art. This feeling for one's profession, a feeling without which no true proficiency in the fine arts is possible, is becoming more and more rare. The arts are now cultivated merely as a means of making money. The painter finishing his picture and the poet concluding his tragedy are only concerned with the reception which their works are to be given in society. Both Canova and Corneille thought of their work in this way, and allowed themselves to be over-influenced by the attractions of society. All classes are now mingled together in France and it is not the richest but the cleverest man who makes the most impressive figure in a salon. This triumph of sociability is fatal to the arts. It is a contagion from which Talma escaped and, escaping from which, derived his own profound feeling for the art of the tragedian. He gave a number of useful hints to actors who are performing today and strongly recommended them to be less bombastic. He had begun himself to feel all the absurdity of the tirade.[1]

New Monthly Magazine, January 1827

[1] The French give the name of 'tirade' to those declamatory passages which occur so frequently in the tragedies of Racine and Voltaire. (Note in the *New Monthly Magazine*.)

STENDHAL

MACREADY AND KEAN ON THE PARISIAN STAGE

Our tragic actresses have grown old and ugly and the public is tired of them. You may therefore imagine how this enhances the reputation of Miss Smithson, who seldom appears on the stage without making the female and many of the male members of the audience shed tears. Mr Kemble has visited us, but has made no impression. He is considered as more or less the equal of our French actors who do not rise above the level of mediocrity. Macready has also appeared, but his Macbeth is not liked. He holds himself as if the pit were full of painters. When he feels that he has found a graceful stance —the grace that is to be found in the vignettes of our editions of *Lalla Rookh* or the *Corsair*—he pauses and remains motionless, as if he wished to give the young artists time to sketch him.

Macready has played Virginius. The tragedy itself was dull, particularly up to the last two acts; these, however, made a powerful impression on the public. Mr Knowles rose in general esteem and Macready was excellent. His acting in this part, however, has been the subject of much discussion. Many critics have blamed the slow and deliberate way in which he kills his daughter. Would an inhabitant of Southern Europe act in this way, or an inhabitant of Rome? In answer to these questions, it has been suggested that Macready shows how an Englishman would be likely to act in similar circumstances; though would a father in London or Edinburgh seem as calm as this, if his passion were so far roused as to impel him to kill his daughter, in order to save her from a tyrant such as Appius?

Be this as it may, however, should not our conception of such a situation be nearer to the feelings of a Londoner than to those of an ancient Roman, whose character was formed by customs and a climate so very different from ours?

Such, in substance, is the principal theme of discussion in fashionable circles. Those who have been to England say, 'Wait till Kean arrives; then you will see something different'. Well, Kean has arrived, but has failed to excite admiration. It is true that Macready, who seemed very inferior to him in *Macbeth*, has only impressed us in the sentimental rôle of Virginius, that is to say in the part of an ancient Roman whom excess of passion almost deprives of motion and speech. Finally, however, it is only Miss Smithson whose success has been consistently remarkable. When she played the part of the widowed Queen of King Edward in *Richard III*, the scene in which she parts with her children left not a single eye in the house which was dry. It should be mentioned, however, that displays of maternal tenderness are quite the fashion in France at the moment; and with us fashion in anything, whether good or bad, is all-powerful.

New Monthly Magazine, June 1828

III
THE CURRENT OF IDEAS

THOUGHTS ON THE PHILOSOPHY OF HELVETIUS
(FROM A CORRESPONDENT)

There was nothing in this world the Emperor Napoleon dreaded so much as public education. Acting on this principle, he was altogether willing that Kant's system of philosophy should be introduced into France. Only this was to go against the old French adage which says that 'anyone who cannot make himself understood is not worth the trouble of having his meaning guessed at'. When it became necessary to abandon German philosophy, an attempt was made to introduce the philosophy of the Scots. In order to smooth the way for Dugald Stewart, a great outcry was raised against Helvétius. It was even, after a time, extremely bad taste to say anything in his favour. Once I spent an evening in the home of a certain well-known and influential lady. Here Helvétius was maltreated in the cruellest imaginable way, so much so that afterwards I wrote in an album that lay on her table the following sentence: 'The greatest philosopher of whom the French can boast was lacking in one single respect. He should have lived in some lonely, secluded spot in the Alps and from here sent his book to Paris. The last thing he should have done was to appear in Paris himself.' The powdered, scented and affected wits of the day, men such as Suard, Marmontel and Diderot, seeing Helvétius so natural and sincere in his behaviour, could not bring themselves to believe that he was a great philosopher. Their contempt for his profound reasoning was genuinely felt and quite unaffected. To begin with, his style and manner of reasoning were clear, simple and unadorned by epigram, the absence of the latter ingredient being an unforgivable offence in France. Then again, the author lowered himself in the public estimation by certain follies into which he was betrayed by the extreme importance he attached to the acquisition of what is known in France as *glory*. He wished to become the idol of his contemporaries, like Balzac, Voiture and Fontenelle. This weakness, however, should never have been visited on his book.

Rousseau possessed too much sensibility and too little reason, Buffon cultivated too much hypocrisy in the Jardin des Plantes, and Voltaire had too much arch, puerile facetiousness for any one of them to be capable of giving a sane assessment of Helvétius' principles.

One of this philosopher's principal defects was a great lack of tact. This led him to call the principle of all action *interest* (a word that should not be mentioned to polite ears) instead of giving it the prettier name of *pleasure*.[1] But what must we think of the good sense of the men of letters of the day, men who allowed themselves to be influenced by so trivial an error, if error it be?

A man of ordinary character and intelligence, such as Prince Eugene of Savoy, if placed in the same circumstances as Regulus on his return from Carthage, would have calmly remained in Rome and laughed at the credulous simplicity of the Carthagenian senate. Prince Eugene would have been following the dictates of his *interest* in remaining, and in the same way, Regulus was following his by returning to be tortured.

In almost all the circumstances of life, a generous mind will

---

[1] Torva laena lupum sequitur; lupus ipse capellam;
Florentem cytisum sequitur lasciva capella;
    . . . trahit sua quemque voluptas
        Virgil, *Eclogues*.
(The lioness with the bloodshot eyes pursues the wolf; the wolf the goat; the goat seeks out fresh clover . . . each one is drawn by his desire.)

perceive the possibility of certain actions, the idea of which a commonplace mind is incapable of understanding. The moment that the possibility of accomplishing these actions becomes apparent to a man of generous sentiments, it is immediately in his own interests that he should carry them out. If he fails to, he feels the sting of self-abasement and, as a result, becomes unhappy. This principle, taught by Helvétius, is true, even in the wildest aberrations of passion, even in suicide. In a word, it is contrary to man's nature and even impossible for him not to do what he thinks may lead to his own happiness, the moment the possibility of doing so is presented to him.

ALCESTE
Paris Monthly Review, April 1822

AN ACCOUNT OF KANT'S PHILOSOPHY

Exposé du système de Kant by Kinker.
Examen de l'ouvrage de M. Kinker by M. de Tracy.

Montmorency, June 10th, 1822.

While I was exercising my corpulent body, walking over the smiling hillsides of Andilly and Montmorency, I plunged into German philosophy and have become completely *Kantified*. You will now have to put up with an account of all I have been reading, which you will find tedious but also useful. I am sending you a *Short Course in Philosophy*, this being nothing more than the assembled notes of a recluse. I crave your indulgence for the work for the sake of its author.

Immediately afterwards, I read M. de Tracy's examination of Kant's philosophy (a memoir seventy pages long to be found in volume III of the memoirs of the Institut Français).[1] Kant himself was not always clear as to his own meaning and it is extremely difficult for anyone else to follow it. When one has at last succeeded, one is left with truths so evident that they seem scarcely worth the trouble of pronouncing in the first place. These truths are mixed up with an immense heap of absurdities that a man of Kant's talent would never have uttered if the language he used had been more lucid.

Nothing is more conducive to good philosophy than a language which, by its very nature, is necessarily clear. A man who is obscure in French, for instance, can have no illusions; either he is deceiving himself or seeking to deceive someone else. M. de Tracy, in his memorandum, is as clear as anyone possibly can be, when he is obliged to pursue his adversary through a gloomy cavern.

All systems of philosophy are addressed to the young. Those philosophers whose self-respect is not too susceptible write what are, in reality, novels for delightful young people to applaud with all the enthusiasm one has at the age of twenty for a good novel. This was the secret of Plato's success in Athens, of Abelard's in Paris during the twelfth century, and today, once again in Paris, of the success of a young highly talented professor.[2]

I am now sixty years old and have read through every system of philosophy. I shall therefore write down thirty lines or so which I hope will be read by the young who are the hope of the nation.

There are really only two sciences[3] that a man can learn. The first of these is the science of knowing the motives of

---
[1] The first four sentences of the article are omitted from the English translation in the *Paris Monthly Review*.
[2] Victor Cousin.
[3] A better word would be *art*. An art always depends on a science; it is the putting into practice of the methods indicated by a science. (Note in the *Paris Monthly Review*.)

men's actions. As soon as you know men's true motives, you will be able to seek to cultivate in them other motives which will lead them to act in such a way as is likely to lead them to bring about your own happiness.

Today, in 1822, men nearly always lie when they talk of their true motives. The most useful science for a young man, the science which at the age of twenty gives the clearest proof of intelligence, is that of penetrating lies of this kind. True politics are nothing more than the art of ensuring that Mr Q—— does not find his happiness in acting in a way which will harm Mr B——. There is a book whose title ought to be *The Art of Discovering Men's True Motives*. This book is *De l'Esprit* by Helvétius.

The second of the two useful sciences is logic, or the art of not going astray in one's pursuit of happiness. The truly ridiculous, that which really causes people to laugh, is the action of any man who makes an error in his attempts to reach his goal, while believing that he is still advancing towards it.

One laughs at the man who wishes to go to Rouen and who scrambles into the stage-coach going to Auxerre. A young man, in the year 1822, wishes to pass for a man of intellect, becomes a pedant and quotes on any pretext Juvenal or Grotius. He is laughed at and ridiculed; he has mistaken the date just as the other has mistaken the road; his pedantry would have passed off as wit in the year 1622.

Logic is the art of not mistaking the road in our advance towards some desired goal.

M. de Tracy has shown admirably in his *Idéologie* that our errors stem always from the imperfection of our memories. At first this discovery is startling; after six months of reflection, however, one learns to rely at every instant of one's life on the facts revealed by experience.

I thus reduce *philosophy* to not misunderstanding the motives of men's actions, and to making no error in one's reasoning, or in the art of advancing towards happiness.

ALCESTE
Paris Monthly Review, June 1822

CHARLATANISM AND THE NECESSITY OF CRITICISM

Dictionnaire des Belles-Lettres, contenant les éléments de la littérature, d'après un seul principe, etc. . . . , par P.-.C.-V. Boiste, auteur du Dictionnaire universel. (*Dictionary of Belles Lettres*, containing the *elements of literature according to a single principle, etc.*, by P. C. V. Boiste, author of the *Universal Dictionary*.)

M. Boiste, the author of this new discovery in literature, seems to belong to that class of inventors and reformers who announce universal remedies for every disease and who attempt to trace out one short, easy road to universal knowledge. The single principle governing the elements of literature of which he tells us is the *association of ideas*. If by this he means simply that we should follow their natural order and observe a clear arrangement in our ideas, analogous to that of whatever subject is under discussion, he is certainly right. He has no right, however, to proclaim this truism to the world as a great discovery concerning the nature of literature. Furthermore, association of ideas is not in itself enough to guarantee excellence of composition; for if the simple ideas that go to form the association are not sound or ingenious in the first place, the stringing of them together will do nothing to change their nature or make the aggregate lucid and excellent, when each component part is obscure and valueless. Indeed, were we to judge M. Boiste's single ideas from the *following* strange association, we should not have a very high opinion of them. As a preliminary to producing anything of value in literature, according to M. Boiste, we should 'feel a flame running through our veins; our nerves should be aroused; each single hair should bristle with a prickling effect on our heads; and we should experience a kind of poetical creeping of the flesh. All these are reliable indications of the feeling of intellectual creation.' This extraordinary association of ideas is not calculated to tempt many to a close perusal of this new dictionary of Belles Lettres. Our sole purpose in fact in reviewing this book has been to warn the reader against being deceived by any such imposing title as *Dictionnaire des Belles Lettres* by the author of the *Dictionnaire Universel, etc.* There is unfortunately a certain degree of charlatanism in the literature of every country; but in France far more than elsewhere. Despite this, those who call themselves the guides of public taste, the critics of the day, instead of denouncing it openly and helping to check its progress, foster and encourage it by the most undeserved praise and intentional misrepresentation. This reprehensible dereliction of their duty towards the public is a result of the system of literary *coteries*, intrigue, cringing and flattery, to which French men of letters so often have recourse. As long as this wretched system exists, it will be impossible to look for anything like sound and impartial criticism in France. This, we are convinced, is one of the main reasons for which a country which contains infinitely more professional men of letters than England, has not been able to produce a critical organ approaching within any calculable degree the *Edinburgh* and *Quarterly Reviews*.

New Monthly Magazine
(Historical Register) October 1823

VICTOR COUSIN AND THE INTERROGATION OF CONSCIOUSNESS

M. Broussais, one of the most fashionable physicians in Paris, has improved upon the system of the celebrated Rasori of Milan, and claims to be able to cure all diseases by bleeding and leeches. One of his patients recently died after the application of eight hundred leeches. This system is so much the rage in Paris that leeches are now brought from the heart of Hungary. Absurd though this may appear, M. de Broussais is nevertheless a man of considerable talent. He has recently published a work entitled *De la Folie et de l'Irritation, ouvrage dans lequel les rapports du physique et du moral sont établis sur la base de la médecine.* (*On Madness and Irritation, a work in which the relations between the physical and the moral are established on the basis of medicine.*) This is an extremely clever work and well worthy of notice in England.

In France, where fashion reigns with despotic sway, there is an incessant craving for novelty. In 1800, Locke and Condillac were admired for the manner in which they explain the formation of our ideas and judgments; but they could not continue to enjoy permanent favour. Towards the end of 1803, MM. Cabanis and de Tracy published their own immortal works. Count de Tracy's *Ideology*, *Grammar* and *Logic* are the most profound and lucid works in the French language on the formation of ideas, the art of expressing them, and on the right conduct of the understanding. However, Napoleon detested the writing of Cabanis and de Tracy. About 1803, M. de Chateaubriand brought the Catholic religion into vogue, while M. Frayssinous, now a peer of France invested with the Cordon Bleu, and M. Royer Collard, now a liberal and President of the Chamber of Deputies, both attacked the philosophy of Locke and Condillac. M. Royer Collard has been succeeded by M. Cousin and the directors of the *Globe*, who endeavour to throw Locke and Condillac into oblivion, and to establish the mystical reveries of the Germans in their place. Translations of the works of Plato, and of Reid, the Scottish philosopher, have been published, while the young men of fortune in Paris have become infected with mysticism and enthusiastic admirers of M. Cousin's lectures, which they pretend to understand. M. Cousin is accordingly lauded to the skies in the journals which are maintained by the subscriptions of his disciples.

MM. Royer Collard and Cousin both take care to say nothing definite and clear on the formation and expression of ideas or on the art of leading the understanding to the apprehension of the truth, in the examination of any particular subject; but they give us a multitude of vague propositions concerning the nature of the Deity, the soul, and the manner in which God created man. M. Cousin claims to have discovered all this in the course of what he describes as *l'interrogation méditative de la conscience* (*the meditative interrogation of consciousness*). This is the whole secret of the new school of philosophy which, so it is claimed, is to supersede the whole of Locke and Condillac. If these gentlemen did not cloak themselves in the obscurity of their style, the inanity of their ideas would be clear to every eye. While interrogating their consciousness, in which they claim to read so many wonderful things, they close their eyes to the clear facts established by Locke and Condillac, and set up ideal speculation instead of facts and experience. Just because it is the fashion among our young men to listen with enthusiasm to M. Cousin's lectures; because a young professor has been denounced by M. Franchet to the King of Prussia as a turbulent spirit and imprisoned in Berlin; and because M. Cousin has stated that he was thrown into a dungeon several feet below the level of the Spree, no professor or journalist will dare presume to comment on the obscurity of his language or the mystical emphasis with which he speaks of God, the soul, and sometimes of the formation of ideas. Men of forty shrug their shoulders, because knowledge of human nature and the world has taught them that what is not clear is not worth attending to. Yet, at the same time, the more obscure and mystical M. Cousin's lectures are, the more they are admired by our young men of twenty. The youth of France is no longer distinguished for its gaiety and levity, as it was before the Revolution. They have become gloomy, meditative and calculating. If the Jesuits had done their work better, they might have become also very devout, for their thoughts are constantly wandering to another world.

It is at this stage in the development of French society that M. Broussais has been bold enough to publish a book full of facts and observations. He attacks the new philosophers formed in the school of MM. Royer Collard and Cousin and gives them the general name of *Canto-Platoniciens*. M. Broussais betrays his anger at the very outset; for he is perfectly aware that all the young men in Paris will rise up against him. He tells them plainly that the figurative style which they so extravagantly admire is that of poetic fiction; that the logic of their masters is a perpetual anthology; and that their language is nothing but a metaphorical phraseology, as obscure as it is bombastic. He also attacks the only intelligible idea which these new philosophers have put into circulation. They assert that 'consciousness is a feeling in itself, and is not felt through the senses'. They pretend that, to hear the revelations of consciousness, it is necessary to wrap oneself up in silence and obscurity, so as to be free from the operation of the senses. In a word, one must 'hear oneself think'. The philosophers of this new school allege that, after being long accustomed to these reveries, they discern an immeasurable perspective extending from man to God. An adept pupil clearly discerns in his consciousness, after closing his eyes for some time, a new world, presenting a multitude of beautiful, singular and sacred facts. These facts are connected by relations, the laws of which may be understood. Finally, and best of all, these facts are entirely distinct from those which are revealed to us through the medium of the senses.

However, I am afraid lest I should weary your patience with these details. I shall therefore conclude my remarks on this subject by observing that all our young Parisians who are neither hangers-on at court nor the dupes of Jesuitical intrigues, are enthusiastic disciples of M. Cousin. Napoleon would have made them all cavalry officers or auditors of the Council of State. M. Broussais tells them, without any ceremony, that their brains have been turned because they lack employment.

I am aware, Sir, that all these remarks concerning the new Parisian philosophy would have little interest for you or your readers, were it not that they serve to show the prevailing cast of mind among the young men who, in ten or fifteen years time, will be peers of France, and employed in all the various departments of the Government.

The corrupt taste and absurd doctrines which are to be found in France at the present moment have already had the most mischievous effects upon our literature. No author can enjoy success, unless by endeavouring to please our newly-enriched provincial traders, or by gaining a reputation among M. Cousin's mystical followers. The author who steers clear of these two shoals will gain but little profit. The only real judges of literary merit, the only judges whose opinions are worth anything at all, are the females of the upper ranks of society and men of about thirty, whose maturity of age secures them against the influence of our current fashionable philosophy. However, fashion, which has plunged us into this state of mental degradation, will probably soon extricate us once again. I have little doubt that Cousin's philosophy will be wholly forgotten in two or three years time. Instead of 'closing their eyes and looking into their consciousness' for the immense chain of circumstances which connects them to God, our young men will once again seek the company of the fair sex. The renewal of war, which everyone in France heartily desires, would speedily convert our young philosophers into gallant officers.

New Monthly Magazine, September 1828

THE REVOLUTION IN LITERATURE AND THE REACTION IN PHILOSOPHY

In France we have four distinct classes of men in politics and literature; first, the triflers of the reign of Louis XVI, who were twenty years of age in 1788; secondly, the revolutionaries, who were only twenty in 1793; thirdly, the Bonapartists, who were fifteen years old in 1800, and who, from 1800 to 1814, were imbued with the love of military glory by reading the Emperor's bulletins; and fourthly, the young men, who, since 1815 and the second restoration of the Bourbons, have been educated for the Church, under the influence of the Jesuits. Many of the sons of our noblest and wealthiest families are educated by the Jesuits at St Acheul, near Amiens, and other similar colleges. Under such tuition they become what is known as men of the world and acquire the great art of serving their own interests by flattering the men in power. The Jesuit colleges have certainly produced many able men; but the youths who now leave them with the reputation of excellent classical scholars, are sometimes unable to understand the simplest school books, and completely incompetent when it comes to construing a page of Horace or Tacitus. The young students of St Acheul have the manners and opinions of the old men who were moving in society twenty years before the Revolution.

Napoleon checked the progress of literature from 1800 until 1814. He bribed men of letters with sinecures and pensions, because he stood in awe of them. The last chapters of the Memoirs of the Duke de Rovigo contain an account of the corruption of M. Esménard, a writer who obtained credit for a certain literary talent during the Empire. It was Napoleon who instructed the Academy to elect M. de Chateaubriand. His object was to have a claim on the gratitude of every man of talent. From the treatment suffered by Mme de Staël's *De l'Allemagne*, however, it is easy to guess the fate that was to be expected by a writer who ventured to express his opinions with any honesty. The restrictions to which authorship was subjected from 1800 to 1814 are sufficient evidence that the Revolution had not had time to extend its influence to literature. The need to defend French territory against the combined sovereigns of Europe occupied our whole attention between 1792 and 1800. Since the return of the Bourbons, the tyranny exercised by the nobles during the reaction of 1816, and the various political manoeuvres which have led to the election of the prudent and reasonable chamber of 1828, have taken the place of all other subjects of interest. However, a great literary revolution is about to take place. Only one department seems to show no promise of rising above mediocrity, namely, metaphysics and logic. MM. Cousin and Royer-Collard (the President of the Chamber of 1828) have set out to abolish the truths established by Locke, Condillac, Tracy, Cabanis and Bentham, and, instead of argument, prefer to send us to the poetic reveries of Plato. The majority of young men, educated under the imperial régime between 1800 and 1814, despise Condillac and admire M. Royer-Collard. The political reputation, and the honour of being President of the Elective Chamber, have enhanced his popularity, and materially helped the reveries of Plato to triumph over the truths of Locke and De Tracy. These circumstances clearly explain the offence that has been taken in certain quarters at Dr Broussais' ingenious work, *De l'Irritation et de la Folie*, which, as I mentioned in one of my former letters, is a bold attack upon Plato.

It is for the reasons here given that the great literary revolution which is about to take place in France, from where it will spread over the whole Continent, will not extend to philosophy (that is, to logic and metaphysics) but will be confined to literature alone. The names of Racine and Shakespeare will be watchwords in the conflict; and the question will be which of these two great poets is henceforth to be the model for dramatic composition.

New Monthly Magazine, December 1828

IV
POLITICS AND SOCIETY

BENJAMIN CONSTANT AND THE NEW PUBLIC MORALITY

M. Benjamin Constant, *De la Religion*.[1]

This book by M. Benjamin Constant is by no means a remarkable one in itself; it belongs in fact to that vast category of literature composed by men of the world who, though not without a certain talent and ability, lack profound views and the power of strict and logical deduction. It is moreover tedious, badly written and lacking in unction, that inward grace and spiritual ingratiation which distinguish, for instance, the writings of the former minister, M. de Chateaubriand. When, in a difficult and abstruse discussion, a man bids adieu to reason and appeals to the *sens intime* of humanity for a solution of the problem, he should write with unction or not at all. He should write, in short, like Chateaubriand who has discovered the art of touching his reader and giving pleasure while at the same time defending the most extravagant lies and absurdities of which it is plain to see that he himself does not believe a word. Constant, on the other hand, succeeds admirably in assuming an air of sincerity; but, with all his talent and all his various qualities, he has a sterile imagination, is lacking in the necessary degree of sensibility and has failed completely in his attempts to flatter.

However, if the merits of M. Constant's book had been either much greater or much less, we should certainly not have drawn our readers' attention to it, had it not been for a reason quite independent of its execution. This work is curious in so

[1] *De la religion considérée dans sa source, ses formes et ses développements* par M. Benjamin Constant. Vol. I, Paris, 1824.

far as it marks a singular epoch in the history of French civilisation, that is to say, in the manners and moral life of the upper classes of French society. Let it not be thought for a moment, furthermore, that, in discussing the moral habits of the French, we are dealing with matters of trifling concern. The extent of their influence must be obvious to anyone who has mixed in foreign circles; while, even in England, where it might be expected to be much less pronounced than elsewhere, its power is well known. Paris is the capital of the continent of Europe. In St Petersburg or in Vienna, the upper ranks of society desire, not only to speak its language, but to adopt its opinions and to believe in its belief. An Austrian prince considers a French duchess as his own compatriot, much more than he does a noble canoness of Paderborn.

Now it so happens that M. Constant's treatise is nothing more nor less than the Gospel of the new religion which certain duchesses and other ladies of the highest rank and leading fashion, who are at the same time perhaps the cleverest of their class, are trying at this moment to promote in Paris.

It may be interesting at this point to cast a rapid glance over the history of morality among the French upper classes during the last forty years. It is a history that is only known today through the faithless medium of the hypocritical novels of Madame de Genlis, or else from the striking remarks on manners which Madame de Staël has scattered over her *Delphine*, *Corinne* and other works. The latter, though sagacious and perceptive, are too often wrapped up in a gaudy and exaggerated style. Moreover, these observations, together with the portrayals of French manners which one finds in the writings of Mesdames de Genlis, de Staël herself, d'Epinay and Campan, represent a period which can be placed round about 1789, that is to say *before* the Revolution. The Revolution has altered everything in France; despite which, together with the rest of Europe, we persist in blinding ourselves to the changes and ignoring, or else simply failing to record, the influence which it has had on the opinions, manners and moral habits of society. Europe continues to think of this society as it was when the last information was published concerning it, which was forty years ago.

The old monarchy of Louis XV bequeathed to the French the corrupt morals of which Lauzun and Mme d'Epinay have given us so faithful and occasionally so repulsive an account. Under Louis XVI the monarchy fell and was replaced by the reign of Terror, during which the women who had been such faithless wives and dissolute mothers proved themselves capable of dying with heroism. Among the thousands of women of the highest ranks of society who passed from the bosom of luxury and the most refined, though by no means the most guiltless pleasure to the scaffold, there was only one, the former mistress of Louis XV, Mme du Barry, who failed to die like a martyr and a heroine. It may be judged from this how far, as a result of the national *trait* of vanity, physical courage is shared in France by both sexes and by every class of society.

The women who were born under Louis XV and who survived the Terror made their way back into society when security returned after the 18th Brumaire and the beginning of the reign of Bonaparte. There is almost no doubt that they retained the moral habits of their youth, their youth which had now faded; but, with the fine tact for which their generation had been noted, they rapidly grew aware of the changes that had taken place and realised the need for a decorum which, under the debonair Louis XV and in the *salon* of la duchesse de Polignac,[1] would have been looked upon as ridiculous and vulgar.

[1] See Bezenval's *Mémoires*. (Note in the *London Magazine*.)

Every woman of superior rank born in France since 1788 has received from an early age an education which is at the same time sensible, judicious and severe. It is altogether different in this respect from the absurd system that was in vogue at the Abbaye de Belle-Chasse and other fashionable boarding schools at the close of the old monarchy. (A description of the education received by Louis XV's daughters in one of these institutions can be read in the memoirs of Mme de Campan.)

As a result of the momentous happenings and violent convulsions which preceded and followed the period of the Terror, every young lady of position had gone through a course of instruction which was necessarily rational and severe. Then, in 1804, Napoleon brought prudery into fashion and by his influence established her on the throne of morality. Whatever had been the previous habits of the Empress Josephine, and with whatever misdemeanours scandal has charged her own daughter-in-law and the sisters of Napoleon, this great man, with his will of iron, wishing to inspire respect for his infant court, declared that it should be moral, and moral it was. The girls who were twelve years of age in 1804 have, as a consequence, been brought up under the domination of this irrevocable law—that no young woman shall ever appear in public unless she is accompanied by her husband.

The austere manners of the new reign were the exact opposite of the usages in vogue before the Revolution. A hundred works of art bequeathed by the former régime bear witness to the truth of this assertion, which outside France appears extraordinary and is scarcely believed. Consider for example *Le Philosophe marié* and *Le Préjugé à la mode* by Destouches. Even today, or rather a short while ago, when Louis XVIII received the ladies of the court, they presented themselves in a manner now become unusual in Paris, *without* their husbands and in the costume of the pre-Revolutionary court, which exposes the neck to a degree unknown today. The *salon* of the King is the only place in the country where such a spectacle may be found. For the last twenty years a young married woman has never been seen in a Parisian drawing-room without one's being certain to find her husband in some corner or other playing *écarté*. This constant presence of the husband is no doubt very praiseworthy and very moral, but it has given a death blow to the art of conversation. What was once known as *l'amabilité française* no longer exists in France. In the presence of her husband the wife loses her independence; he is the established authority; and, although he may be inclined to wear his honours meekly, yet his real power imposes restraint. It checks that abandonment of the spirit out of which spring pleasantries, delicate allusions and *jeux d'esprit*, innocent enough in themselves, but which can never flourish in the presence of the authority established by law. In wit, satire and gaiety, in short, in the comedy of social life itself, there is invariably something of the spirit of opposition. There are even those who play upon established authority, those who are by their very nature rebellious. Apart then from the cramping effect that the eternal presence of the same person must inevitably produce, who will be able to tell a story even or relate an anecdote in the hearing of someone who, you know full well, is taking note of the little details that you have chosen to add for the sake of effect, someone who is liable, at any moment, to introduce into the conversation, with an air of complete spontaneity, the brilliant observations that you yourself have spent the day preparing and collecting for the evening? How are you to shine under the eye of a man who has perhaps shared your own preparatory labours? When the husband enters the room, the art of conversation inevitably flies out of the window.

To return to our original theme, however, upper-class life, from 1804 to 1814, was extremely austere and dull, compared with the good old days of the past. In many ways, nevertheless, the change was for the better. Virtue was in fashion, morals were pure, mothers carried out the duties imposed upon them by nature with the most scrupulous fidelity, and fathers reflected upon the dowries they could give their daughters, upon how little they themselves could live, and in what way they could best manage their own fortunes. Every lady was the nurse of her own children and every gentleman was his own steward. It may appear strange that virtue should have infiltrated downwards from the throne. It is uncommon for this to happen in any country and in France it was almost without precedent. Since the time of François I, the French kings had been the impudent corrupters of public morals and had bequeathed nothing to posterity in the way of virtue apart from the names of their mistresses. Before François I, there was nothing that could properly be called a court. The residence of the king was little more than the headquarters of a general, most of whose time was taken up in waging war. Astonishing then though it may appear, the first sovereign to effect a reform in the morals of the French people was General Bonaparte who found it to be in his own interests as the despotic founder of a new dynasty. The Bourbons in 1814 brought back the reign of the priests and the mistresses. Nothing could be more like the reign of Louis XV than that of Mme du Cayla. There is probably not a girl of eighteen in all Paris who is not perfectly familiar with the name of that lady, and who, prior to the death of Louis, did not know her functions and envy her for them, for the place she occupied gave her an income of a million francs a year.

Fortunately, however, the Bourbons have no influence on public opinion. The late king was old, very infirm, and never rode on horseback. He was incapable, that is, of making a spectacular public appearance, though, if he had been, the situation may very well have been different. It is as if his government had said to each class of society in turn: 'Turn out the greatest fools among you'; and, when the order had been obeyed, appointed them to the leading positions in the state. This seems to have occurred, not only in political departments, but in the army, in science, in law and in medicine. Perhaps, as we have suggested, this system would have met with little opposition if we could have turned the king, for a time, into a brilliant young man who appeared before the public on horseback. But Louis XVIII was lame, moribund, and the prey to a thousand diseases. It is true that he was an author and published the *Voyages à Coblentz*. This did a great deal for his prestige, though it was of little weight on its own. Today, for the first time in the history of France, the moral example of the court has no perceptible influence on the general manners of the people. A few duchesses, it is true, tried to show that in their virtue and morals they were conforming to the traditions of the court of Louis XVI, but public opinion left them stranded. They are talked about and their names are quoted, but no longer as models of elegance or *bon ton*. The host of young ladies who have since then come out in society formed a barrier against the dissoluteness which characterised the intimate court circles surrounding the late king and the Duchesse de Berry. It proved almost impossible to overthrow such a barrier, in spite of the brilliant drawing-rooms to which the advocates of the old system could appeal, and in spite of the dullness which reigns in these drawing-rooms at the present moment. In the most splendid *salons* to be found in Paris the women, as often as not, are abandoned to their own resources and left to assemble in a corner while the men sit apart discussing politics or played *écarté*. Nothing is more common in the leading circles of French society than to see eight or ten handsome, well-dressed young women sitting sadly in a group, exchanging from time to time a cold monosyllable and never for an instant attracting the attention of a man. So low are the mighty fallen that, unless the most trustworthy evidence is to be refuted, we may now pronounce the dwelling place of the spirit of *Ennui*, which Frenchmen are said to hate above all things, to be the very meeting-place of French society.

An extensive society made up of these unfortunate neglected women who have talents, spirit and religious convictions grounded in habit, for they all learned their catechism under Bonaparte, is excellent material for the founding of a new sect. They have imagination and they have the passions and feelings of twenty-five, that age which is so avid for emotion. All this is controlled and subdued by the prudery of the existing code of behaviour, but at the expense of considerable boredom and disgust. Moreover, since 1820, the triumph of the priests and the impostures perpetrated by the Jesuits of Montrouge and St Acheul, who secretly govern France, together with a thousand petty, sanctified villainies and annoyances, have turned the more generous souls away from Papism in disgust. The priests have put the ladies completely out of love with their own catechisms. Here then is the moment for the founding of a new sect. 'My *salon* shall be famous throughout Paris. I shall be at the head of something; at least they will talk about me.' A gospel and a creed are all that is wanting. It does not take much to turn a French head. Only how is one to establish a new religion in Paris of all places without being covered in ridicule, the ridicule which extinguished the theophilanthropy of La Reveillère-Lépeaux twenty-five years ago? A happy thought suggests itself. Our friend Benjamin Constant is about to publish his history of religious sentiment. He shall be the St Paul of the new church. His politics are on the wane; he will be only toopleased to take the lead of a new school. He shall first prove to the world that religious sentiment must have a *form*, that is, a form of worship. Then, with that skill and dexterity which allow him to say anything and be understood by anyone without getting laughed at, he will demonstrate the vices inherent in all the existing forms. After which, having convinced his readers that all the existing forms are bad, he must stop. It is at this moment that I will open my salon. Everything, however, must be done slowly and with caution. Benjamin shall publish this work volume by volume, tread slowly but surely, and, like St Paul in his epistles to the Corinthians, take measure of their spiritual needs.

If Mme de Staël had not been overtaken by the sudden death which deprived the world, almost in the flower of her age, of the most extraordinary woman it has produced, one who has carried French conversation and the brilliant art of improvisation on any subject that may arise to the highest degree of perfection, she herself would have taken the lead of the new religion. Unable to dazzle by her beauty and no longer capable of exerting that charm which made up for its absence, Mme de Staël had found to her chagrin that her birth prevented her from playing any conspicuous rôle at a Bourbon court. At the moment of her death she had been on the point of opening a rival salon in opposition. The standard flown by this salon was to reveal, when unfurled before the astonished eyes of Europe, the word *religion*. It is probable that the disrepute into which the Jesuits have fallen in recent years, as a result of a number of scandalous intrigues, would have done much to enhance its popularity.

Mme de Staël, twenty-five or thirty years ago, tried to persuade M. Benjamin Constant, who was then her intimate friend, to write a study of religion. It is the first volume of this work which M. Constant has just offered to the world. If we are to believe the reports of scandal, M. Constant has changed his opinions on this important topic three times during the long interval of thirty years. When he began his study in Berlin, he was undergoing the exaltation of German mysticism. The figure of Jesus Christ filled the work from one end to the other. We believe in fact that a special revelation of the person of the Redeemer was promised to the true believer. At present, it is with the utmost difficulty that we can find his name anywhere within the four corners of the volume. In all probability the work would never have appeared at all had not the circumstances of which we have spoken above created a need for it. It is the text book, or it was intended to be, of the witty, handsome and seductive young duchesses who want something to do, and who, for the sake of diversion, are about to open a *salon*, where their guests may converse on serious subjects and take steps towards the establishment of a new faith. It was in this way that Mme Guyon, the friend of Fénelon, made her name under Louis XIV. It is true that she chose a favourable moment in which to create a new sect, for, at that time, persecution was all the fashion. The only persecution from which the new religion will suffer is that of ridicule.

There is perhaps no man in France, however, who is more perfectly capable of placing his opinions beyond the reach of ridicule than M. Constant. He offers us the history of every religion, but, in order to treat this vast subject in four volumes, he was obliged to write, not a detailed history of every religion, but the history of religious sentiment. It is this which he discusses in the present volume. What, however, is this religious sentiment? After the Battle of Waterloo, Napoleon, while discussing in the Elysée the various courses that were open to him, exclaimed, 'Ah! if only I were my grandson, I would retire towards the Pyrenees and all France would rise for me.' What then is this peculiar charm which would have led the French to slaughter for the sake of an insolent despot, merely because he could name a king or two among his ancestors? This singular feeling can be easily explained, although the grave Germans find it very mysterious. It is one of the effects of *imagination*, which is as much part of the human organism as the eye or the hand. Every man who is properly formed possesses the power of imagination, and it is this which, after every deluge, earthquake or thunder-clap since the beginning of time, has revealed to every group and race the existence of the gods. This is what M. Constant describes as religious sentiment.

Sixty years before the discoveries of Franklin and the age of conductors, a storm, accompanied by a frequent discharge of electricity and a number of noisy peals of thunder, would awaken in the minds of most Europeans an idea of the infinite and terrible power of God. Today we see nothing more in thunder than an ordinary phenomenon which we can explain with perfect ease. On this subject M. Constant writes: 'The belief of every people takes shelter beyond the circumference of its knowledge.' The entire section of his work in which M. Constant develops this idea is borrowed from M. le Marquis de la Place. This great man in his *Mécanique Céleste* has developed the truth on which we have just touched with a strength and clarity of logic, which, to us, is far preferable to the pretty sentimental phrases of M. Constant. Perhaps it is for this reason that he has omitted to mention even the name of La Place.

We must not overlook the fact, however, that the apparent end of M. Constant is to give the history of religious sentiment, independent of the forms with which men have invested it, and it is true that he offers an ingenious explanation of the origin of these forms, that is to say of the origin of external worship. It is a well-known fact that the more strong and sincere a man's feelings are, the more intolerant he becomes towards those who do not feel as he does. The mere sight of someone who doubts what he himself believes shakes to some extent the steadfastness of his own belief, deprives him of the serenity which this belief affords him, and, as a result, irritates or even enrages him.

Religious sentiment leads then to the establishment in different countries of the *forms* of religion which give one man the pleasure of seeing that all men think as he does. If a passionate lover dared, and had the power, he would compel every other person to speak of the woman he adores only on his knees.

After speaking of what he describes as religious sentiment, M. Constant gives us a little refutation of the philosophy that has reigned in Paris for the last thirty years. This philosophy teaches us that man is invariably determined in his actions by the prospect of some immediate form of pleasure and that, unless it is to procure this, he can never be induced to act. The French claim that this is true, even in the case of a man who blows out his brains with a pistol, even in the case of Regulus when he left Rome and returned to Carthage to perish in dreadful torment. Though no one can regard the blowing out of his own brains as a pleasant operation, he may prefer it to some even greater pain. The balance of pleasure may be in favour of priming and loading. Regulus was perfectly conscious of the tenpenny nails that were awaiting him in Carthage, but he had a higher pleasure to gratify: the pride of marching out of Rome with the respect and admiration of all those he left behind and the assurance of an immortal place in the history of his country.

M. Constant begins by saying: 'The natural effect of this

system of philosophy is to make every individual his own centre. Now when everyone is his own centre, all are isolated. When all are isolated there is nothing but dust. When the storm comes, the dust ... is turned to mud.' (Preface, p. 37.)

This exquisite form of reasoning of which M. Constant gives many other examples is altogether worthy of M. de Boulogne or any other fanatical preacher in or out of Paris.

The manner, at once frivolous and presumptious, in which M. Constant refutes a philosophy which, to most educated Frenchmen, is considered as borne out by everyday experience, will probably be one of the greatest obstacles to the sucess of this book among the coteries of Paris. M. Constant contends that the theory of immediate pleasure fails to explain a *generous sacrifice*. He does not recall, however, that the philosopher who first brought this theory into vogue in France gave as an example the very instance of Regulus voting at Rome against peace with Carthage and then returning to Carthage to meet a dreadful punishment, an action whose generosity, down to the time of M. Constant at least, has never been questioned.

Two men are walking along the bank of a river. A child falls into the water and is carried away by the stream; it is in danger of drowning. One of the two witnesses is content to deplore the accident; the other reflects that he could jump into the river and save the child. The moment that the latter conceives the possibility of this generous act, his pleasure compels him to jump in and attempt to carry it out. If he fails to jump, he knows that he will be pursued by remorse at having contributed to the death of the unfortunate child and by his own self-contempt.

This is the form of reasoning, plausible enough it may have been thought, which in France is accepted as a commonplace. M. Constant undertakes to refute it by means of mystical arguments borrowed from that unfortunate German philosophy which is the laughing-stock of Europe. It is strange that so skilful a writer as M. Constant should be ignorant of a truth which a thousand instances go to confirm, that is to say that in France nothing that is obscure can ever hope to succeed. A Frenchman, restless for novelty and variety and accustomed to the striking clarity with which Voltaire illuminates every proposition which he puts forward, will always be afraid of being taken for a dupe if he gives even momentary assent to something which is not universally intelligible. We admire as much as anyone M. Constant's delicate and epigrammatic wit. His speeches in the Chamber are as embarrassing to his adversaries as they are entertaining to the reader. His genius abandons him, however, as soon as he attempts to grapple with the great questions of higher philosophy. It is as if we were to see an insect on a Seville orange losing itself in the valleys of which the peel is formed on account of its own infinite tinyness. It travels laboriously over the immense body investigating its form and, at last, boldly concludes that an orange is not round.

Whatever justice there may be in the comparison or whatever scope M. Constant's philosophy may exhibit, nothing is more obscure than the style of reasoning in which his work is composed. We conclude this article by setting out some of the more lucid passages for our readers' instruction and in order to save them from hunting them out in the work itself. The work is one that might have been called *The Errors of a Man of Talent*.

London Magazine, November 1824

GENERAL SEGUR ON THE CAMPAIGN OF 1812

Histoire de Napoléon et de la Grande Armée en 1812 by General Count Philippe de Ségur.[1]

It was mentioned in the letter from Paris in our last number that two remarkable works had just been published in France. The first of these is entitled *Histoire de Napoléon et de la Grande Armée pendant l'année* 1812 by M. le comte de Ségur. The second is called *Manuscrit de* 1813 and is by M. le baron Fain, one of Napoleon's secretaries. These two interesting historical productions show clear signs of a judicious imitation of Sir Walter Scott. This celebrated novelist has caused a revolution in French literature. Without being conscious of it probably or aspiring to the honour, he is the head of what is known in France as *le parti romantique*. All the women adore him and there is no literary name which so frequently falls from their lips as his. Moreover, the strong attachment felt or feigned by Sir Walter Scott for all that smacks of ancient institutions, and his consequent lack of enthusiasm for those innovations and improvements which tend to ameliorate the present social state of mankind, have made him a distinguished favourite with the *ultra* party, to which at least three-quarters of his female readers belong. The History of the Dukes of Burgundy by M. de Barante, and the two works mentioned at the beginning of this article, will find their way into every château in France, as they are calculated to excite strong emotions without exacting from the reader any great effort of historical acumen.

[1] The writer of this article was himself an officer of the Grand Army and had peculiar means of observation. (Note in the *London Magazine*.)

The difference of merit in these three compositions, however, is immense. M. de Barante is an adroit rhetorician who has taken care not to give offence to the powers that be by unpalatable deductions. He was at one time an under-secretary of state, and now writes only to fill up his enforced leisure, until some favourable opportunity throws another *portefeuille* in his way. While we read him we are given the irresistible impression that we are in contact with a man endowed with all the patriotism of one of Bonaparte's prefects, together with the frankness and candour of a diplomat. M. Fain writes history as if it were a report to go before the royal and imperial eyes of his late master, while M. de Ségur is a writer *sui generis*, and displays the independence of character and depth of thought which, in the nineteenth century, are indispensable to any writer who wishes to secure a distinguished place in the republic of letters. To produce a book which is correctly written is now, because of the spread of education, something which lies within the capacities of seven-tenths of the richer members of society. There are hundreds who, like M. Villemain, the king of modern rhetoricians, can string together a set of fine phrases; the difficulty is to attach any thoughts to them.

The History of the Campaign of 1812 by the Comte de Ségur is by far superior to any other attempt that has been made to treat this subject. It is a true and sublime account of one of the greatest trials to which the heart of man has ever been submitted, the retreat from Moscow. Having myself taken part in that deplorable catastrophe, I am able to testify to the unerring fidelity of M. de Ségur's narrative. I witnessed certain events that he describes from a different vantage-point. This would in no way induce me to doubt M. de Ségur's veracity, however, or the pains which he must have taken to procure accurate information concerning the unforgettable march from Moscow to Koenigsberg. It is clear that M. de

Ségur adores the great man in Napoleon and, at the same time, that he perceives and condemns the various moral disorders which were engendered in his elevated mind by despotism and by the exclusion of all truth from his own immediate circle. M. de Chambray, an officer in the royal guards, published about a year ago an account of the same campaign. This officer, a man of intellect and acquirements, would have willingly told the truth, had his pen not been checked by hopes of promotion under the Bourbons. He was obliged to avoid doing justice to Napoleon in order to affect ultraism, and, as a result, the veracity of his account undergoes various eclipses. It would be an interesting exercise, particularly for military men, to compare the two accounts, that of the officer playing the rôle of an *ultra* and that written by M. de Ségur. In the former there is almost nothing apart from military details, these being the only ones in which the author felt free to tell the truth. In M. de Ségur's History, which is more philosophical and political than military, these details are not always to be found. It is a work, nevertheless, which, like Mignet's History of the Revolution, ought to be translated into every civilised language. It is unquestionably more engrossing to read than *Redgauntlet* and contains a far more intriguing leading character in Napoleon than the poor pretender Charles Edward.

Having said as much and with perfect sincerity of the author's merits, we must now, however, deal with his failings. M. de Ségur has too closely imitated Rulhière's *Histoire de l'Anarchie de la Pologne*. Until 1815, this work was undoubtedly superior to any History that had appeared in France during the previous fifty years. The French mind, emasculated by the puerile refinements and morbid taste of the court of Louis XV, had been able to produce nothing apart from those insipid writings which make French literature between the years 1756 and

1789 seem so unnatural and effeminate. The stunted and pigmy intellects of the period had been altogether unable to grapple with great historical questions. Voltaire alone, through the force of his wit, rose above the mist which covered the literature of his country. General de Ségur's own father, a former Grand Master of Ceremonies in Napoleon's court, may be taken as representative of the men of letters of the time of Louis XV. He has compiled an interminable Universal History in thirty octavo volumes, and employed throughout the style that was in vogue before the Revolution, a style as colourless and inanimate as that used by the Abbé Millot and the other intellectual leaders of the period. Typical also of the period are the petty vanities and affectations which the Comte de Ségur, Grand Master of Ceremonies, manages to exhibit. He has prefixed, for example, to his enormous compilation a facsimile of his own handwriting. Rulhière, in his *Histoire de l'Anarchie de la Pologne*, sought to imitate the style of Seneca. The work was not published for several years after his death, for the manuscript belonged to the government, which had paid him a pension of eight thousand francs for twenty years in return for writing it. It would probably even then never have seen the light of day, had it not been for the rupture between Napoleon and the Emperor of Russia. Napoleon, after this, caused it to be made public in order to dishonour the Russians in the eyes of the world and to give civilised Europeans some idea of the barbarians who were threatening to over-run them. M. Daunou, one of the three or four writers of first-rate talent who has till now refrained from selling himself either to Napoleon or the Bourbons, was Rulhière's editor. Unfortunately, however, the Jesuits, who are to be met with everywhere and on all occasions, had previously censored the original manuscript and either effaced completely or considerably mutilated the strongest passages. In passing, it may be said that whenever you hear of an outrage of this kind taking place in France there is little chance of your being mistaken if you set it down at once to the activities of the villainous sons of Loyola. I have spoken at such length of Rulhière's work for two reasons; in the first place, because it forms an appropriate and almost necessary introduction to General de Ségur's own History and, secondly, because it is the model which M. de Ségur seems to have had most constantly in mind, and which, unfortunately for his own literary reputation and his reader's pleasure, he has closely imitated. Apart from this, I cannot help objecting to the obscure metaphysical speculations concerning Napoleon's character in which M. de Ségur all too often loses his way, and again to his endeavours to prove the immortality of the soul from the fortuitous events of the Russian campaign. Last of all, I feel obliged to deplore the affected brevity of his style, which leaves the reader convinced that it is the result of considerable labour. In the very first sentence of the book the author commits a grammatical error in his attempts to write with the conciseness of a Seneca: *Depuis 1807, l'intervalle entre le Rhin et le Niémen état franchi et ces deux fleuves devenus rivaux.* These blemishes are more than made up for, however, by the varied and novel information contained in the work and by the many passages written with a great force both of style and expression. The only really ridiculous passages are those in which an affected and mock-pathetic dedication is made to the veterans of the Grand Army to whom, like Caesar in his commentaries, M. de Ségur refers as his 'companions'. This lapse of taste was probably necessary if the work was to be favourably reviewed in the *Constitutionnel* and other liberal journals, who find it in their interest to flatter the partisans of Bonapartism and without whose aid no literary production can ever hope to succeed.

This dedication has a certain interest, however, in that it

can be taken as an example of the way in which the French army was accustomed to speak of itself. We are given a spirited and faithful account of what this boasting manner was like in the first volume. The soldiers themselves, though influenced by it, were not unaware of its absurdity, and always referred to it as *blague*. To make oneself understood when speaking to them, or even to most of their officers, one was obliged to express oneself in this way. Marshal Augereau was a perfect master of this detestable mode of declamation, which is the exact opposite of the natural, straightforward style used by English officers in their dispatches or in addressing their troops. The secret of *blague* is for the speaker to talk in unmeasured terms in praise of himself and his men. The truth is that the French soldier would remain altogether unmoved by the plain, matter-of-fact address of an English general. A philosopher like Catinat would be powerless at the head of a modern French regiment. Only a ranting actor, like that madman, the brave and foppish Murat, could lead it on to the cannon's mouth. M. de Ségur explains very clearly how the jealousy which Napoleon was weak enough to feel towards Marshal Davout led him to be influenced by the *gasconading* Murat. Davout was the only one of Napoleon's generals who foresaw the precise species of obstacle that was to prove ruinous to the Russian expedition, whereas it was Murat's 'brilliant' manoeuvres which caused the loss of fifty thousand horses before the army reached Moscow. Among the other unskilful advisers by whom Napoleon was surrounded, M. de Ségur has ventured to refer only to Prince Berthier and to two or three others now deceased. As those who have survived do not enjoy the sunshine of the court's favour, M. de Ségur has generously abstained from further adding to their gloom by his reproaches. The author does full justice to the firm, frank and *ungasconading* character (this last quality a very rare one in

France) of Messrs Caulincourt, Daru and Ney. General de Ségur, as the son of the Grand Master of Ceremonies, was able to acquire the fullest information concerning what went on within the court itself; consequently his account of Napleon's diplomacy, both preparatory to and during the campaign, is singularly interesting and entirely new. One of the drivellers whom, in the pride of his despotism, Napoleon had about him in numbers, dissuaded him from sending Talleyrand, the most skilful intriguer in Europe, on a mission to Constantinople and Stockholm in order to secure the co-operation of the Sublime Porte and of Bernadotte, who was then Prince Royal of Sweden. I do not know if Talleyrand would have succeeded in these missions, but this I do know, that if Napoleon had possessed the *unspoiled* qualities of greatness which he displayed in 1796, if the habit of despotism had not made him prefer talentless sycophants to men of energy and tact, he would have left no effort untried to secure the support of Bernadotte, and more particularly, that of the Sublime Porte, without whose co-operation the right wing of his army was doomed to destruction. The presence of Talleyrand at Constantinople was then a most indispensable preliminary, and the Emperor was most grievously punished for not sending him there by the disasters at the Berezina. All that section of M. de Ségur's work dealing with diplomatic details and the intercourse of Napoleon's court is a masterpiece.

In his description of these interesting matters the author throws much new light on the character of Napoleon. He declares his profound admiration for the greatness and extraordinary qualities of his hero, but in a very different style from the undiscriminating and childish adoration of Las Cases, the perfect type of the chamberlain. We learn from his work a number of singular and interesting details concerning the severe attacks of illness, which he made a policy of concealing from the army, but which frequently reduced him to a state of utter feebleness in the very moment when he most needed all his physical and mental energy. This was the case, for example, on the day of the Battle of the Moskowa. The author in another passage shows that despotism, which is commonly considered to be useful and even indispensable in commanding an army, often defeats its own ends. Napoleon's jealousy of Davout, the Prince d'Eckmühl, convinced the other generals that the Emperor was unwilling to see any of them evince talent superior to his own. They considered it more prudent therefore, to act as mere automatons and abstain from acting on their own initiative, even where circumstances urgently required it. How different this is from the methods of 1796 during the immortal Italian campaign when everyone, fired with Republican enthusiasm, obeyed with zeal, and at the same time, when the commander-in-chief's orders failed to arrive, had the courage to act on his own. The debasing effects produced by Napoleon's wilfulness cannot fail to strike the most inattentive reader in the account of the Battle of the Moskowa on September 7th, 1812. The battle might have been won five times over if Napoleon had been on the field, or if his generals, at the same time so brave and so timid, had ventured to take upon themselves the risk of following up their successes. Napoleon was a league distant from the field of battle, suffering from an attack of fever. Under these circumstances, if the Russians had been commanded by a Blücher, who would have recommenced the battle on the 8th, the French army would have met with the same fate which they have since known at Waterloo. Then, however, as they were ninety-three leagues from Poland, not a single soldier probably would have escaped the just revenge of the Russians. The only complete *corps d'armée* that the Emperor had with him at the time was his guard, which was about twenty thousand strong and mostly composed of young recruits unable to stand the shock of the Russian onslaught. If this disastrous eventuality had taken place, it would have been solely attributable to the timidity which the Emperor had inspired in his generals. It was the absence of such timidity which enabled the foolhardy Murat to play so brilliant a *rôle* in that campaign

On the field of the Moskowa Napoleon was eclipsed as a great captain by the superior conduct of two of his marshals. One of these was Ney, who has since been put to death by Louis XVIII, in violation of the capitulation of Paris and, as is commonly said in France, with the connivance of the Duke of Wellington aided by the abject subservience of the Chamber of Peers. The other was Davout, the Prince d'Eckmühl. In Egypt he gave very few signs of talent, but between 1800 and 1812 he showed himself a man of genius both in war and espionage. It was Davout who won the Battle of Jena in 1806 and who, at the Moskowa pointed out to the Emperor, at the same time offering to carry it out in person and in two hours time, a manoeuvre which might have saved the lives of ten thousand Frenchmen. Napoleon, on this occasion, behaved like a drunken captain of grenadiers and ordered his troops, not to turn the lines of the savage Russian army, but to attack them on their front. One word will suffice to show the murderous effects of such a system of attack; forty-three generals were either killed or wounded on the field. M. de Ségur is too much of a Bonapartist to record this truth. However, every reader of his book gifted with the spirit of deduction and who examines at all minutely the military details of the campaign will draw this inference from the facts, which M. de Ségur sets down with impartiality even if he fails at times to bring out their implications.

Ney was a truly great military leader. On September 7th

at nine o'clock in the evening after the victory of the Moskowa, if such a frightful battle can be called a victory, his first words to Napoleon were, 'Sire, you will have to withdraw'. In giving this frank advice, his behaviour was highly honourable, all the more so when one considers Napoleon's state of extreme irritation as a result of his illness and his awareness that the frightful losses he had just sustained were largely the result of his own lack of generalship. All, however, was not yet lost, for if, four days after the Battle of the Moskowa, Napoleon had marched on Smolensk, a distance of eighty-three leagues which he could have covered in twenty days, he would have found himself on October 6th on the banks of the Borysthenes. Until then the sun would shine brilliantly and the cold air would be bracing rather than unendurable. In making such a move he could have made Poland his own and the next year marched on Moscow during the summer with only ninety-three leagues and two or three battles between him and his goal.

Prince Eugène de Beauharnais and King Murat presided over the frightful butchery of the Moskowa, like men who seemed to think that there was no such thing as death. Murat braved it out like a ranting actor and with a constitutional gaiety which, though a little *de mauvais ton*, was all-powerful in its effect upon the troops. The extravagant costume of this theatrical king, the plume of feathers two feet high dancing above his casque, and his headlong valour made him their admiration and their rallying point. The bravery of Prince Eugène, who always had something about him of the *marquis* of the *ancien régime*, was cold, unaffected and in good taste. It was noticed that his refinement of feeling was greatly shocked when, at one point during the day, finding himself on foot, he was compelled to walk ankle-deep through the pools of blood that had spread over the plain. Seeing his finest regiments mown down like grass, he sent to the Emperor for aid, informing him that his troops could hold out no longer. 'I cannot remedy that', was Napoleon's reply. He was endeavouring at the time to quench his fever thirst with copious draughts of tea. Napoleon had considerably increased his illness by passing the night of the 6th until four in the morning on horseback reconnoitring the enemy's position within gunshot of their lines. It may be said in fact that, upon this memorable occasion, Napoleon was a general only during the eve of the battle. His principal fear, as well as that of his army, was that the Russians would escape a second time.

I intend to bring this article to an end with extracts from the work of M. de Ségur. Many of them inspire so deep an interest, that it would be in vain for me to expect that anyone, after reading them, would want to pay attention to further reflections of my own. I shall therefore, before presenting them, put forward a few of the observations and reflections that M. de Ségur's work has awoken in my mind. Though reluctant to speak of myself, I ought, in order to recommend myself to the reader's confidence, begin by saying that I served in a regiment which took part in the action of the Moskowa.

All the strategic blunders that despotism had given rise to in Napoleon's great mind were tripled in their fatal consequences for the army by the astonishing incapacity of the chief of staff, Berthier, Prince de Neufchâtel. The physical force of this poor man was almost exhausted, while mentally he was nearly in his dotage. Eight or ten leagues on horseback would leave him unfit for further exertion. Many of the disasters for which this campaign will be remembered would probably have been avoided if he had fallen sick at Dresden and been replaced by Marshal Soult, Duke of Dalmatia, the same man, let it be said in passing, who today, in December 1824, is seen every morning on his way to Mass with a huge missal bound in red morocco carried before him. Under Napoleon he was a great general, but under the Bourbons he has become a hypocritical and ardent worshipper before the power of the Jesuits.

To resume, however—a change as desirable as that of Soult for Berthier was inconceivable at the time, for Napoleon had come to detest all outstanding merit. Senile or plodding mediocrity was the quality which found most favour in his eyes, and unfortunately his prejudice was a secret to no one. He was seen at Dorogobouge, I believe, half-way between Moscow and Smolensk, red with suppressed rage at having been forced to appoint, as Marshal of the Empire, Gouvion St Cyr, one of the greatest military figures of whom modern France can boast. At Vitebsk, where he commanded and where he was ably seconded by Count Amédée de Pastoret, St Cyr gave battle twelve times to the Russians, who were seeking to break the French lines of communication and cut them off from Poland and France. These engagements cost the Russians more men than General St Cyr had under his command. Since the Restoration, Marshal St Cyr has been Minister of War, a post in which he has conducted himself with scrupulous honour. In 1822 he published the memoirs of his campaign in Catalonia, a work as remarkable for its good sense as for its simplicity of style. He has just concluded a similar work on the Moscow campaign, which, when it is published, will cause considerable scandal to the Bonapartists; for the writer both asserts and demonstrates that, during the fatal year 1812, Napoleon not only proved to be incompetent as a general, but gave signs of thoughtless folly which seemed, to all appearances, to be that of a mind turned by pride. Marshal St Cyr has made no mention, however—why, I do not know—of the Emperor's frequent indisposition. Napoleon was of an unusually highly-strung disposition, and sickness would prostrate his bodily and nervous faculties to such a degree that he would become almost an inert mass. On these occasions he sometimes slept for twelve hours straight off, and, on awakening, would try to stimulate his faculties by drinking large quantities of tea in which a small portion of brandy was mixed. Subsequently, however, as misfortunes thickened around him, this tea became brandy punch, so strong that a single glass of it was enough to send the honest Duroc to sleep. On certain occasions the Emperor has been known to drink as much as two bottles full of this beverage. When Marshal St Cyr calls Napoleon a *mediocre* general, he seems to forget the Italian campaign of 1796 and the battles in the neighbourhood of Paris in 1813. It is true that the bodily powers of the great man failed him at Brienne and at Montmirail, however. On this last day, in order to rouse his sinking powers, he drank three bottles of brandy punch. Of this the army suspected nothing, for those around him would have considered it base treachery if it had been known.

The only men who, at the Kremlin, when Moscow was burning, had the courage to speak truthfully to the Emperor were the Count Daru, then Secretary of State, and the Grand Marshal Duroc. The harsh and abrupt observations of Daru irritated Napoleon at the time, even while they impressed him, whereas the persuasive reasoning and long-tried friendship of Duroc almost certainly had more effect on his mind. Nevertheless, the servile flattery of several individuals still living, but whom I shall not name here, together with the blind wilfulness that goes with despotic power, led the Emperor to stay in Moscow until four days after the conflagration. He entered that extraordinary city on the 14th of September; the army was by then perishing for want of food as a result of the inadequate precautions that the head of Commissariat, Count Dumas, had taken for its support. The city continued to burn throughout the 14th, 15th and 16th; and, when the conflagration had ceased, a large store of good fried fish was found in the cellars and so much excellent wine that the best claret was sold for three francs a bottle. The soldiers of the guard were given the privilege of looting, and it was they who carried out the trade in wine and fur pelisses, which the more far-seeing took care to provide themselves with. The army, thus refreshed, could and ought to have left the city on the 19th of September. They did not go, however, until the 19th of October. On the Berezina and in the environs of Wilna, they paid dearly for this fatal delay. Rather than stay at Moscow it would have been better if they had marched on St Petersburg. The Russian army could scarcely have caught up with them until they were half-way there, and once arrived, it is not improbable that the inhabitants of the city, who are much more self-seeking and less patriotic than the citizens of Moscow, would have opened their gates to them like those in Vienna and Berlin. To march on St Petersburg would certainly have been an act of folly; so would it have been if the army had spent the winter in Moscow under Davout's command, while Napoleon made his way to Paris. Either course was less hazardous, however, than setting out on the 19th of October for Smolensk.

It was at this juncture that the imbecile incompetence of the Prince de Neufchâtel became disastrously evident. He alarmed the entire army by directing its attention to the six hundred weary leagues that separated it from France, After the 12th of October, straggling groups of thirty or forty deserters, their baggage and arms tied on the backs of the little horses known by the soldiers as *coniats*, began to leave Moscow and set out for Smolensk by way of Borodino and Dorogobouge. Berthier lacked the firmness of character necessary to have the first man who abandoned his eagles and left for home *en voyageur* summarily shot. Instead, he authorised this infamous desertion, or as good as authorised it and Napoleon, who had acquired the habit of maltreating those who revealed to him the truth, either knew nothing of what was happening or lacked the energy to put a stop to it. These are the principal causes of the unheard-of desertions that accompanied the retreat. They are mainly to be attributed to the Prince de Neufchâtel and to the fops in red pantaloons who were his aides-de-camp. During the fatal march, the Russians committed the most extraordinary tactical errors. Posterity will in vain try to understand the excess of stupidity which prevented these barbarians from destroying the bridges and causeways over the marshes of the Berezina. Had they done so, the whole French army would have met with a fate similar to that which overtook General Partouneaux's division. I was with that army and yet I do not hesitate to affirm that it would have been fortunate for France if Admiral Tchitchakov or General Tchaplitz had possessed half the military skill of an ordinary English or French colonel. If this had been the case, Napoleon's downfall would have been inevitable. So conscious was he himself of the perils of the situation that he thought seriously of committing suicide. This time, furthermore, he would not have attempted suicide in vain, as on the occasion when, at Fontainebleau in April 1814, he drank the mixture of stramonium which had been invented by Cabanis and tried successfully by Condorcet. Napoleon once dead, the army would have been made prisoners. The great majority of them would have perished of cold and hunger; but the barbarians would never have ventured to cross the Rhine which, at that time, formed the frontier of France. The King of Rome, under the direction of Cambacérès and a well-chosen regency, would have enabled the Senate to recover its influence and today France would not have to deplore the debased condition into which she has fallen, governed as she is by the Jesuits and compelled to follow behind the chariot of the Holy Alliance.

London Magazine, February 1825

BENJAMIN CONSTANT IN THE CHAMBER OF DEPUTIES

Letters from Paris by Grimm's grandson, no. iv

Paris, March 18th, 1825

My dear friend,

The most remarkable volume which has appeared this month is, beyond any doubt, the one containing three speeches by M. Benjamin Constant, General Foy and M. de Girardin protesting against the projected law by which the returned *émigrés* hope to pocket the equivalent of more than forty million pounds sterling. You will frequently find in M. de Girardin's speech the pungent irony of Voltaire and the caustic humour of Pascal. The main theme of this masterly attack, delivered by a disciple of Jean-Jacques Rousseau, is summed up in the following sentence: 'Gentlemen, in this Chamber composed of four hundred and thirty members, of whom three hundred and seventy are entitled to the proposed indemnity, are you going to have the effrontery to flaunt every sentiment of honour and decency, every feeling which must surely compel you to stand out against your own interests, when you are called upon to vote a thousand million francs to the returned *émigrés*?'

General Foy's speech was magnificent to hear. This copious and eloquent speaker rose to the level of Mirabeau, whom I remember having seen during the last year of his life.[1] Unfortunately, however, all that he said was based on a supposition which was all too evidently false: he attributed to his listeners a certain generosity and a few remnants of honour. True eloquence merely seems ridiculous when it is addressed to complete and unshakable egoism. The present Chamber is made up of old men of sixty, libertines during their youth, and now stupid, self-seeking bigots, incapable of acquiring a single new idea. It is obvious that the sublime and potent eloquence of Demosthenes and Mirabeau would be totally misplaced with such an audience, and to adopt towards it a tone so inappropriate is almost to betray a lack of ordinary good sense. General Foy managed to give this impression to almost everyone, and his speech, as a result, was almost completely deprived of any effect.

If, then, in this competition for pre-eminence between three men of the highest talent, M. Benjamin Constant finally carried off the palm, this may be attributed to his having adopted a tone suited to his audience. Addressing both the Chamber and the nation by whom his speech would be read the following day, he succeeded in making the partisans of the bill *swallow contempt* in all its forms. You know perhaps that we have a proverb according to which *contempt can be swallowed, but cannot be chewed*. Be this as it may, M. Constant succeeded, with consummate art and skill, in covering with ridicule the three hundred and seventy wigged heads which decide the destiny of France. To complete his triumph, the triumph of the subtlest wit and most adroit strategy which have been seen anywhere for a good many years, M. Constant never once allowed his opponents time to interrupt him. They would begin to understand the bitter irony of one sentence, only

[1] Mirabeau died in 1791, when Stendhal, who had not yet left his native Alps, was a child of eight. (*Editor*.)

when the orator was in the middle of the next. The *Constitutionnel* which reported his speech was obliged to bring out a second edition, a thing which normally will not happen as often as three times in one year. It was eagerly sought all over Paris, as soon as it was known that it contained a faithful account of M. Constant's terrible reply to the *émigrés*' constant boast of heroic fidelity. He demonstrates, with the utmost clarity, at this point, that, after returning under Bonaparte in 1801, after crowding into his ante-chamber and after swearing allegiance to him, they can scarcely boast of their fidelity and still less of their heroism; simply of their prudence. This passage, which it is impossible to read without laughing, and which I do not quote because it is too long and too closely related to what precedes it, is unquestionably equal to the finest passages in Pascal's *Lettres Provinciales*. It would be to the advantage both of the public and of M. Constant himself if his own works on religion were written with the same fervour and the same talent.

The great merit of these three speeches is that they have awoken public opinion to the actual quality of the present Chamber of Deputies. What we find, after a little examination, is that, without any exception, this is the most *stupid* Chamber that has been seen anywhere for the last thirty-five years. The deputies are supreme; they have plundered the nation and taken a thousand million francs, and now they do not know how to divide the spoil. For a good three weeks, they have had the wildest notions of what they are about. Three or four times in the course of a debate, M. de Villèle, or his aide-de-camp M. de Martignac, have to mount the tribune in order to prevent them from resolving the same question in two opposite ways. In one of the more recent debates, they insisted for three hours that it was expedient to decree the consequence of an article of law *before* the article itself was adopted. M. Ravez, their president, M. de Villèle and M. de Martignac all failed completely to make them see reason. At last, thoroughly worn out by the effort, they were obliged to break up the sitting, and adjourn the discussion till the following day. M. de Talleyrand, despite his old age, was delighted by this farcical exhibition, and observed in his salon the same evening: 'They are like savages who have killed a hare, but who can neither skin it nor cook it. Each savage in turn approaches it, turns it over from head to tail, looks at it for some time, and at last goes away, not knowing in the least what to do with it.' According to M. Séguier, a peer, first president of the Royal Court of Paris and, above all, a man of talent, all these deplorable absurdities in the Chamber could lead to a second edition of the present list of *émigrés*. The Englishman who is curious to understand the full extent of the Chamber's ridiculous behaviour would do well to read M. de Montrol's *Histoire de l'Emigration*. It is factually correct, impartial and perfectly devoid of talent.

Two books, both with the same title, *Histoire des deux derniers Stuarts, Charles II et Jacques II*, have been widely read in Paris since they were published. Their authors, M. Boulay de la Meurthe, counsellor of state under Napoleon, and M. Sauquaire-Souligné, both sat down two years ago to present this period of history with a view to pointing its moral for the benefit of the Bourbons. What they said in effect was this: 'You are doing exactly what the Stuarts did. You are going to cause such alarm among the nine million purchasers of national domains and, you are going to allow your provinces to be so overrun by priests and nobles, that you will be brought down like James II.' I myself am very far from sharing this opinion. In the first place, where are we to find a man of genius like William III? And secondly, the Bourbons are evidently as unpopular as they are because of their fidelity to the cause of the nobility. There are no great nobles, as a result, who would find it in the least to their advantage to call in a new sovereign. There are the people themselves, to be sure, but they seem to lack entirely the necessary courage. As soon as three Frenchmen are together, they become convinced that they are talking in front of a spy. Nevertheless, the danger which threatens the Bourbons, even though it was never so much as thought of last September, is beginning to attract attention.

M. Dumesnil, a Jansenist and a man of great courage, has published, sword in hand, so to speak, a pamphlet against the Jesuits in which he has had the boldness to tell the whole truth. He first brings forward general proof of the iniquity of the above-mentioned good fathers; he then quotes the base flattery which L'Abbé de Lammenais and M. de Boulogne, the gallant bishop of Troyes, addressed to Napoleon. This pamphlet inspired another *bon mot* from M. Séguier: 'How is it that the kings fail to see that, until 1789, the Church may have sustained them, but that now it will get them hung?' This, as you will see, is an allusion to the *line* of your Lord Norbury.[1]

M. Séguier has similarly induced the magistrates of the Royal Court of Paris to defy the government by prosecuting three clerks who had set up a shop for the sale of Crosses of St Louis and Légions d'Honneur. The latter cost the equivalent of sixty pounds, while the Crosses of St Louis could be obtained for little more than thirty. Half the crosses that you see in Paris are obtained by these means. The Cour Royale, I should add, have had the absurd pretension of wishing to revive the pre-revolutionary *Parlement*.

M. Séguier also threatens to prosecute a number of M. de Villèle's clerks who, it is said, are selling tax collectorships for an equivalent of four thousand pounds. He has reprimanded a certain M. Genou, who calls himself M. de Genoude, from the chair of justice itself. This gentleman, who is the *âme damnée*

[1] See Appendix J.

of the Jesuits, is editor of *L'Etoile*, a ferocious publication very much in the style of your *John Bull*, though written with the good taste and breeding of *Blackwood's Magazine*. *L'Etoile*, however, is read by every one as soon as it comes out; it always appears at eight in the evening, and contains all the news that the ministers are willing to divulge.

I shall conclude this long political gossip with a reflection of a literary cast. If Voltaire could return to life, he would not write tragedies; he would try to get himself elected as a deputy, for there is not a village in France in which Benjamin Constant and General Foy lack admirers. I very much fear that, in the future, politics will become the vampire of literature, and, as the details of any country's internal affairs can scarcely be of interest to a foreigner, that we shall cease to maintain our traditional rôle as the entertainers of Europe.

While I am on the subject of Europe, I have forgotten to mention to you a pamphlet which the booksellers here proclaim as a masterpiece. It is called *Coup d'oeil sur la France et l'Europe en 1825*. It is empty and emphatic and very similar in manner to the works of Guizot. If it is successfully puffed, it will inform the multitude of a truth which has been self-evident for a long time to our veterans of the Revolution: very few people in France care much about *liberty*, but everyone adores *equality*. Nobody likes a republic. It was perfect folly to adopt a form of government so foreign to all our tastes and so opposed to all our national instincts. The idea, in fact, has never gained ground, except among the Protestants in the seventeenth century. Religion, at the moment, is very much the fashion. The people enjoy having a king who is a good horseman, who gives gay feasts and who keeps a mistress. French vanity, however, abhors inequality and the insolence of the petty nobility of the provinces, or the country gentry, as you call them. If ever the Bourbons fall, it will be thanks to their priests and nobles. If Charles X would only curb their arrogance and pretensions, the nation would only too gladly grant him a civil list of a hundred million francs.

London Magazine, April 1825

A CHATEAUBRIAND OF THE MOB: BISHOP FRAYSSINOUS

Conférences sur la Religion, by M. le Comte Frayssinous, bishop, peer, Chief Almoner and Grand Master of the University. 5 volumes octavo.

Towards the year 1802, Napoleon conceived the most violent fear of the Republicans whom he called Jacobins. Although they were, for the most part, men of courage, while the more devoutly inclined citizens were cowards, Napoleon endeavoured to conciliate the latter and seek their support. Volney was speaking for every reasonable Frenchman when he offered Napoleon the following advice: 'Do not persecute the priests of any religion; think of them merely as one particular class of citizens. But, at the same time, take care never to spend any public money on any one of them. Let every assembly of believers pay for its priest itself.' This advice put Napoleon into a passion of rage. He broke out into the most violent invectives against Volney and Lafayette, as soon as these two great and excellent citizens had left his presence. By his express command, the church of St Sulpice was given over to a poor priest, wholly devoid of talent and who spoke with a strong Gascon accent. This priest was Frayssinous. Every Sunday, he delivered what he called a lecture, that is to say, an imaginary dialogue between himself and Voltaire or Rousseau; and, in these dialogues he naturally, like Harlequin, took care to put the most pitiful arguments into the mouths of his unfortunate adversaries. As one needs very little money to live in France, Paris swarms with idlers who are always ready to attend any meeting or to cry bravo at the entry of any prince. M. Frayssinous had the merit of killing two hours every Sunday for a large regular audience who found his way of knocking down Helvétius or Rousseau highly diverting. They thronged to hear him say, 'Well, are you silent, Rousseau?' or 'Have you nothing to say, Voltaire?' The dramatic form of his compositions amused his audience and everyone tried to attend at least one performance of this farce.

M. Frayssinous was known as the Chateaubriand of the mob. After the Restoration and the consequent triumph of the priests, M. Frayssinous, like his fellow workman, M. de Chateaubriand, had every dignity of the state showered upon him. Not content with these, he thought that, as Chateaubriand had a seat in the Academy, he should have one too. There was no difficulty in getting himself elected; the difficulty lay in not being hissed by the public, and, in fact, when he was elected, the hisses were so loud and so general that the Royal Courts of Justice were called in to avenge the insult. Journalists were sent to prison for an offence against *Christian morals*, because they said that, never having published a book, he had no right to be an Academician. At the same time, however, the reproach was so cutting that M. de Frayssinous had his lectures corrected by someone who knows how to write French and has just published them. The work, such as it is, is altogether despicable. His eloquence and his reasoning are both equally adapted to the taste and comprehension of the populace. His invariable practice is to assume as a fact the very thing he ought to prove. He is at an immeasurable distance from the d'Abadies, de Hautevilles and others who were hired by the clergy before the Revolution to defend religion.

London Magazine, July 1825.
(from *Letters from Grimm's grandson, no. vii.*)

COMMENTS ON A REPLY TO GENERAL SEGUR

Examen critique de l'Histoire de la Retraite de Moscou de M. le comte Philippe de Ségur, by General Gourgaud, aide-de-camp of the Emperor Napoleon, 1 volume in octavo.

Here is another work addressed to the Bonapartist faction. Unfortunately the few remaining members of this party can scarcely read. Twenty-two thousand copies of M. de Ségur's book have been scattered over France in every direction. But, despite their powerful influence over public opinion, the *Constitutionnel*, and the *Courrier Français*, which were themselves Bonapartist till six months ago, will find it difficult to secure a sale of 1,500 copies for M. de Gourgaud's panegyric. From 1814 until 1815, M. de Gourgaud was attached to the general staff of the Duc de Berry, and was even a sort of favourite. In 1815, he fought courageously at Waterloo, and obtained permission to follow his master to St Helena.

Three quarters of the officers engaged in the Moscow expedition are referred to in M. de Ségur's History, but, according to the partisans of the nation's honour, he has said things which ought never to have escaped the lips of a Frenchman. As a historian, he has ventured to tell the truth. He says, for example, that there was a secret agreement between Napoleon and his army. This army was mowed down by the cannon as rapidly as the English armies which you send to Ava or the Cape are wiped out by tropical diseases. The French armies submitted to this horrible lottery, and, in return, Napoleon promised them not only the advantages of pillage (that would have been a peccadillo) but licence to murder the citizens on whom they were billeted (the baker in Cassel is one example), to murder the *maires des communes* in France; and to pillage their own wagon train, as they did in Spain in 1809, thus causing the defeat of the French army. M. de Ségur has committed a crime which the army will never forgive him: he has directed the attention of the French to the military leprosy introduced into France by Napoleon. His object may have been merely to tell the truth, or it may have been, at the same time, to flatter the Bourbons and the aristocracy and thus gain some lucrative position under Charles X. In any case, this is something that we cannot tell and that we will only know after three or four years. The crimes that were committed in the army of the Emperor would never have been tolerated in the army of the Republic. The years from 1793 to 1800 saw the truly heroic age of French bravery, and its representative figure is the sublime Desaix.

In attacking M. de Ségur, M. Gourgaud has adopted a simple tactic. Whenever, on the testimony of witnesses living in Paris, or men of sense such as M. Daru or M. Mathieu Dumas, M. de Ségur relates an incident which shows Napoleon in an unfavourable light, M. Gourgaud exclaims that the Emperor possessed too great a mind and too firm a character to descend to such weakness. Occasionally, it is true, he quotes instances in which Napoleon gave proof of the sublime energy for which he was pre-eminently distinguished; but it is clear enough that this proves nothing against M. de Ségur's argument, in which, we are reminded, furthermore, twenty times over, that the Russian campaign was altogether an exception in Napoleon's career. M. de Ségur would have had no difficulty in pointing out the names of a thousand Frenchmen, now living in Paris or the outskirts, who were in the retreat from Moscow; he would have been able, had he chosen, to place eight or ten questions in the hands of notaries and invited any number of them to answer yes or no. M. de Ségur's style, it is true, is open to a great many objections; it is the style of a gloomy and bilious man trying to imitate Mme de Staël. His book contains three or four hundred sentences which are ridiculous on account of their exaggeration and emphasis.

But then to what do MM. de Chateaubriand, de Lamartine, Delavigne, Hugo and Mlle Delphine Gay owe their success, if it is not to emphasis taken to the last degree of absurdity? As a general rule, M. de Ségur speaks the truth, but he has chosen to ascribe some brilliant feat to each of his friends and he has tried to avoid giving pain to two or three persons who are still alive and who, in 1812, occupied important posts, and, by their repeated acts of folly, contributed to many of the disasters of the defeat from Moscow. If the author is still alive in ten years time, he may bring out an edition of his work stripped of the deliberate lies that he has inserted. I say *lies*, because I feel that M. de Ségur has too perceptive a mind to believe many of the stories he relates. As it stands, his book is a masterpiece. We have had nothing at the same time so interesting and so accurate for the last forty years. M. Mignet has shown as much talent and much more sincerity and philosophy in his History of the French Revolution. He thought it proper, however, to compress this immense body of material into two volumes and failed, as a result, to inspire the intense interest which M. de Ségur's tragic narration must surely hold for every reader, whether he be French or not. Two men surpassed Napoleon in the retreat from Russia: for prudence, Davout, and for strength of character and promptitude of execution, Ney. Without any intention of flattering my readers, I ought to add that, if Napoleon had had a division of six thousand English troops under his command, he would have been able to prevent the worst calamities of his retreat. The complete absence of discipline was the cause of by far the greater number of the disasters by which the army was overtaken.

The French are never conquered, unless through lack of discipline or a ridiculous display of personal bravery. This has been demonstrated continually from the Battles of Agincourt and Montlhéry down to Waterloo, as may be seen if one reads a curious work called *Mes Rêveries* by Marshal de Saxe.

London Magazine, August 1825
(From *Letters from Grimm's grandson, no. viii.*)

CHATEAUBRIAND, DARU AND THE DUC DE MONTMORENCY IN THE FRENCH ACADEMY

February 10th, 1826

Sir,

England can offer nothing comparable to the spectacle which we enjoyed here yesterday. The object of the ceremony to which I am referring was truly ridiculous; it was the election to the French Academy of the Duc de Montmorency, a man who possesses neither talent nor literary distinction. The duke, nevertheless, is a man of the most polished and graceful manners, almost entirely free from what one might call the ferocity of the middle ages. This ferocity has not yet altogether disappeared from the French character, unless among the natives of Paris. The grace of French manners does not entirely preclude energy of character, if we can be said to possess energy in the first place. A bold character in France, observed the Abbé Siéyès, is an iron hand in a velvet glove. In other countries and especially in the north, a bold character is a hand of iron, the surface of which has been smoothed with a sharp file. I am sorry to have to speak ill of the Duc de Montmorency; but he was guilty of an unpardonable fault in allowing himself to be elected, with the aid of two or three intriguing academicians (MM. Roger, Auger, Chateaubriand, etc.), to a position to which he is entirely unsuited.

It was precisely on account of this unsuitability, which ought to have excluded the first Christian baron from the Academy, that the upper classes made a point of sanctioning his election by their presence. Ridicule soon wears thin in France. Here it is not enough that a joke should make one laugh; there must also be somebody to tell the joke. During the last two months there has been so much laughter at the expense of the French Academy because of its folly in accepting the first Christian baron as one of its members, and the folly of the baron in accepting the choice, that anyone who ventured a joke on the subject in the hall of the Academy would himself have been laughed at for retailing the sort of witticism that had been made in the morning's newspaper. In London you do not have, as we do, nine daily newspapers whose sole object is to make jokes at the expense of everyone from *Robin Hood*[1] to M. de Sosthène, and you can have no idea of the effect that this can produce.

I am afraid too that I shall be unable to give you any adequate idea of the delightful spectacle which we witnessed yesterday at the Institute. The hall is an elegant rotunda lighted by a

[1] The king.

dome. This rotunda, which is not very large, is surrounded by seats and the middle is set aside for the members of the Institute. Yesterday, as early as two o'clock, and with that disregard for order which invariably attends every ceremony in France, these reserved seats were occupied by about two hundred ladies of rank, almost all of them remarkable for their beauty and all elegantly dressed. Another circumstance which was to render this sitting so extraordinary, was that all these beautiful women came from that class of society most distinguished for its talent in this highly intellectual nation. The dread of ridicule banishes from the hall of the Institute all those who are incapable of understanding the obscure hints and allusions of which French academic eloquence is composed. Amidst this choice assemblage of beauty and fashion, a few men were to be seen here and there, and on enquiring who they were, one was sure to find that they were all distinguished by their talent or their rank, all either members of the class known for its historical names or anxious to be included in it. Apart from the few who were attracted to the Academy out of mere curiosity, none were to be found there but persons of repute. Mademoiselle Delphine Gay, who has assumed the appellation of the *Nation's Muse*, was seated opposite the illustrious Mme de Cayla; while Mademoiselle Mars found herself facing the Abbé Feutrier, the most witty and gallant of all our bishops. Next to the pensive Mademoiselle Gay sat Mme Belloc, who is no less beautiful than the French Muse and whose charming work on Byron is more often read than the emphatic and somewhat meaningless verses of her fair neighbour. I could mention here more than twenty beautiful young women who are the grace and ornament of Parisian society; but I have determined to name only those who are known in literary circles, and among the men, only those who are connected in some way with the Academy.

STENDHAL

For the space of an hour the most animated conversation prevailed in the hall of the Institute, until suddenly the words, 'Gentlemen, the sitting is opened', pronounced in a loud voice, produced general silence. The announcement was made by M. Daru, who was Napoleon's minister during the Russian campaign. On his right was M. de Chateaubriand, his brow still clouded with the ill-humour occasioned by his expulsion from the government; on his left, M. Renouard, secretary of the Academy, who in the past enjoyed a year or two of public acclaim, but who is now the willing instrument of authority and a worthy colleague of the censors, Lemontey, Auger and Lacretelle. No sooner had M. Daru announced the opening of the sitting than a man with a remarkably pale complexion and handsome features, but whose face expressed nothing but weakness of character, rose from his seat. From the numerous crosses which adorned his black, green-embroidered coat, it was easy to recognise the Duc de Montmorency, the general of the short-robed Jesuits and the tutor of the young Duc de Bordeaux. He could almost have been taken for one of those ghastly objects which the professors of medicine in our hospitals raise from their beds and lead to the lecture rooms in order to explain to their students some singular and incurable disease. The Duc de Montmorency read out a printed speech of which the following extract is the opening:

'Gentlemen. Ever since the day when your voices called me to accept an honour that lack, or rather a total absence, of literary distinction had forbidden me to hope for, my eyes turned necessarily towards the day when I would have to thank, from the ranks of the Academy, those whose admission was not like mine, generous and undeserved, but the proof and the reward of their labours and their glory.'[1]

---

[1] See the *Moniteur*, February 16th, 1826. (*Editor*.)

On hearing this extraordinary yet perfectly just confession, rendered necessary by the jokes that have amused Paris for the past two months, everyone very naturally wondered how, if he really was so conscious of his own lack of qualifications, the new academician could, in all honesty, accept such a position. It is a position which, since 1814, has not been much to be envied, it is true; nevertheless, it should go by right to those unfortunate men of letters who are weak enough to want it, and who have been intriguing for twenty years to obtain it. The only reproach we intend to make concerns the Duc de Montmorency's lack of honesty; but for a man of honour surely this in itself is very grave. The seat in which the duke has just been installed is M. Etienne's who, although he is our best comic poet, was driven from the Academy by Vaublanc, an indifferent writer himself and the instrument of the Bourbons' fury. It belongs by right to M. Etienne, to M. de Lamartine, to M. Lebrun, to M. Béranger, to M. de Barante and to a dozen others whose claims might be variously estimated, but who would evince no lack of honesty in allowing themselves to occupy it. Another circumstance which indicates the insincerity of the present age is that, while committing a theft, the only theft that *could* be committed by a Montmorency, a duke, and a man earning a hundred thousand francs a year, this same duke, the leader of the saints, delivered, instead of an academic address, a sermon on *virtue*, which he extolled above talent of any kind. Such hypocrisy reminds one of the worst days of Louis XIV's dotage. Heaven defend us from any reaction such as was seen in the way of life adopted under the Regency!

Next to the Duc de Montmorency sat M. Lally-Tollendal, whom Mme de Staël humorously described as the fattest and most feeling man she had ever known. He smiled throughout the whole of his colleague's tedious sermon, despite the gloomy silence that reigned over the assembly and the general weariness and dissatisfaction. Why did he go to the trouble of smiling, you may ask. Because, for the past ten years, he has been soliciting the *Cordon Bleu*. Finally the duke's tedious oration, which was written in a style of perfect elegance and delivered with an air of languid good humour, came to an end. He concluded with an eulogy of the Emperor Alexander, a prince whom the King of England did not even deign to mention in his speech to Parliament, and whose death has been regarded by all Frenchmen, except for those of the name of Bourbon, as a signal and unhoped-for cause for rejoicing. Mention of the Emperor's name succeeded merely in increasing the general boredom and irritation of his audience.

An interval of a minute or two followed during which the whisper seemed to go round: 'So this is the man who is to form the character of the future Henri V.' Then the Comte Daru, a peer of France and president of the Academy on the unhappy day chosen for the duke's election, rose to make his reply to the tutor of the Duc de Bordeaux. The unprecedented success of some of the speeches made by the former minister of Napoleon may be ascribed to his having expressed the sentiments which animate the public and to his having uttered them in a tone of perfect moderation and yet with all the spiritedness which is naturally excited by the spectacle of vice triumphing over virtue. The most vehement applause, continually renewed and continually repressed for fear of losing a single word, accompanied the whole of this magnificent address. Like every French man of letters who, when he obtains a hearing of three-quarters of an hour, turns to every subject on which he can possibly speak and lays open the whole storehouse of his ideas, M. Daru touched directly or indirectly on every topic of conversation which is at present going around Paris. Alluding to Napoleon's Minister for Religious Affairs, he observed, for example, that 'the office he filled in no way diminished his tolerant spirit'. You will not perhaps seize the cutting sarcasm conveyed in these few words, but they were no sooner uttered than the hideous gloomy countenance of M. Frayssinous, Bishop of Hermopolis, who is our present Minister for Religious Affairs and a member of the French Academy, was suffused with an incriminating blush. He crossed his arms indignantly and cast a haughty glance in M. Daru's direction. All eyes were turned towards him and the whisper went round, 'Bravo! That is indeed courageous.' The sarcasms directed at the Duc de Montmorency were no less obvious and severe, even if they were more guardedly expressed. They were at all events much more entertaining, for the hypocrisy and fanaticism of our priests, Gallican and Anti-Gallican (that is, Jesuit), have now become too evident to call for any direct reference from a speaker like M. Daru in the presence of an intelligent audience alive to every allusion. Only imagine the pleasure and enjoyment of a company composed of the flower of French fashion, among them so many beautiful and accomplished women, as they sat in judgment for three-quarters of an hour on the sarcasms directed at a despised power controlled by odious priests—sarcasms so delicately turned that a numbskull or a man from the provinces might have taken them for real praise. In the course of the speech delivered by the author of the *History of Venice*, the minister, who at Moscow had the courage to tell Napoleon the truth, a moral principle would occasionally be unfolded which interrupted the sequence of ironies, and yet was itself a sarcasm. Imagine the state of intellectual excitement produced by the combination of so many elegant pleasures, and tell me whether they could be enjoyed anywhere but in Paris; tell me too whether I have been wrong to spend so much time on the subject. Such entertainment is unique in Europe and in the world, and I will boldly affirm that any educated man, whether he be born in Edinburgh, New York, Stockholm or London, will be unable to estimate a hundredth part of the advantages given by ten years intercourse with polished society and twenty years of classical studies, unless he has been present on the sort of occasion I have described in the French Academy. Such sittings, however, are of very rare occurrence. Suppose, for instance, that M. Auger, M. Roger, M. Lacretelle, M. Lemontey or any other member who has sold himself to the Jesuits, had been president on the day chosen for the Duc de Montmorency's election. Both the sitting and the business performed would have been trivial and uninteresting. I was present at several sittings of the French Academy before 1791, and I have not missed one under Napoleon or since the restoration of the Bourbons. I can safely affirm, however, that I have seen none comparable in interest to yesterday's. The genius of the French people is, like that of its language, essentially *moqueur* and *naïf*. A really interesting sitting of the French Academy could never have taken place under a clever despot like Napoleon, but only under a government which is guided by an erroneous system and which is the creation of violent and ridiculous prejudices. In this respect, it must be acknowledged that we have all that can be wished for. A striking example of these prejudices is the refusal by the government to allow the remains of the painter David to be brought back into France.

If I wanted even better proof of the spirit of derision and gaiety which is so much part of the French character, I should find it in the composition of the elegant assemblage in whose presence the Duc de Montmorency was enrolled among the members of the Academy. Among those present were all the duchesses of the Faubourg Saint-Germain and many peers; in a word, an immense majority of men and women of aristocratic birth and *ultra* convictions. In spite of this, however, the applause always went to the passages of M. Daru's speech which were most imbued with the spirit of Voltaire or of modern philosophy. Yet this did not prevent almost all the men who were there from voting for the most odious and absurd laws the following day in the Chamber of Peers, among them the law establishing the right of primogeniture and the law of sacrilege. This inconsistency in the French character, which makes it indispensable that one should be always witty and never dull or ridiculous, is precisely what has always made the French the most lively and agreeable people in the world. The folly which a Frenchman commits at three o'clock in the afternoon in voting in a certain way in the Chamber does not oblige him at five o'clock to applaud a similar folly in the Academy. We have as much venality as any other nation, but only the indispensable degree of human folly. What does a Columbian, a Swede or an Englishman care if a French deputy sells his vote for a hundred thousand francs a session? The main thing is that the deputy should not appear dull or stupid. Now that America is securing for herself the most reasonable of all forms of government, it is plain that in three hundred years time she will have plunged into one common abyss of contempt all the nations of Europe which are at present, to some extent or other, degraded and enervated by despotism and aristocracy. When this happens, the French alone will remain to provide an inimitable model of wit and elegance. The French privilege of being pusillanimous with a good grace was strikingly exemplified about a week ago, when the King of France gave a reception at which three hundred or so ladies were present. The conversation on this occasion had a distinctly Voltairean tint, and doubtless exhibited a singular contrast to the conversation which takes place in royal circles in England. Your English peers, however, who are very rich, are never reduced to the necessity of selling their votes any more than your ministers are obliged to gamble with the public funds. Poverty often forces us to do what is blameable, but we contrive despite this to render ourselves agreeable. How is this? Because we are fortunate enough to be inconsistent. A short while ago, I saw a man laughing heartily at one of M. Leclercq's comedies which painted in forcible colours certain acts of meanness which the very man who was laughing was known to have committed three years before. Furthermore, half the audience who were laughing with him knew that he had been guilty of the sort of conduct which was being so finely ridiculed by M. Fiévée's friend.

I should be neglecting the best literary composition to have appeared in Paris since my last letter, if I failed to mention the historical analysis of the Roman emperors from Caesar to Augustulus which was read at the Academy by M. de Chateaubriand, after M. Daru's reply to the Duc de Montmorency. Throughout the whole of his delightful speech, M. Daru was so guarded in his language that there was not a single sentence, perhaps, which fully expressed what he really meant. The tyrants whom M. de Chateaubriand depicted, however, in a style worthy of Montesquieu, have been long since dead and buried beneath contempt. The speaker therefore endeavoured to give the utmost clarity and brilliance to his ideas. The unexpected contrast between a liberal statesman, continually obliged to veil his thoughts, and the disappointed colleague of M. de Villèle seeking to give the utmost bitterness to the contempt with which posterity looks back on the Roman tyrants (even though these are no more ridiculous in fact than those of St Petersburg and Vienna), afforded inexpressible amusement to the audience. The most curious circumstance is that M. de Chateaubriand, when he was in the government, praised those very despots of St Petersburg and Vienna who, today, would be fortunate if they could resemble the most insignificant of the Roman emperors so ironically portrayed in his survey. Do not imagine, however, that anyone was displeased at this species of recantation. There were not ten members of the audience who would not have recanted in the same way for a Prefecture.

The pusillanimities and *capucinades*[1] which M. de Chateaubriand printed in the *Conservateur* (a journal of 1819), with a view to getting into the government, have had no other permanent effect than that of inspiring a distaste for his *unction* and for the sentiments of virtue which he professes continually, but which only a man like M. Daru, who has never sold himself, has the right to affirm with any boldness. The word *unsold*, for which France is now paying a million francs to the children of General Foy, will soon be the rarest title that can be inscribed on the tomb of a Frenchman. Yet even if M. de Chateaubriand's conduct had been a hundred times worse than it was, what would it really matter? He would still be one of the cleverest men in France, and his first address to the Academy would not have excited any less admiration. It was an order of Napoleon's in 1810 which obliged the Academy to elect him to the place left vacant by the death of Chénier, the same poet who has recently been so cruelly treated by the *Edinburgh Review* and *Blackwood's Magazine*. Chénier, the brilliant disciple of Voltaire, was an infidel, however, and M. de Chateaubriand, who wished to make his fortune by allying himself to the clerical party, refused to pronounce the customary eulogy of his predecessor. As a result, he never in fact took up his place. Napoleon was weak enough to tolerate this act of defiance, and it is thus that we now have the Jesuits. It is as the precursor of the latter that Napoleon is most particularly disliked or rather

[1] See footnote to page 29.

pitied in France. This is the great flaw in the otherwise glorious reputation which he enjoys. Whenever he is praised, the answer is invariably: 'Yes, but had it not been for Napoleon we should not be plagued today with the Jesuits and the Bourbons.'

It is with these considerations in mind that the public has given its judgment of the historical analysis with which the author of *Atala* made his first appearance on the tribune of the Academy. M. de Chateaubriand presents in glowing colours the historical facts which have now been settled by the erudite. Not once, however, does he perceive or unfold anything new. When he is obscure it is because he is being mystical and theological; not because he is expressing new ideas which are not immediately clear to his auditors. He is, in short, a painter and not a thinker. Throughout three-quarters of his life and three-quarters of his writings he has been uttering untruths. In this way he continually wearies the patience of his reader, who will exclaim: 'Oh! the hypocrite!' but never: 'Oh! the numbskull!'

Chateaubriand's falsehoods are shown up sometimes as so barefaced, because of the information which he betrays in spite of himself, that they become quite unreadable. I have never known a man of ordinary intelligence who has been able to read through the *Génie du Christianisme*, while knowing the author's opinions on monarchy and religion to be the exact opposite of those given in his first work published in London. The latter was printed in Paris in 1823; but the bookseller dared not try to sell it for two reasons: firstly, because he was afraid of being prosecuted for an attack against religion and secondly, because he was afraid of M. de Chateaubriand's friends.

I here quote from M. de Chateaubriand's historical summary, a work which strikes me as better written and less tainted by hypocrisy than any of his previous productions.

Alluding to Caesar he says:

> 'Caesar is the most complete of historical figures, because he combines the triple genius of statesman, writer and warrior ... if he had lived in the days of morality, he would have been the rival of such men as Cincinnatus and Fabricius, for he was capable of vigour and strength in all their forms. When he appeared in Rome, however, virtue had gone; he found nothing left but glory, which he assumed for want of anything better.'[1]

This passage, which is amusing, ingenious and truly French, was applauded for two minutes. M. de Chateaubriand then went on:

> 'The morals of Tiberius were worthy of the rest of his life; only nothing was openly said of them, for to assist his vices he invoked his crimes; and terror would answer the challenge of contempt.'

The applause was renewed for this last sentence, which might have been taken from an unpublished manuscript by Montesquieu.

M. de Chateaubriand powerfully depicted the profound dissimulation of Augustus; the hideous cruelty of Tiberius; the violence of Caligula; the imbecility of Claudius; the bloodthirsty nature of Nero; the misfortunes of Galba; the debaucheries of Otho and the orgies of Vitellius. When he came to the reigns of Vespasian, Titus, Domitian, Trajan, Adrian, Antoninus and Marcus Aurelius, he gave incontestable proof that the Roman Empire could never have been saved, even by that line of princes whose names are consecrated by antiquity.

> 'Every imaginable species of merit appeared among the leaders of the Empire; those who possessed these qualities, furthermore, were able to undertake any course of action

---

[1] See for this and the following quotations, the *Etudes Historiques* of Chateaubriand, Paris 1833; volume I, pages 134-204. (*Editor.*)

they chose; there was no impediment to their power; heirs to an absolute authority, they were free to turn it to good account, where before it had been used for evil. Yet what was achieved by this despotism of virtue? Did it bring about a reform in morals? Did it re-establish liberty? Did it save the Empire from its downfall? No. Human nature was neither improved nor changed. Firmness reigned in Vespasian, moderation in Titus, generosity in Nerva, greatness in Trajan, the arts in Adrian and piety in Antoninus. Finally, with Marcus Aurelius, philosophy itself was placed on the throne; and yet this fulfilment of a sage's dream brought no solid benefit. For nothing is durable or even possible when everything comes from good will and nothing from the law.

★ ★ ★ ★

With Marcus Aurelius the era of Rome's happiness under imperial authority comes to an end, and with Commodus begins that fearful period of history which is to end only with the division of the Empire and the transformation of society. The virtue of Marcus Aurelius contributed no more to the public good than it did to personal happiness; it bore no fruit even in his own household. Commodus was an odious sovereign, and, once more during his reign, the Romans plunged into depravity, though, this time, with such ardour, that one might have taken them for men newly restored to liberty; in fact, they were emancipated merely from the moral standards established by their rulers.

One may observe two effects of absolute power on the human heart.

It never even occurred to those good princes who governed the Roman Empire to doubt the legality of their own power, or to restore to the Roman people the power which their predecessors had usurped.

That very same absolute power corrupted reason itself in the worst rulers. Nero, Caligula, Domitian and Commodus were truly insane. It was as if heaven, in order to save the earth from an excess of horror, had added madness to their crimes, like a mask of innocence.

Commodus, meeting a man of unusual corpulence, cut him in two to prove his strength, and to enjoy the spectacle of his victim's entrails. He called himself Hercules; he wanted Rome to change its name and assume his own; the memory of this whim has been perpetuated by shameful medals. Commodus died by the poison served to him by one of his concubines, and by the hand of an athlete who concluded the effect of the poison by strangling him.'

As M. de Chateaubriand approaches the age of Christianity, he begins to assume the emphatic, vague but elegant style of the *Génie du Christianisme*. It is a style, however, which, though it appeared so novel in 1803, has been degraded by his disciples and imitators, MM. Marchangy and d'Arlincourt. Having described the various invasions of the barbarians, M. de Chateaubriand continues his interesting summary as follows:

'Famine and the plague destroyed all those who had been spared by the sword. The previous race of men was annihilated and the plains, scattered with the bones of the dead, were covered over with forests. The wilderness, as if it had been drawn there by the barbarians and had travelled with them from afar, stretched over the face of what had once been the most fertile provinces, and in the districts which had at one time teemed with innumerable inhabitants, there remained nothing but the earth and the sky.

When the dust raised by the feet of so many armies and by the crumbling of so many monuments had at last settled; when the colums of smoke from burning towns had disappeared; when death had silenced the groans of its countless victims, and when the sound of the fall of the Roman colossus had ceased to resound, then was a cross revealed to the eyes of men, and at the foot of this cross, a new world. All was now changed: men, religion, customs and language. From among the tombs, a few priests, seated on the ruins with the Gospel in their hands, brought about the resurrection of human society, like Jesus restoring life to the children of those who had believed in him. . . .

Let us pause a moment to contemplate this strange world, and consider two men.

One of these is the son of the secretary of Attila, who, after the fall of the Empire, had left Rome for ever. He resides in an old country house which had once belonged to Lucullus, without a thought of the importance attached to its name and without realising what lessons and memories are in the future to immortalise its site. The other, crowned by his flowing hair and with an axe for a sceptre, has conquered a small town called Lutetia.

The son of Attila's secretary is Augustulus; the barbarian king is Clovis.'

A number of elderly gentlemen who were present at yesterday's meeting of the Academy condemned M. de Chateaubriand for his lack of historical dignity. I should like to know, however, if any of the elegant women who graced the assembly with thei presence cared a fig for Commodus, Claudius or even Caesar. A narrator, faithful to the dignity of the past, would have bored his listeners, whereas the author of *Atala* never failed to entertain and even instruct his audience. If you can find a good translator, and if the taste of the English public should correspond to that of the French, I should strongly advise you to have the whole of M. de Chateaubriand's address translated. This depends, of course, on whether the author consents to have it printed.

Nero and the other demented rulers of Rome decimated their courtiers. M. de Chateaubriand, however, says nothing about the degree of happiness enjoyed by one hundred and ten million subjects under the Roman despots. Were these millions more unhappy under the consulate of Cicero or under the empire of Nero? And would not this dangerously controversial and rather Jacobinical question be an apt one for the *friend* of the Emperor Alexander to ask himself today? Only three years ago he was boasting of this friendship in the Chamber of Deputies.

New Monthly Magazine, March 1826

THE JESUITS AND THE ARISTOCRACY

The Jesuits and their Jubilee have afforded every class of society a certain amusement during the past month. On Good Friday they lost their general, Duke Mathieu de Montmorency, the leader of the short-robed Jesuits, who number one hundred and eight adopted members in the Chamber of Deputies. Last year the Duke was very active in petitioning his fellow peers to approve of the death penalty, which the Jesuits succeeded in introducing into the Law of Sacrilege, and his assiduousness in this direction has been spoken of in a number of the eulogies which have appeared on the occasion of his death. The Jesuits were even successful in getting some of these eulogies into the English press. I dare say you may have noticed that, in the enumeration of the various posts to which M. de Montmorency was appointed by the Bourbons, and the various rewards conferred upon him, no mention has been made of the title of Duke, which he received after the Congress of Verona. The reason for this ostentatious omission is that the Jesuits disapproved of the distinction, and considered its acceptance as an act of vanity on the part of their leader. Who is likely to be his successor? Where can one hope to find a man of such illustrious birth, who is able to plead for the death penalty in such a mild and gentlemanly way?

People were still speculating on the difficulties which the short-robed Jesuits would encounter in finding a suitable successor, when the duel between Marshal Soult and Marshal Law de Lauriston[1] suddenly attracted attention. Marshal Soult is considered, next to Gouvion St Cyr, as the most able of our French generals; but he is dying of disappointment at having no position, not even that of a peer. Some time ago, he dressed himself in full uniform, with four or five sashes across the front of his coat, and followed by eight lackeys, went to receive Holy Communion in his parish church. To justify a parade of this kind, a man's name must be Montmorency or La Tremouille at the very least. Such absurd ostentation in a man like Marshal Soult became the talk of every salon in the Faubourg St Germain.

As soon as he learned that Charles X intended to take part in the Jubilee procession, Marshal Soult wrote to Marshal Law de Lauriston to ask whether the Marshals were expected to join the procession too and whether there was a place reserved for them. Marshal Lauriston holds the sinecure of *Grand Veneur*, and is not master of ceremonies. He replied, however, that he believed that a place was in fact to be assigned to the Marshals and that he himself intended to go in undress uniform. Marshal Soult accordingly made his appearance on the chosen day in undress uniform, and with a lighted taper in his hand. This provoked the laughter of all the officers, and to complete his misfortune, he discovered that there was no place set aside for the Marshals. The Jesuits had never ventured to hope that any marshal would be foolish enough to sacrifice his popularity without the prospect of some tangible advantage to

---

[1] A descendant of the famous Scots Law. We thus have now two Marshals of Scots origin, Macdonald and Lauriston. (Note in the *New Monthly Magazine*.)

himself. For the space of two hours, therefore, Marshal Soult paraded the streets of Paris amidst the jeers of the spectators. Next day he addressed a letter to Marshal Lauriston, demanding satisfaction for his having deceived him by his intimations that he would be given a place among the others. Marshal Lauriston, who is a man of unquestionable courage, replied that he had had no intention of giving offence to his unfortunate comrade, and that he certainly had no intention of fighting him. A second challenge was sent, to which a second refusal was returned. This challenge has been the talk of Paris for the last week. M. de Villèle has also refused a similar challenge, this one from General Sebastiani.

There is another incident connected with the famous Jubilee procession and which I hardly know how to describe to you. It concerns two distinguished personages who are paid out of the budget and whose names I would be perfectly justified in disclosing to you on account of the important posts which they occupy. If I were to name them, however, and if my letter should be opened at the Post Office, as it usually is, it would stand a good chance of being thrown in the fire. To avoid any risk, therefore, I shall mention no names. In the first place, you need to know what is known by every Frenchman, even those of the most exalted rank; that is, that *Enseignement Mutuel* (Mutual Instruction) begins with an E. Many houses in Paris are insured against fire by private insurance companies, and on the doors of these houses plates are fixed with the initials A.M., which stands for *Assurance Mutuelle* (Mutual Insurance). While the procession was passing along the Rue St Jacques, an illustrious personage was observed to glance at the above-mentioned plates with a marked air of uneasiness. At length he called over M. Sosthène de la Rochefoucauld, and the following dialogue took place: 'This seems to be a very disloyal quarter of the town. These initials A.M. which are so conspicuously displayed on the doors of houses stand, I take it, for *Enseignement Mutuel*.' 'I suppose they do', was the reply. 'You count on the left hand side and I'll count on the right, and we'll see how many there are.' They soon counted up to a hundred and twenty-two. No sooner was the procession over than the illustrious personage in question sent for the Bishop of Hermopolis. 'So', he exclaimed, 'I find that the Rue St Jacques is full of establishments for mutual instruction. Why have they not been suppressed gradually and by gentle means? Are not the people sufficiently jacobin and impious already, without being taught to read Voltaire and Rousseau?'

I shall not relate the rest of a curious conversation in the course of which the Bishop had the embarrassing task of explaining that the word *Enseignement* begins with an E and *Assurance* with an A.

The barefoot expedition of the Marchioness d'Au——t, the adventures of Marshal Soult and the discussion concerning the insurance plates have given Paris abundant entertainment over the past few weeks. As a result, the Marchioness d'Aumont, whose initials are the same as those of the famous barefooted pedestrian, has found it necessary to print a notice in the papers stating that it was not she who performed the memorable pilgrimage. At present the Jesuits are the object of general derision. M. de Montlosier's terrible manifesto of which I spoke in my last letter,[1] instead of being seized, has now reached its sixth edition within the short space of a month. The government is, in fact, so much in awe of public opinion that the reply to M. de Montlosier's book by M. de la Mennais has been seized and prosecuted instead. The King desired that a letter should be sent to M. de la Mennais directing him to go to Rome; but M. de la Mennais, who is a former officer and a man of spirit, refused to leave the country.

[1] See too page 276 of the present edition.

It is curious to observe that the Royal Court, over which M. Seguier presides, is condemning the Jesuits, not because they are fanatics or because they recommend thirty thousand young priests to read M. de Maistre's book on the Pope.[1] Its hostility has nothing to do with M. de Maistre's maxims, but is due above all to the fact that a third of its members are Jansenists. This madness was scarcely to be expected. The Jansenists are perhaps more fanatical in their way of thinking than the children of Loyola.

Some of our balls have recently opened in a very curious way. The company arrive about nine o'clock. The young ladies, all elegantly dressed and provided with bouquets, range themselves round the room with downcast eyes and in complete silence. When the party is assembled, a gentleman with his hair combed straight over his forehead, in a way which distinguishes the short-robed Jesuit, takes up a book, opens it and immediately shuts it with a loud clap. At this signal, a priest enters from an adjoining room, and with great solemnity commences a pious exhortation. The Jesuit, who is always a handsome young man, delivers his address in an effeminate voice and with a mild and melancholy air; then, after three-quarters of an hour or so, he makes his departure. No sooner has he gone than the ladies raise their eyes, take out their bouquets which till then have lain concealed, and as soon as the violins have been tuned, begin dancing.

In 1810, during the reign of Napoleon, who would have ever thought of seeing so comical a spectacle in Paris? The versatility of its manners must render the French nation extremely curious and amusing to the eye of a foreigner.

This spectacle would be far less ludicrous if people really believed what they profess. But the Catholic religion, as

[1] M. de Maistre affirms that the Pope may dethrone kings, and change governments; and this doctrine was maintained in the official journal of Rome, about the end of last year. (Note in the *New Monthly Magazine*.)

conceived by the Pope, is not believed in by three men or twenty women in a hundred. If Napoleon had not been defeated at Waterloo, we should now have the tyranny of the epaulette. Jesuitical tyranny is, after all, the best, because it is necessarily the least likely of the two to last. Napoleon's soldiers possessed physical courage, a quality which is incompatible with hypocrisy, and one that is at present very fashionable in France. The Jesuits, on the other hand, have nothing to recommend them, for they do not even have any claims to learning or instruction. M. Grégoire, former Bishop of Blois, M. Lanjuinais and two or three eminent scholars are always pointing out the ignorance betrayed in the religious pamphlets which the Jesuits publish every year, and which are talked of by all, though read by none. Something more amusing is to be found in the *Report on the Constitutions of the Jesuits* made to the *Parlement* of Brittany in 1761 by the celebrated La Chalotais. This is not dull reading like the works of Mme. Lanjuinais and Grégoire. M. la Chalotais is a man of the world. He does not, to be sure, express himself very well in his mother tongue; but he has a considerable share of talent and firmness. He is not an empty talker like the Abbé de Pradt; nor is he kept in check, like M. de Montlosier, by the fear of losing a pension.

A fact which appears to me to prove the advantages that would be derived from rendering politics a purely experimental science, like chemistry and natural philosophy, is that the sale of judicial offices, a financial measure suggested to a rapacious king by a corrupt minister, produced the formation of the most respectable body of judges ever assembled in modern Europe. Before the Revolution, men such as d'Aligre, Molé, Séguier and Malesherbes, who possessed an income of one hundred thousand francs a year, besides their annual emoluments of fifteen hundred francs, rose at five in the morning and laboured assiduously and conscientiously in the administration of justice. They were rewarded by the respect of the public. M. de la Chalotais, who was born in 1700, was a man of exceptionally firm character, and in this respect, one of the most remarkable men of his century. In 1761, he made a report to the Parliament of Brittany on the spirit of the various constitutions of the Jesuits. Of this report, four editions have been published in Paris within the last month. M. de la Chalotais was a nobleman and we cannot suppose him to have been influenced by revolutionary principles. His book is therefore calculated to make a profounder impression on moderate men than all that has been written by MM. de Pradt and Montlosier. The Jesuits had sufficient power to have M. de la Chalotais thrown into prison on the following grounds: The English made a descent on the coast of Brittany and a battle was fought at St Cast. The Duke d'Aiguillon was in command of the French troops, and M. de la Chalotais was imprudent enough to write to a friend by post: 'Your general got himself covered with flour, and not with glory.' It is affirmed that the Duke d'Aiguillon, on the approach of the enemy, really did conceal himself in a mill. The Duke, who was protected by the court, joined the Jesuits. Chalotais was accused of writing anonymous letters; and on this and other pretexts, he and his son were thrown into prison. They were not set free until the year 1775, when Louis XVI came to the throne and made Chalotais a marquess. I send you these particulars because they are not perhaps generally known in England; though, for the past month, they have been the main topic of conversation in Paris. The *Etoile*, which is the *Père Duchêne*[1] of Jesuitism, has recently been heaping the most furious abuse at Chalotais, whose family has replied by legal measures and an open prosecution.

[1] The title of an infamous newspaper of the time of Robespierre. (Note in the *New Monthly Magazine*.)

The city of Rennes has sent its best lawyer, M. Bernard, to defend the memory of La Chalotais. Bernard speaks very much in the style of Phillips, the Irish barrister. His speeches are florid, and highly coloured, full of personifications and apostrophes and quite the reverse, as a result, of the calm and restrained style which MM. Berthe, Merilhou, Dupin and some of our best Parisian lawyers have adopted through their fear of ridicule. M. Bernard's speech has been much admired, and this admiration has proved a fresh mortification to the Jesuits, who have experienced nothing but misfortune since Good Friday, when their General, Duke Mathieu de Montmorency, died. The florid eloquence of M. Bernard of Rennes has excited no small degree of attention here; for, throughout the last two centuries, Paris has been the headquarters of the dread of ridicule. In matters of taste, the Parisians always seek to moderate, as far as possible, the extravagance of her provinces. The great writers who have been natives of Paris, such as Molière and Voltaire, are distinguished for having ridiculed the excess of energy.

Amidst all the absurdities which the Jesuits have occasioned in France and which a wise government might put an end to in a month, one thing is particularly remarkable, namely, the air of dissatisfaction and uneasiness evinced by most of our young noblemen.

Lord Byron probably rendered himself unhappy, because he was proud of being a lord, and at the same time proud of being a great poet. Of these two qualities, which are, in certain respects, irreconcilable, it was necessary to choose one; and it has been observed by certain of our French critics that Lord Byron never had the strength of mind to make the choice. The same is true of our young noblemen. They are proud of their high birth, while, at the same time, they read the *Constitutionnel* and admire America. They see their school friends, who are not the sons of noblemen, become lawyers, physicians and manufacturers, and see them thus enjoy the happiness of being consistent. They hear these same companions utter truths which appear to them self-evident and yet which they dare not repeat; while at home they hear the most extravagant praise lavished on the absurd writings of MM. de Bonald, de Maistre, and de la Mennais. Many of these young men have been in the army. They have been to Spain and seen a country which was tolerably happy under the Cortes, rendered miserable by the introduction of the principles of French ultraism. These young noblemen lack the courage to avow openly their secret desire to see all who are not noble themselves sacrificed to the interests of the privileged classes to which they belong. At the same time, they dare not profess open liberalism, like the Marquis de Lafayette. It is no doubt very agreeable for a young man to find himself regarded as a drawing-room oracle, merely because his ancestors fought in the Crusades. It is very convenient, when one is at a loss for a reply, and when one's interlocutor is a man of plebeian origin, to take refuge behind the privilege of birth, and throw out hints about vulgarity.

But this paltry triumph is paid for by the sacrifice of happiness. Our young noblemen wish to be both marquesses and liberals, and thus are neither one nor the other. This is the most wretched condition imaginable. They do not, like MM. de la Mennais and de Maistre, acknowledge the omnipotence of despotic authority; nor do they, like MM. Royer-Collard, Benjamin Constant and Jeremy Bentham, admit the right of examination and the necessity of judging the legality of all laws solely according to their degree of utility to the majority of the people.

To complete their frustration, the Bourbons do not even gratify them with a war, which would, at least, afford them an opportunity of proving their courage and gaining promotion. The Congregation proposes that they should become short-robed Jesuits; and they know very well that, without the aid of the Jesuits and despite their illustrious birth, they may very well remain lieutenants all their lives.

New Monthly Magazine, May 1826

A CHARITY CONCERT AT THE VAUXHALL

Paris, May 20th, 1826

The other day I met an old friend of mine, an English gentleman, who had just arrived from London. He told me that no one in England knows of the existence even of the order of the Jesuits in France. If this is truly the case, some of my recent letters must have struck you as very absurd. While Louis XVIII was on the throne, there was still a bare possibility of describing to a foreigner the state of our literature without touching on politics. But with Charles X, we had the three per cents with a threat of extinguishing the fives,[1] the indemnity granted to the emigrants, and finally, not merely the existence, but, if we except their not being in the government, the omnipotence of the Jesuits. The talent of the nation now seems to have no employment other than that of deriding the Jesuits or of hinting to the Royal Family, in every possible way, that

[1] A reference to the system devised by de Villèle's government and voted in the two legislative chambers in 1825 to provide indemnities for the *émigrés* whose property had been confiscated during the Revolution. The interest on government stock was reduced from 5 per cent to 3 per cent and it was out of the economies thus realised that the indemnities were paid. Charles X, in a speech from the throne, described this measure as one which would 'close up the last of the wounds left by the Revolution'. (*Editor*.)

it may soon expect to be sent on a journey similar to that once taken by James II of England. In looking over the weekly catalogue of books printed in France,[1] I do not find one worthy of attention which does not bear some relation or other to the Jesuits or to politics. It is therefore no fault of mine if, contrary to my wishes, these letters, which ought to be confined to literature and society, assume a very political hue. For that you must blame a ridiculous and feeble government, at the expense of which everyone has a laugh or a sarcasm to make. For instance, the phrase which is going the rounds at the moment was originally uttered by Chateaubriand, who, on setting out for Switzerland, observed, 'I very much fear that on returning to Paris in six months time, I shall miss the Bourbons.' I do not need to point out to you the exaggeration of this remark. While I am on the subject of M. de Chateaubriand, I should point out what a triumph and honour it is for literature that 550,000 francs should have been given for the copyright of his works. They have been bought by Ladvocat, the greatest *puffer* of all our booksellers. Subscribers, however are slow to come forward and the writings of the great Bourbon panegyrist are being found rather too hypocritical for the present moment. When men of property find the intrigues of Jesuits carried so far that even their servants are turned into spies, they are not disposed to look with the usual indulgence upon declamations in favour of Catholicism, such as fill the pages of *Le Génie du Christianisme*, and which serve to illustrate the proposition that 'eternal motion springs from eternal rest'.

The principal event in the annals of fashion over the past month has been the concert for the benefit of the Greeks, which was at first advertised for the 21st of April and which eventually took place on the 28th. This concert afforded the

[1] This eatalogue, which forms a journal, affords a striking example of the accuracy of M. Beuchot. (Note in the *New Monthly Magazine*.)

first instance for the last twenty-six years of the upper classes assembling in opposition to the government. In England such an event is fairly common, and in America the papers would scarcely pay attention to it. Here in France, however, this concert given for the benefit of an oppressed people has acquired a certain historical significance. The plan was first broached timidly by the Duchess of Dalberg and a number of other ladies who trembled lest the massacre of Chio should be renewed at Missolonghi. The Government opposed the measure by a hundred little indiscreet measures. No clerk in any of the public offices dared purchase a ticket; and so great was the fear of giving offence that it was feared at one stage that not a thousand tickets at twenty francs each would be disposed of. Suddenly, however, a number of *ultra* ladies of rank began to evince symptoms of compassion, and in a day or two it became quite the fashion to patronise the concert. An English gentleman paid three hundred francs for a ticket, and the seller immediately presented the sum to the general funds. This bargain, which was struck on the Exchange, immediately completed the vogue, and the rage rapidly increased. The Duc de Doudeauville, minister of the King's household, and one of the short-robed Jesuits who had opposed the concert by every means, found himself reduced to the necessity of paying five hundred francs for two tickets. Rossini, who it is said received orders not to direct the concert, took great pains in supervising the rehearsals of the Duchesses, Marchionesses and Countesses who vied with each other for the honour of singing in the choruses. To help the ministers out of their difficulty, Rossini, who receives a handsome salary in Paris for doing nothing, declared that, being a subject of the Pope, he would incur the danger of persecution in Bologna, where his property is situated, if he ventured to direct a concert for the benefit of subjects in revolt against their legal sovereign. That nothing might be wanting to complete the *éclat* of the entertainment, news was received on the morning of the 28th of April that the Turks had been driven from Missolonghi, which, for a week past, had been assumed to be in their power. Some friends of Colonel Fabvier stated during the performance that they were reliably informed that Lord Cochrane intended to leave for Greece, and that he needed only eight steam vessels of two hundred tons each to destroy all the Austrian and Egyptian ships.

You may consider that I have spoken too lengthily of this concert. I assure you, however, that for the last fortnight, nothing else has been talked of in Paris. The Salle de Vauxhall is built on the model of an ancient circus. It is oval in shape and the singers, who were placed in the centre, were in the lowest part of the hall. The centre is surrounded by steps which rise to what might be called the outer space, while a row of columns a few yards further back support a gallery. The full orchestra of the *Opéra Comique* was on the steps behind the singers. Every other part of the hall was crowded with ladies and gentlemen of fashion. The drawing-rooms of the Faubourg St Germain that evening were empty and the Court was even duller than usual. The audience seemed to be astonished at its own numbers, as well as at its courage in opposing the government. The little narrow street leading to the Vauxhall was completely choked with carriages and it seemed as if every private vehicle in Paris was trying to find room. It was thought that the doors of the concert hall would be surrounded by the agents of M. Franchet,[1] so that the names of every member of the audience might be noted in the police files. On seeing the vehicles that thronged the Rue des Marais, however, one could not help thinking that the police would have done better to send round to the concierges, who in Paris are nearly

[1] The Director of the Police, and a violent Jesuit. (Note in the *New Monthly Magazine*.)

all spies, and enquire for the names of all the notable personalities who stayed at home. The sense of the triumph which the concert represented over the government party increased the joy which had been excited by the good news of the morning. About half-past eight, the hall was completely filled, and everyone was saying to himself, 'What is there left for the Bourbons?' If the Duchess de Berry had appeared at that moment, she would have been received with enthusiastic applause, and this concert, which will certainly mark an epoch, would not have been hostile to the reigning family.

The performance began with the *Preghiera* from *Mosé* (which in England is given in the opera *Peter the Hermit*). This extract was very appropriately selected. It is a prayer for divine protection offered up by a whole nation on the point of being massacred. It was admirably executed by the singers of the Italian Opera and a chorus of twenty-four voices, in which several ladies eminently distinguished by their rank and their talents took part. Colonel Brack sang the solo part in what may be said to be Rossini's masterpiece in the pathetic style of composition. Afterwards the Countess Merlin, wife of the Lieutenant-General of that name, gave an exquisite rendering of the grand aria from *Zelmira*, and the wife of Colonel Dubignon, a lady who possesses the best contralto voice in France, sang an air by Nicolini. This she did in the finished scientific style which she has learned from her well-known master Crescentini. Mme Dubignon's triumph and the triumph of the concert were complete. All the wits of the Faubourg St Germain were on the alert to catch a false note or anything else that would provide them with a pretext for mockery. But this was one gratification which they were unable to enjoy. Everything was arranged in the most perfect taste by the Baron de Staël and twelve members of the committee. The proprietor refused to accept any remuneration for the use of the hall, which was illuminated for nothing by the *lampiste* of the establishment. Finally, the venerable General Lafayette, who had scarcely recovered from a severe attack of gout, made his appearance and was greeted like a father by his children. Among the multitude of lovely women who were assembled for the occasion, English beauty had a worthy representative in Miss Fox, a name which is held dear in Paris.

The last Jubilee procession, held on May 3rd, offered a complete contrast to the concert in aid of the Greeks. The Jesuits were piqued at the manner in which they had been treated by the Royal Court and the Chamber of Peers, both of which had ridiculed the invitation to take part in the first Jubilee procession, a procession which had been honoured, however, by the presence of Charles X. They therefore contrived the following stratagem. They announced an expiatory ceremony and the laying of the foundation-stone of the monument to be erected on the spot where Louis XVI was guillotined. Nothing, however, could have been less wise. Every day diminishes some of the sympathy that we feel for this king, of whom M. de Talleyrand has observed that he evinced the courage of a woman in child-birth.

M. de Villèle, our Prime Minister, did not approve of the procession; but Cardinal de Latil, the King's confessor, who will sooner or later take his place, obtained his Majesty's full permission. There is no way in which a sovereign can be brought more closely in contact with his subjects than by joining a procession. Charles X, with his head uncovered, made his way slowly on foot through the most thickly populated streets of the capital, that is, from Notre Dame to the Champs Elysées. The Parisians are fond of gay uniforms and dislike the priests because they have a dirty appearance. The procession was led by a thousand seminarists walking two by two. These future priests are young peasants of about eighteen or twenty years of age who would rather kneel in a church than till the soil. They were instructed to walk with their eyes fixed devoutly to the ground; but found it impossible not to glance from time to time at the ladies stationed at the windows. The ladies pronounced them to be all fearfully ugly. It is said that each of these young priests costs the nation a thousand francs and that the money would be better spent on providing a thousand more officers for the army. Whatever may be the opinion of the upper classes, who execrate Napoleon and admire mystical philosophy, the general opinion, as it was expressed on the day of the procession, was favourable to the regimental and hostile to the canonical.

In France nothing is so rare as religious faith. Evey one is afraid of being taken for a dupe, a word which explains everything to anyone who knows the French character. To crown the mortification of those whose interests might have been promoted by the procession, the old courtiers who preceded Charles X were declared to be very unprepossessing. The three Cardinals, MM. de Croy, de Latil and de la Fare, were readily distinguished by their red robes, but presented on the whole an extremely mean appearance. On the other hand, M. de Quelen, Archbishop of Paris and a former officer under Napoleon, won the admiration of the entire female portion of his flock—many of whom did not know who he was—by his handsome appearance and dignified deportment. The ceremony was a splendid one, and highly entertaining. Two hundred thousand of the wealthiest citizens in Paris were stationed at their windows to enjoy the spectacle. The day was extremely warm and the procession moved very slowly. The pavilion erected in the centre of the Place Louis XV was in good taste and decorated with violet-coloured flags, violet being the colour of royal mourning in France. Everything conspired to reveal the true opinions of five hundred thousand

Frenchmen, and these struck me as unanimous. During the two hours which it took to reach the Place Louis XV, not a single *Vive le Roi!* was heard. The courtiers were extremely mortified at this. Some of them were pleased and some of them shocked at the absence of the Duke of Orleans, whom the King refused to invite because his father had voted for the death of Louis XVI. Charles has given instructions that the Place Louis XV shall henceforth be known as the Place Louis XVI, the slight to the former being perhaps a punishment for his having signed the order banishing the Jesuits. If I had not already said enough about the procession, I would tell you in addition how M. Bellart, who rendered himself so notorious at the trial of Marshal Ney, threw himself at the King's feet[1] and entreated him not to irritate any further a nation which does not love the Bourbons. Charles X merely replied, 'I am sixty-nine, and would fain not be damned'.

New Monthly Magazine, June 1826

THE WOMEN OF ITALY

Though the political degradation of Italy may be traced to a variety of causes, the deepest and most poisonous has never been sufficiently insisted upon. It is to be found in the toleration, or, to speak more correctly, in the privileges granted to those who infringe the sanctity of marriage and who belong to the more aristocratic or wealthy classes of society. This has long been the case and has frequently been commented on, sometimes with more severity by Italian writers than by foreigners. Foreigners, if they are less severe, fall, nevertheless, into the general error

[1] This is a phrase of the French court newsmen, and must not, like our kissing of hands, be literally understood. It merely signifies speaking to the King. (Note in the *New Monthly Magazine*.)

of subjecting all the women of Italy to one undiscriminating censure; they cannot distinguish between the classes to which corruption is confined and those in which circumstances combine to preserve the virtue of wives and mothers. We have still not found any writer, whether native or foreign, who has traced the causes of the present customs in the history of the country, or who has pointed out how greatly it has contributed in the past, still contributes and will continue to contribute to its subjection. Viewed in any other perspective and treated with any other intention, the subject would scarcely be worthy of our attention. After seeing the way in which it has been treated by other writers, we hope to turn it into something both new and useful, free from the gossip, licentiousness or cant with which it has been tainted—this, according to the author's opinions or disposition, in every classical or unclassical 'Tour of Italy' which has so far appeared.

The system of *cavalieri serventi*, though it may, at first sight, seem worthy of nothing but ridicule and contempt, has always been like one of the negative powers of mathematicians, condemning the more active powers to inertia. The system was brought about by religious circumstances, though the reasons for its continuation were political. The anomalous figure of the *cavaliere* disappeared almost at once throughout the north of the peninsula on the arrival of the lovely daughter of the King of Bavaria, who reigned as the wife of Eugène Beauharnais and the model of every domestic virtue. The influence of her own example, however, would probably have been less pronounced and taken longer to make itself felt, if she had not refused outright to receive any lady at court unaccompanied by her husband. Where will you find any woman who would not prefer to give up her *cavaliere servente* rather than her place in the royal court? The results of this attempt to employ vanity as a corrective to domestic vices could only, nevertheless, be superficially apparent. Its effects, as a result, were altogether transient, while, in the southern states, established customs underwent no change whatever. This was particularly the case in Rome, where the celibacy of the priests, who are at the same time sovereign princes, causes adultery to be considered as an incorrigible and necessary evil. This is the part of Italy from which almost every account which is given of national customs—whether real or imagined—is taken, and in which most of the exaggeration and declamation of those who write about Italy are inspired. It is to Rome that women flock from every country in Europe, when they have been too much or too little favoured by fortune in their ties of love or marriage. They fly southward, as if to a peaceful sanctuary; and, when their days of gallantry are over, beguile their old age, either by talking unrestrainedly of the pleasures of their youth, or by displaying their virtuous zeal in vehement indignation at their successors in a similar career. These ladies, whose nature is embittered by exile, domestic loneliness, mutual jealousy and, above all, old age, regularly meet in little *coteries* and *conversazioni*, into which each of them will introduce any traveller or fellow-countryman whom she may happen to encounter. It frequently happens that the traveller is wandering over the face of the earth with little other purpose than that of writing a book. And so it happens that, by giving an attentive and credulous ear to all the gossip going on around him, he achieves two separate ends: he pays for the favour of an introduction, and, at the same time, he collects profitable material with which to fill several volumes. These volumes will invite his fellow-countrymen to compare their own virtues with the vices of another nation; they can thus be relied upon to flatter national vanity. Lord Byron, who was the most accurate and impartial observer of the English and Italians, from this point of view, has traced, with the grace of a poet and the rigorous truth of a historian, the origin of the numerous stories which are now forgotten in Italy, but repeated continually to all Europe in the volumes written by travellers.

> The pleasant scandals which arise next day;
> The nine days wonders which are brought to light
> And why no husband sues for a divorce,
> Soon find their way to London press of course.

We quote from memory, and will therefore have to ask our readers to forgive us any unintentional misrepresentation of the famous poet. We trust as well that it will not be put down to any merely puerile admiration for his genius, for his acute perception of the truth and his manly courage in asserting it, if we subscribe to the sentiments he expressed, when writing to a reverend correspondent: 'That all our words, manners, religion, morals, our whole mind and existence in modern Europe, turn upon one single hinge, which the English in one expressive word call cant.'[1] It is certain that, if the demon of cant had been as omni-present among the ancients as it is among us, they would have raised altars and temples to it.

'Why an Italian husband does not sue for a divorce' is a question which, one would imagine, had been finally settled by the gypsies in their tents in a way which is equally valid for any other savage race. The Italians, however, are a civilised people, and, among civilised peoples, their customs form a distinct peculiarity. To understand them perhaps we should first consider what it is that makes them different from women of other climates. Eustace's remark[2] that 'in Italy the beauty of the sex seemed more connected with sentiment than in our colder climates' strikes us as incontrovertible. The most moving spectacle which Nature can present to the heart or eye of man is a young mother with her first-born at her breast or a young

---

[1] Letter from Lord Byron to the Rev. C. Bowles on the poetry and character of Pope.
[2] Eustace: *Classical Tour*.

girl who has the frank and cordial smile of her age and at the same time the shy and thoughtful expression of deep sentiment. The former spectacle is rarely seen among the ladies of Italy; but in no other country does love so early influence and exalt the heart of a woman. Passion, as they know it, is never confused with romantic fancies or arithmetical calculation. Their love is love pure and unmingled; the only other feeling with which it is ever identified is that of religion. Their upbringing, so different from that of English girls, enhances the natural temper of their hearts. Society is closed to well-brought-up young women till after their marriage; the retirement in which they are accustomed to living concentrates all their thoughts and sentiments on this one passion. At first it merely takes the form of attachment to some single individual. Love springs up vague and undetermined in their ardent and simple hearts, and their affections meanwhile rapidly find an object to which to attach themselves. With true feminine instinct they almost invariably guess who it is that loves them most, and single this person out as the object of their preference. Even then, however, the intercourse of the heart is carried on only with the eyes, and the opportunities even for this are very infrequent. The exchange of letters is neither easy nor safe, surrounded as they are by mothers, aunts, grandmothers and governesses, who aggravate their passions by the excessive anxiety with which they watch over them. If by chance a girl should meet her love, or if he should call at her father's house, she is compelled by decorum to respect an unwritten law according to which young ladies must be seen but rarely heard. It is a law that she is all the more careful to respect for fear lest a chance word should excite suspicion and endanger her secret.

Mme de Staël's observation, that female beauty in England attracts attention at once, while, in Italy, with slower but more magical effect, it kindles passion, is perfectly true, and goes far to explain the pre-eminence of painting and sculpture in Italy.

In England, all the warmth of a woman's feelings is expressed without fear or restraint and is apparent in her every word and action; whereas, in Italy, it is always being suppressed and is always striving to break free, always glowing instantaneously from the face and eyes, before it is checked and restrained once more. England would often provide the artist with more beautiful and graceful models than Italy; but the serenity of an Englishwoman borders on imperturbable coldness. In Italy, nature and upbringing have combined to produce an expressiveness in the female face which gives the work of her painters and sculptors a captivation and soul that are elsewhere inimitable.

Nevertheless, the future virtue and happiness of an Italian girl (though let it be remembered that I am thinking all the time of the daughters of wealthy and eminent families) almost invariably depends on a husband who has been approved of, not only by her, but by her parents. It frequently happens that the husband is chosen and the marriage contract settled, before the girl knows anything of the matter at all. Refusal to sign is an act of disobedience which compromises her father's honour, and all that happens, if she insists on choosing her own husband, is that she is obliged to spend the rest of her life in a convent. Almost always, her consent is registered in the marriage contract with due form and ceremony and everything is carried out as in a business partnership, based on no other consideration apart from pecuniary interest and law. It is not difficult to imagine how such a union comes to be embittered by hostility, coldness and perpetual suspicion. And

> ... marriage is a matter of more worth
> Than to be dealt with in attorneyship.

At the time of the *Spectator*, writers on domestic morals were obliged to avoid any reference to the opinions expressed by Shakespeare on marriages at which the only presiding deities were arithmetic and law. Some traces of poetic sentimentality still survived, and these might have led to an abuse of the great poet's text and the disregard of every dictate of sober reason. Today, however, that danger no longer exists, least of all among the daughters of wealthy families. The genius of our age, which is completely mercantile, leads them to consider marriage as a means of acquiring capital to protect them against the assaults of fortune or the contempt or indifference of the world. The ancient allegorical conception of love would today seem ludicrous, if even the greatest of modern poets were to attempt to revive it. It is barely tolerated in the masterpieces of painting or sculpture. The most girlish fancy no longer thinks of love as a wicked urchin laughing secretly to himself while he feigns to weep; he is not even

> A little, curly-headed good-for-nothing,
> And mischief-making monkey from his birth . . .

Whatever the reader may think of this excursion into metaphysics, he will at least agree that Cupid, even in his modern guise, still retains many of his former habits and plays many of his former tricks. These are none the less mischievous for being less gay than they used to be. His laughter is no longer joyful but malicious. His impudence is veiled beneath hypocrisy, and his prattling lies turned into set speeches of systematic imposture. The result is that sometimes he might be taken for a Jew, sometimes for a Jesuit, and sometimes for a diplomat.

Love, as we know it today, has the grave physiognomy and deportment of a wise man. He no longer runs about naked as he used to, but is clad from head to foot in the clothes of a lawyer. His quiver has become a blue bag, and his arrows deeds and settlements, these being by far the most powerful weapons with which to strike down men and women. This idea was already implicit in the personification of Cupid conceived by the Greeks. When the god wished to inspire an unsuccessful passion, he tipped his arrows with lead; but to kindle a triumphant flame, he made use of gold.

As philosophers and prudent men, however, we are obliged to confess that love is an inconstant and capricious passion which vanishes with youth. The calculation which romantic heads have misnamed avarice thrives with the years and is at its most vigorous in old age. These two passions, when they neutralise one another, produce a third, which is very useful to the state of matrimony.

Another still more striking change which has come over love, and thus over marriage, is the need now felt by all rich and fashionable couples for the amusements and pleasures of society.

There used to be a proverb which had been handed down from generation to generation all over the world and according to which 'two lovers are sufficient to themselves'. They admire nobody else, speak to nobody else and care for nobody else. Nowadays things are arranged differently and the tender bonds of marriage are strengthened by a mutual desire to escape from the retirement of domestic life and make one's way step by step into the higher circles of society. As there are a good many steps to climb, each of them more difficult and important than the last, the joint undertaking requires a considerable amount of money, great perseverance, and a faithful offensive and defensive alliance between husband and wife. It necessarily follows that a matrimonial union calculated to introduce and establish a couple in the best society, helps to preserve a harmony and understanding which would be impossible if it were to depend solely on conjugal affection in the seclusion of domestic life.

Now among all these considerations prompted by experience

in countries like our own, there is not one which ever occurs to the mind of a girl in Italy. A young lady in Italy knows very well that the man she loves can never be hers, unless by some extraordinary accident which she desires, but for which she never dares to hope. She persists in loving, however, and the more noble her nature, the more ardently does she persist in her attachment. Every passion, nevertheless, which is starved of all hope will either lead to madness or the grave, unless it yields beforehand to time and reason. She accepts, at length, marriage with a man whom her tyrants have chosen for her, and her revenge is to refuse him any place in her heart. Marriage in Italy does not subject the young wife, as it does in England, to closer supervision and a more conventional restraint and decorum; it invests her, on the contrary, with complete liberty, so that now, with greater facility and far less innocence, she can converse with her first love and see him where and whenever she pleases. Some few, out of a feeling of self-respect or piety, rather than go to the altar with perjury on their lips, prefer the melancholy fate of dying alone.

A young Englishwoman of good family who fails to find a husband is always free to move wherever she chooses in society, and enjoys the privilege of being accompanied by a chaperon. This sort of protection, though not very pleasant to young ladies who have only just 'come out', is enjoyed by those whose first youth is over; it is a sign that they are still liable to be seduced or abducted, particularly if they are heiresses to a large fortune. Even if they remain spinster ladies all their lives, there is nothing to prevent their opening their homes to *conversazioni*, or to giving parties, balls and dinners. It rarely happens that anyone openly exhibits the contempt which is commonly felt for a woman who goes through life unmarried and childless. In Italy, on the other hand, a woman is scarcely twenty-five years old before she begins to see the utmost disdain in every face and before the conversation she overhears and the advice of her friends tell her that it is time she left the world. Nor can she hope to enliven her seclusion with those occupations which deaden or distract the passions, overcome the sense of isolation and nourish one's self-esteem— we refer of course to literature and science. A learned woman in Italy is the chosen victim for the jibes of the vulgar, or more particularly of those who, in every other country, are tireless in their endeavours to render women ridiculous. A single lady cannot, as in England, take shelter either in her own literary reputation or in that of the learned and distinguished men who frequent her house.

Whether female education, carried as far as it has been in England, is likely to contribute to the virtue and peace of society, is a question which has often been discussed, but rarely settled:

'Tis pity learned virgins ever wed
With persons of no sort of education,
Or gentlemen, who, though well born and bred,
Grow tired of scientific conversation.
I do not choose to say much on this head;
I'm a plain man and in a single station.

Another great poet, who could not boast of being single, taught his wife that Eve's desire to steal the fruit of the tree of knowledge condemned posterity to toil through one hell in order merely to die and go to a worse. Another, having been persuaded by his wife to teach her Greek, began by explaining the word Δαίμων, daemon, and told her that, in the masculine gender, it means *genius*, and in the feminine, *a devil*.

True or false, just or unjust though these stories may be, it is certainly true that English and Italian customs and prejudices, as far as the education of women is concerned, stand at opposite extremes. The Italians do not exactly debar women from literary and scientific acquirements; it would be more accurate to say that they treat them as the Spartans treated their children and compel them to satisfy their appetite by stealth and theft. Italy, nevertheless, has had a number of female professors. Not long ago, Signora Tambroni occupied the chair of Greek in the University of Bologna; while the talent for improvisation, which is peculiarly Italian, has brought fame to two or three eminent female bards. As far as the latter gift is concerned, it might have been generally agreed that the sweetness of the woman's voice, the mobility of her imagination and the volubility of her tongue would give her a peculiar advantage over a poet of the other sex. Such women are looked upon, however, with less respect than wonder. They are thought of as monsters of talent and enjoy no protection against the inexorable persecution of ridicule. If a woman decides to engage in literary pursuits, she is forced to decide whether to conceal her acquirements at the outset or expose herself to the lash of epigrams. Either course presupposes a complete sacrifice of her vanity. In England, an occasional blow to her pride is more tolerable to an authoress than the insignificance and obscurity of single life. But in Italy, satires fall on learned women like hailstones; even the humblest citizens, who are remarkably observant, attack them pitilessly in every conceivable way. [They are treated as pedants in a country in which pedantry is considered, not only as an intellectual, but a social offence.][1] In any city throughout the peninsula, a writer who has pretensions to using the national tongue, in preference to the local dialect, will find himself in the same predicament as the poet who recently attempted to write in Greek hexameters. As for the alternative to social persecution, however, that of amassing a fund of literature and science, unknown to any other human being, and with no

[1] My own insertion. (*Editor.*)

other object than secret satisfaction, this demands a resolution and a vigorous high-mindedness which human nature has never yet exhibited, even among the greatest philosophers. We will scarcely be accused of excessive severity towards the other sex, moreover, if we say that, however great a woman's intellectual powers may be, the value they hold for her in her own eyes will be all the less if they do not excite the applause of admirers and the envy of rivals.

In any other country, even without ambition or the consolations and charms of literature, an unmarried woman of thirty who is not excessively bad-tempered or embittered, and who possesses a few novels, a pianoforte, a harp, a portfolio of drawings, a garden, a horse or two and a pet lap-dog, can live long and die in solitary happiness, like the fairy creature of Spenser:

> Making sweet solace to herself alone;
> Sometimes she sang as loud as larke in ayre,
> Sometimes she laught as merry as Pope Jone;
> Yet was there not with her else any one
> That to her might move cause of merriment:
> Matter of merth enough, though there were none
> She would devise, and thousand waies invent
> To feede her foolish humour and vaine joliment.

Among her other privileges, we ought not to forget that of being the owner of a mansion, a country house or a cottage residence like those to which so many independent spinsters return after the gay season has ended in London and in which they can reign over their parishes like little queens. Even if they have no house of their own, the hospitality of their fellow-countrymen is extended more graciously to them than to any other class of person. They may travel, if they wish, from house to house and rusticate among their various relatives and friends, in the perpetual enjoyment of society and with almost no sense of their isolated condition.

An Italian lady, in the same situation, however rich her family and however numerous her connections, cannot even imagine having a house of her own, as long as she remains unmarried. Nor can she avail herself of the hospitality of others. The life led by Italians, furthermore, is not a rustic life—they live almost constantly in the great cities. They pay considerable attention to the architecture and embellishments of their country seats, but their visiting them is a mere matter of state and ceremony, and is only for a few weeks in the year. They take no delight in excursions, whether long or short, so that a journey to the neighbouring province is considered as a more serious undertaking than a tour through France and Switzerland would be to an Englishman. Finally, the same reasons of propriety which impede an unmarried woman's free introduction into society, forbid her even more strongly to spend as much as three days under any roof other than the parental one. These domestic regulations go with popular prejudices and time-hallowed customs. No young unmarried woman would dare to violate them, even if every circumstance were combined to ensure her complete independence.

Until she finds a husband, therefore, she must live like a burdensome ward in the house of her father, elder brother, or whoever happens at the time to be the head of the family. She must always live, act and speak under the supervision of the mistress of the family and the servants. Meanwhile, the prospect of her becoming herself the mistress of a family grows more remote with every year and her relations' doors are opened to her with increasing reluctance. There are very few who are able to endure for long this most exquisite form of torture, which is like a state of solitary confinement in the midst of society and in the company of brothers and friends. They almost always return to a convent.

We use the word *return*; for they receive their first education within its walls. They enter the convent almost in their infancy and it is there often that they learn all that they are ever to know of the world—that is, its name. After the French Revolution, and more particularly during the reign of Napoleon, this practice fell, in great measure, into disuse. The number of religious schools, which till then had been thickly scattered throughout the peninsula, was considerably diminished, while, at the time of the expedition to Russia, every establishment and congregation of monks and friars was abolished. Without them, if the act had been properly carried out, the religious houses for women would have exercised a more useful, or to speak more accurately, a less pernicious influence. Finally, the *Code Napoléon* decreed that the property of the father should be divided into equal portions at his death, among all his children, whether male or female. It is not difficult to see that, if these measures had been rigorously enforced, they would, in the course of one generation, have totally changed the system of upbringing and marriage among the noble and wealthy families of Italy. They would have improved morals in general; for, as we shall presently have occasion to remark, the principal effect of the system was to demoralise, necessarily and completely, the grown-up sons, all of whom, with the exception of the eldest, were predestined to a life of celibacy. However, the governments which succeeded Napoleon's dictatorship did not find it in their interests to retain any of his laws, apart from those concerning finance. His civil and criminal codes were therefore summarily abolished or else, in certain provinces, partially retained. They were retained with so many important modifications, however, that they became virtually inapplicable.

The number of convents for women is now growing to be as great as ever, while there are more monasteries than before. Many of the congregations which have been revived had been abolished, even before the Revolution, by either the Emperor or the Pope. The result is today that the number of youthful victims of hypocrisy, fanaticism and avarice; the number of adulteries excused by necessity and sanctioned by custom; and the number of priests, friars and laymen condemned to celibacy and all equally dissolute, have increased in the same ratio. What sense of domestic virtue, what energy can be expected from a nation in which the influence of religion and of every wealthy family combine to produce such base profligacy of mind and morals? The consequences which we have deduced will strike any man who has known the inner life of a patrician household in Italy as true and inevitable. Not one word on this topic is to be found in the accounts of Italy written by tourists. It is probably a subject of investigation in which the tourist's innate curiosity has always till now been baffled. We could, perhaps, at the risk of making a number of unfounded assumptions, assert positively how matters stand in this respect at the present moment; but, if we describe these customs accurately, as they existed before the changes introduced by Napoleon, we shall not be far from the truth. It is perfectly safe to conclude that the restoration of old laws and governments will have given rise to the same customs as existed thirty years ago. We shall therefore attempt to describe them with as much brevity as is compatible with accuracy.

For many centuries, children have been considered as a means of financial speculation by their wealthy parents. A reasonable ancestral pride has always induced them to grant to every daughter a marriage portion which is suited to her rank, and of course very burdensome to their own estate. As this could not be bequeathed in real property, which was all entailed on the eldest son, the daughter's inheritance had to be paid in money. The daughter, however, could claim no right to the smallest fraction of this sum until after her marriage. Refusal, therefore, to accept the husband proposed to her, left her necessarily at the mercy of her family and completely dependent on their charity.

A young woman, in order to have any right at all to dispose of her own portion, or to choose a husband for herself, must be sole heiress, that is to say, must find herself in circumstances which are extremely rare in a country in which estates are entailed exclusively in the male line of descent. Normally she receives only a nominal bequest, which is administered by trustees who are under no obligation to render an account, and who generally dispose of it for the furtherance of their own interests. The head of the family will always leave the bulk of his property to the elder son, thus hoping to transmit it with increasing value from one generation to another, to the aggrandisement of his name. From time immemorial, therefore, to avoid the granting of numerous dowries, an infallible expedient had been employed for preventing the marriage of all but one of the daughters, this one invariably the youngest. The elder sisters, educated from their earliest years in the cloister and directed in everything by their reverend governesses and holy father confessors, grew up having been schooled to abjure nature. At the same time, their young girls' proneness to fall in love was alternately soothed and excited by the most alluring representations of the fairest of spouses, the name given to the Redeemer himself. They were exhorted to promise him their fidelity until the time should come for them to join him as brides in Paradise. In plain language, they were persuaded, from the earliest age, to take the veil, only to repent when every word or sigh of repentance would be taken by their tyrants as an act of sacrilege or apostasy. It was from this combination of religion and sensuality that arose that immense dissoluteness of the imagination which is so repulsively evident in old legends and the descriptions of beatific visions. Many of them were current during the lifetime of the illustrious Fénelon, and he himself, though a man of a purity of heart and a good faith far removed from any of the knavish hypocrisy of friars, often fell into this strange form of mysticism.

To avoid going into the details of this cult, and, at the same time, to prove our own good faith and lack of exaggeration, we refer our readers to the *Life of Scipion Ricci* and the documents which have recently been published in the same edition in Belgium, thus outraging the Jesuits in every country, above all in France.

The prelate whose life is described in this volume devoted his life, within living memory, to correcting the abominations committed in the monasteries of his own diocese in Tuscany. In this he received the powerful protection and co-operation of the Emperor Leopold II, despite which, his reforms proceeded with the utmost slowness and were afterwards abruptly repealed. This was so that the various congregations of monks and friars might return to indulge, under the cloak of religion, their four dearest passions, namely, sensuality, proselytism, dominion and avarice. Today once more, mother superiors, who have learned by experience to make the best of a bad situation, together with their directors of conscience, aid the heads of rich families to impose religious vows on their daughters. In so doing, they acquire new minions for themselves, secure the protection of men of power and influence and increase the number of religious communities. Every nun who makes her final vows pays into the treasury of the convent either a lump sum or an annuity for life. In either case, this dowry, so to speak, is about ten times less than their full inheritance or the income they would have derived from it if it had been banked or invested.

It sometimes happens that one of these girls, doomed to celibacy from the cradle, finds a lover who is willing to marry her either without any dowry at all, or else with a very small one. But generally this is only a widower or aged bachelor, full of years and money, who buys a young girl under the pretext of marriage. He enjoys the illusion of being about to spend many years of happiness with her, while she, naturally enough, longs for the day when she may bless his memory for having placed his whole fortune at her disposal. If she revolts from the idea of bargaining herself in this way, her refusal to accept the offered marriage will be considered as an act of open rebellion and a disregard for the sacredness of her father's promise. The punishment she may expect is to be sent back to the convent, with no hope of ever leaving it.

Many novels and sentimental dramas have treated this subject with great power, especially in France and Germany. Even without the aid of the imagination, however, the forcible sacrifice of a young, beautiful and warmly affectionate girl, under the pretext of religion, offers a situation in which nature herself speaks with all the necessary eloquence. Many of the events reported factually in Italian chronicles are capable of producing the strongest emotions, even though they are written in the rugged style and with the dry simplicity of two centuries ago. From that day to this, Italian writers of the greatest genius have used every means, including ridicule, to shame their fellow-countrymen out of the practice of trading in their own children. One example we quote is an extract from a famous poem of the age of Leo X, the intermediate period between our own and that in which we find the first records of the system in Italy:

Duro, per certo, e da non sopportare
Che fra gl'altri animai della natura,
La donna sola s'abbia a maritare
A modo d'altri, e non alla ventura,
O per dir meglio, a propria elezione,
Come le fiere fan, che han più ragione.
Han più ragione, ond'hanno anche più pace.

. . . . . .

Ditemi, padri, che avete figliuole
E v'ha Dio d'allogarle il moto dato
Onestamente, qual ragione poi vuole
Che le date ad un vecchio, onde al peccato
La tarda penitenza poi le mena?

. . . . . .

Un altro, sotto specie di severo,
Ma con effetto d'avaro e furfante,
Metteranno una frotta in Monastero,
E vorrà, che per forza elle sien sante.
Ell'aran, fate conto, altro pensiero,
(Come han le donne quasi tutte quante)
E si provederan di preti, e frati,
Ed ecco in susta i Vescovi, e gli abbati.[1]

(*Orlando innamorato*, book II, canto 26 and 27.)

The last line, however sentimental it may sound, is in no way an exaggeration of the truth. It suggests the root of the whole execrable system, with all its poisonous ramifications, the

---

[1] It is certainly hard and not to be endured that, out of all Nature's creatures, the woman alone should have to marry as others wish and not as destiny, or rather she herself, decides. Why can she not marry as wild animals do? They are wiser and more reasonable than human beings and therefore more content....

Tell me you fathers who have young daughters and to whom God has given the natural desire to see them decently married, what sort of reason is it that makes you give them up to an old man, and thus to the sin into which they are led by remorse, which comes to them too late?

... Another, under the appearance of a just severity, but in fact out of rascally avarice, will send a whole band of his daughters into a convent and hope that force and oppression will turn them into saints. Make no mistake, they will have other ideas (like most women). They will provide themselves with priests and monks and, lo, once they have got the bit between their teeth, they will have abbots and bishops. (See Appendix I.)

root of which is to be found in the celibacy of the clergy. The evil today admits neither of remedy nor palliatives. The system is one in which Rome reigns triumphant in every part of Europe which is subject to its ecclesiastical discipline, for the discipline is in the hands of a hierarchy which is itself condemned to celibacy and which has legions of monks and friars in its train. It is in no way surprising that the governments of Italy co-operate with the Church more willingly than do those of other nations. These governments consist either of powerful foreign princes or petty Italian ones compelled by treaties and armies to govern their subjects at the good pleasure of a foreign power. It is in their own interest consequently to ensure the demoralisation of any powerful family, and, in so doing, to produce that state of enervation which destroys every spring of public virtue and paralyses every effort that might be made to restore the national independence.

Let us now consider the condition of a noble Italian girl, married according to the usages of the country. In the first place, the two heads of each contracting family arrange the marriage, often through the intermediary of old ladies, without giving the slightest hint of their intentions to either the bride or bridegroom-to-be. We have already mentioned the fact that the couple, with few exceptions, consists of the eldest son and the youngest daughter of two rich houses. Equality of age, rank, education and fortune may seem to promise a happy union; but the young couple are impeded in any attempt they may make to contribute towards their own mutual happiness. They may have had the good fortune to escape the dangers which usually accompany an engagement for life undertaken by two people who have no previous knowledge of one another's character. Even then, however, there is the insurmountable difficulty arising from the fact that, for years after their marriage, they have no house of their own. The bridegroom is obliged to take his bride to his father's home; and it sometimes happens that, while he is keeping an establishment for his mistress, he takes a young girl from a convent, swears fidelity to her at the altar, and then, at the accustomed hour, returns to his mistress leaving his wife under the guardianship of her new father and mother-in-law. Other husbands, who would prefer to behave with more honour, or at least with more decency, are unable to. Every son in Italy is a minor, as long as his father lives, and cannot emancipate himself without risking the loss of much of his inheritance.

Hence it follows that the greater the affluence a noble bride finds in the house in which she is established, the less right she has to call any part of it her own, or dispose of it as she pleases. She can never employ herself in household economy or provide for the domestic comfort of her husband. She is not mistress of her servants, and she sits at table as an invited guest. All the children of her father-in-law, whether male or female, all the unmarried uncles and aunts and every other member of the family generally inhabit the same mansion and eat at the same table. The community is a tiny state over which the mother and father reign like absolute monarchs, while the administration is carried out by confidential servants, who are the ministers, privy councillors and secret inspectors of police. The jealousy of power which, in old men, increases with the years, and the repugnance inspired in every young woman conscious of the dignity of her position by the subjection to which she is reduced, embitter the relations and the conversation between every member of the household. This is evident from the very outset, so that the bride has scarcely entered the house before she feels the necessity of seeking consolation out of doors.

The young husband has neither the power nor the experience to adjust these domestic differences; he grows weary of them, becomes as disgusted as his wife, and finds no other way of avoiding them than in dissipation and vice. The political situation of his country, rendered desperate by the inaptitude of the aristocracy for public affairs, condemns him to a life of complete indolence and insignificance. Hence the bad habits, the follies and incurable moral diseases of which he becomes the victim and which, in their turn, affect his youthful, almost childish wife. When the intellectual and moral pleasures cease to hold any attraction, the human mind necessarily abandons itself to the dreams and excitements of vanity, and to every species of sensuality. It is then that every artful coquette, every courtesan and every opera dancer begins to hold more attractions for a man than a modest innocent girl. As he has assumed the role of husband merely in order to obey his parents and promote the interests of his family, he considers that, in indulging his inclinations, he is exercising a natural right. He soon becomes a libertine by profession, without principles or heart. Who then can blame his wife if, sooner or later, she begins to imitate him? Where is the country in which the women would sacrifice every feeling and passion of their nature for the sake of a husband who does everything in his power to show his disregard for their mutual obligations?

Public opinion is the most powerful instrument in any country for influencing the actions of the great; law is almost inoperative as a remedy against their vices; while religion, which ought to correct them, is turned into a means of corruption. The evidence of servants would bear little weight in a court of law in Italy; against master or mistress it would rarely be admitted. Yet, without such testimony, the wife's adultery could scarcely ever be proved, and, even if it were, the husband would never be able to receive satisfaction in the form of money. In England, proceedings of this kind are instituted with the sole intention of obtaining divorce, whereas, in Italy, even if the proceedings were successful, they would cause the plaintiff to incur an intolerable expense. Marriage being a sacrament, its annulment depends exclusively on the oracles of the pontifical court of Rome, and these can only be consulted with the aid of exorbitant gifts. Remission of sins, on the other hand, can be obtained with the utmost ease from any priest or friar. Husband and wife, therefore, confess their infidelities, not to each other, but to their father confessor. The latter, every year, half-year or quarter, weighs their accounts in the balance of the recording angel, equalises them by means of holy absolution, and enables both parties to draw on their respective consciences at three, six or twelve months date. However dissipated the life of a Catholic woman may seem, and however much she may laugh at the censure of the world, her thoughts and feelings are like mercury in a thermometer, rising and falling according to every impression they receive from her confessor. The latter need only adhere to one simple principle, that being to keep her passions in a perpetual state of oscillation, to inspire her at one moment with the terrors of hell and, at the next, lull her with the hope of forgiveness and salvation. In this way, he can obtain sure control over her mind, a control all the greater since he is the guardian of her closest secrets, and, as far as she herself is concerned, the infallible dispenser of the mercies of God. The daily application of this principle soon teaches spiritual directors how to apply it according to the character, circumstances and inclinations of each individual; also to employ it in the precise degree to which it is required. It was for this purpose that the graduated scale of the casuistical Jesuits was so ingeniously contrived. It set out by being extremely indulgent towards the dreams of Platonic love in order to nourish them and, in the course of time, turn them into a form of positive sensuality. However, the theological distinction best calculated, both to bring about adultery in the first place and then gloss it over, is to be found in the two words, *sin* and *scandal*. With the aid of the scriptures and the canonical texts, a confessor is able to prove that sin is harmful only to the individual, while scandal involves the whole of society. He can thus render sin inevitable and habitual by presenting it to the penitent as the lesser of two evils. In so doing, he acts as a mediator between husband and wife, until the day comes when the latter agree to dissemble each other's offences and to live in peace. This is so that their mutual infidelities may remain private, and in order not to awaken the malignancy of the public or encourage it to follow their own unfortunate example.

While a young wife is being goaded and disciplined to be unfaithful, she is surrounded by admirers more numerous and attractive than the suitors of Penelope. As it is the eldest son alone who ever marries in a noble family, all his brothers are provided for by means of the slenderest of allowances, together with the undisputed right to live under the same roof as the father and elder brother and to enjoy all the comforts and luxuries of the establishment. This is a privilege which they forfeit for ever by marrying. Superficially the life led by this race of bachelors has a great deal in common with that of the fellows of rich colleges in English universities. Their position renders both the Italian bachelor and the English *fellow* egotistical, cantankerous and epicurean while, at the same time, restless and indolent, subject to all the caprices of the passions and possessed of few means of satisfying them. As far as gallantry is concerned, however, the fellow of a college would have to hide his head; he is a mere bashful boy. His Italian counterpart does not have to pretend even to lead a life of erudition. He rarely has any hope of advancement; and, even if he has, the example offered by the handsome Braschi (Pius VI) or the gay and gallant Cardinal della Genga (Leo XII) go to prove that a youth spent in the indulgence of tender passions is in itself no obstacle to the winning of a mitre, a red hat or the triple crown. These, however, are the exception rather than the rule. A better and more practical reason for the licentiousness of the Italian bachelor is to be found in the absence of that formidable ally of reason and virtue, the English institution of damages.

As for the Church, in spite of its numerous and opulent hierarchy, it is hardly able to employ one out of every hundred of these unfortunate young men. Those who do enter the ecclesiastical profession, however, flock to Rome, usually from every corner of the peninsula and, once established, without taking holy orders, adopt a clerical silk gown, obtained by family prestige or interest, and assume the titles of prelates or *monsignori*. A few of these, by dint of talent, study, but, above all, intrigue, obtain lucrative employments and the highest dignities of Church and State. Sometimes they win the highest dignity of all, that which gives its possessor the power to dictate infallible oracles from the chair of St Peter and to cast anathema on the kings of the earth. It was in Rome that the spectacle of Italian ladies surrounded by men such as this prompted Eustace's forceful and eloquent description—'Beauty in the sex is blended in Italy with intelligence, with benignity, animation of feature, dignity of gesture, a language all music, quickness of remark, a fine tinge of religion—every female attraction is theirs, except perhaps the best. But alas! can modesty be expected in a state where celibacy sits enthroned and fills every post of authority and instruction? Must not the interest, the animal wants of the governors, discourage fidelity in the sex? Must not a government of bachelors of necessity form a nation of libertines?'

If Caesar could justify himself by saying that he would never have violated his oath except for the sake of acquiring the supreme power, the same excuse can scarcely be denied to the ladies of modern Rome. Though ostensibly administered by dignified priests, many government departments are, in fact, entirely in the hands of their mistresses. Furthermore, in a country in which men, once they marry, must abandon every hope of rising by their own merits, the favours procured for them by the merits of their wives are necessarily accepted with less repugnance than elsewhere. This is true, however, only of the states ruled over by His Holiness. In the rest of the peninsula, women are never exposed to the temptations of ambition or avarice. Their lovers, who are legion, have nothing but the worthless privilege of being called noblemen, marchesini, contini or cavalieri. Their political influence is less than nothing. Their fortune consists principally in having the right to be perpetual guests beneath their father's roof. Their occupations, as far as the public interest is concerned, are completely negative. The army and navy, in the few states which are able to maintain them, are too small to employ so many young men. The law offers even fewer openings, both on account of its not being, as it is in England, a genteel profession, and because of the Italian mode of procedure which fails to stimulate either talent or ambition. Any kind of commerce would be considered as a contamination of the purity of their blood and an act which would arouse the souls of their ancestors and bring them cursing them from their tombs. They grow up, therefore, and spend their lives, unfit for any occupation other than that of visiting as many ladies as they can. Their custom is to visit them in their drawing-rooms, during the morning, and, in the evening, in their boxes at the opera. These same ladies are no sooner married than they endeavour to assemble a troop of admirers around them; and the drawing-room or box filled with assiduous visitors is an object of universal envy.

From the facts now stated, the reader will be able to infer that every lady of rank is doomed by the circumstances in which she finds herself placed to live a life of unending intrigue. This goes on until every principle of virtue which nature has implanted in her heart is worn away, until passion is an excitement necessary to her existence and a habit which only ends with her life. When she has reached a certain age, she begins to think seriously of providing herself with a lover known as a *cavaliere servente*. She generally chooses him from the numerous band of bachelors who are now grey-headed, but who, in days gone by, paid her their court. Her choice will probably fall, not to the most fortunate, but to the most persevering, the one who was the most willing to submit, without complaint, to the presence of some casual favourite. A true *cavaliere servente* is a constant guest at his mistress's house; he acts as her steward and superintends her household; he always stands behind her while she sits at the pianoforte, and punctually turns over the pages of her music; he sits by her and assists her in her embroidery or other work; he never goes out without her; or, if ever he does walk out alone, it is to exercise her lap-dog. Finally, as soon as the lady's eldest son marries and brings home his bride, the mother-in-law lends her her own *cavaliere servente*, who now accompanies her into society, initiates her in the ways of the world and reports officially on her conduct. It often turns out, however, that his attractive young pupil manages to convert her mother-in-law's informer into her own trusted secretary and the best and most useful friend of all the lovers who begin to flock around her.

It is in this way that, in a country in which nature has endowed her daughters more liberally perhaps than in any other with the qualities of heart and mind best calculated to make them the mothers of free citizens and the nurses of patriots, bad government and consequent bad usages have so corrupted them that the life of the home destroys every seed of virtue in the children. We hope that we are false prophets; but it strikes us as evident that, until such an abominable system of marriage is wholly extirpated, the aristocracy and the great landowners of the country will continue to be contemptible both to themselves and to others; they will remain inert and unfit to liberate their country; their lives will continue to be spent in intrigue, their minds stupefied by idleness and their souls corrupted by sensuality. Who can expect men who are indifferent to their own honour to undergo toil or danger for the honour of their country?

We cannot conclude without adding that, although the class we have been describing exerts a greater influence than any other on the political life of the country, our observations would be quite inappropriate if applied to society as a whole, and afford no criterion by which to judge the character of Italian women in general. Those to whom wealth provides both the stimulus to indulge ungoverned fancy and immunity from its consequences, and those, at the other extreme, who are driven into vice as a result of necessity, ought, when we talk of any country, to be considered as exceptions to the general rule. Virtue is always to be found in those classes of society in which mediocrity of fortune is accompanied by moderation, discipline and domestic decency. These classes, although widespread throughout Italy, are those which are the least exposed to the eyes of foreigners. Eustace, fearing lest the dissoluteness which is so apparent should be attributed to the Catholic religion, sees virtue in every Italian home. Another author complains that Mme de Staël in her *Corinna* has given a picture of Italian women which is not only exaggerated but false, and observes that 'Those who do not travel with pretensions to move in high life, could alone bear witness how strangely the fair sex in that part of the world has been calumniated. It would be absurd to deny that there were, or that there are at present many frail women in Italy; but the proportion is much smaller than the joint influence of climate, religion and government, might have warranted one to expect. The generality of females are perhaps more respectable than elsewhere. I pity those whom particular circumstances have led to think otherwise: and I am extremely glad to have opportunities of forming a more favourable, and, I am sure, a more equitable judgment'.[1] As this traveller was a Swiss and a Protestant, he may be regarded as a credible witness as to the general character of the women of Italy.

London Magazine, October 1826

THE FRENCHMAN'S KNOWLEDGE OF ENGLAND

As a general rule, very few Frenchmen ever travel to England. The difficulty of speaking your language in a way you find intelligible is a great obstacle to foreigners. But what deters Frenchmen above all is the fear of dying of boredom in the evenings, as a result of the great difference between the social manners of each country. In France, every man above the lower class is accustomed to spending his evenings in company which invariably includes women. This, perhaps, cannot be very easily done in England, for it is impossible to consider a rout as an agreeable party. A rout is the abuse of social intercourse and neither its equivalent nor its perfection.

[1] Galiffe's *Travels in Italy*, vol. ii, pp. 82-3.

In Paris a party is considered to have sufficient guests if there are five or six ladies and about a dozen gentlemen.

But whatever it may be which usually prevents Frenchmen from crossing the Channel, I have observed with pleasure that the curious spectacle presented by your elections has tempted many of my fellow-countrymen this summer to travel to England in preference to Switzerland. Before our Revolution the French knew nothing about your country. Your customs, which differ so essentially from our own, occasionally provided our men of wit with the material for a joke, but that was all. Even Voltaire, whenever he speaks at any length about England, is puerile and soon becomes absurd; as, for instance, when he accuses the English of horrible cruelty because of the execution of Admiral Byng.

Since 1814 we have had our elections, and we now choose, well or badly, the members of our own House of Commons. Seven or eight years went by before we properly learned to understand our own elections. We have no bribery, it is true, nor do we give huge dinners to the electors; but a great deal of roguery and deception is practised by the president whom the Government appoints for each electoral assembly.[1] Our Chamber of Deputies has yet to feel its own strength; it is of the same age, so to speak, as your own House of Commons under the reign of Queen Elizabeth. But our Chamber of Deputies is duly acquiring importance, and most of our young men of education are beginning to regard it as the instrument destined to bring about mighty changes in France. To obtain a reputation for talent in Parisian society, it will no longer be sufficient to have written some agreeable poetry, or a few articles for the Journals, as was the case before 1780. A man

---

[1] One of our French election tricks consists in counting the number of votes for any particular candidate, and taking away twenty votes, for example, from the opposition deputy, and giving them to the deputy on the ministerial side. (Note in the *New Monthly Magazine*.)

will now have to be a member of the Chamber of Deputies and deliver one or two tolerable speeches a year. None of the young men of fortune who reside in Paris have clearly discerned the turn of events which I have described; but they all feel it.

The younger portion of Parisian society (for I do not speak of people of fortune over fifty years old) is fully prepared to understand England. Between 1715 and 1815 the French made no progress towards understanding the institutions of the most singular, and at that time, the freest country in the world. The various travellers' accounts published about the year 1810 were no less frivolous than the works of the same kind which appeared during the reign of Louis XV. I remember very well that, about the year 1800, a man would have been looked upon as an original,[1] if he had ventured to make in company a simple reflection such as the following: 'Look at the British Isles on the map; they are so small as to be scarcely perceptible, and yet, because of the persevering industry of its inhabitants, they impart life and activity to the two extremities of the globe, and are equally feared in Copenhagen and before the walls of Seringapatam.'

For the last two or three years we have been beginning to understand England. This fact is evident from the success enjoyed by the letters on the English elections which have appeared in the *Globe*. *The Times*, which is regarded as the organ of public opinion in England, published a condensed version of these letters some time in early September and acknowledged the general correctness of the author's views and the accuracy of his descriptions. These little sketches have therefore been approved on both sides of the Channel, which is unusual for articles of this kind. They have been attributed

---

[1] This was considered an insulting term in the language formed for the French nation by the monarchies of Louis XIV and Louis XV. (Note in the *New Monthly*.)

to M. Duvergier, a young man of means, whose name is already well known in the literary world. In one respect they will mark an epoch; for henceforth, whenever English customs are spoken of in Paris, it will no longer be considered legitimate to confine oneself to a few more or less witty epigrams like those written by the travellers who endeavour to imitate Voltaire's *Lettres sur l'Angleterre*.[1] Do not imagine, however, that the letters attributed to M. Duvergier would induce us to admire everything English. You have a dangerous rival in America. In the course of a discussion on England, occasioned by the letters in the *Globe*, M. de Pradt, Archbishop of Malines, made the following remarks: 'With respect to liberty, we are like a savage who has walked all his life bare-legged. He finds it very comfortable to wear stockings and he introduces the custom into his own country; but would he be so absurd as to buy needles and teach his fellow-countrymen how to knit them, when he might purchase and import a stocking-machine which can make a hundred in the time that it takes to knit one by hand? We must not therefore imitate institutions which, some hundred years ago, procured a certain degree of liberty for England. We must borrow from the Americans the more simple and efficient methods by which they manufacture liberty on a large scale. We ought to approximate the French to the American elections, and take good care not to imitate the English ones.'

The Times and the *Morning Chronicle* are much more widely read in Paris this year than they were last. This tendency, which every sensible person will regard with satisfaction, would be diminished, however, if we were to find many observations printed in the English press as futile as those published by *The Times* recently on the profound excitement

---

[1] Beyle is obviously referring to Voltaire's *Lettres Philosophiques*. (Editor.)

caused in France by the Portuguese constitution. *The Times* wrote approximately as follows: 'Every Parisian newspaper is speaking of the Portuguese constitution with truly French exaggeration and passion. In England alone have the sensations aroused by this Revolution been those of reason.' *The Times* would be very embarrassed if its editor were obliged to answer the following question: Will Don Pedro's grant of a constitution hasten or retard the emancipation of the Irish Catholics, will it hasten or retard Parliamentary reform, and will it have any influence on the Corn Laws?

At present, matters as important to the French as the emancipation of the Irish Catholics or the disputes over the Corn Laws are to the English, will be accelerated or retarded by the granting of a constitution to the Portuguese. I have drawn attention to this erroneous interpretation of French affairs, because errors of this kind occur frequently in the most highly esteemed English publications. Not long ago, the *Edinburgh Review* affirmed, with the utmost gravity, that the celebrated poet Joseph Chénier (the imitator of Voltaire who most closely resembles his own model) was partly responsible for the death of his brother André. Such mis-statements appear all the more ridiculous when they are put forward in a tone of ill-humour and jealousy, a tone which does not become one great nation when speaking of another. England and France are the fountain-heads of the world's civilisation. If anything can throw doubt on the place held by Great Britain, it is the feeling of jealousy and envy which she cherishes towards France. Unfortunately, too, the French are very quick to feel the slightest effects of wounded vanity. You cannot imagine how much we have been entertained in Paris by an article in the *Quarterly Review* on Baron de Staël's *Lettres sur l'Angleterre*. One of Sheridan's best comedies could not have made us laugh more heartily.

It is by such articles as these that insignificant writers impede the intellectual intercourse of two great nations—an intercourse which is as advantageous to both as the exchange of French wines for Birmingham cutlery. We are at the present moment deriving considerable profit from that intellectual commerce which the manner adopted by the *Quarterly* and *Edinburgh Reviews* tends to check. No French writer over the past twenty years has afforded us anything like the pleasure we have derived from the works of Lord Byron and Sir Walter Scott; and this we freely acknowledge. I have observed that the English newspapers carefully record all the offences tried in our assize courts. You perhaps recall that the president of the court recently, during the trial of a man accused of seducing a young girl, observed that he was 'another Lovelace'. Some of your English readers may not recall the character of Lovelace in Richardson's *Clarissa*, but you may see from this that the reputation of your great novelist is still alive in France.

Apart from the letters on the English elections published in the *Globe*, the Frenchmen who are at present travelling in England must have transmitted privately to their friends a good many descriptions of what they have seen. The French, in any case, have never been more interested in England than they are at the moment. Our *ultras* are busy getting Cobbett's *History of the Reformation* and Lingard's *History of England* translated and *puffed* in all the right-wing journals. Lingard attempts to diminish the horror which is naturally excited by the massacre of St Bartholomew's day, and this has made him a favourite with the Jesuits. One French writer, who is literally pensioned by the *ultras* and by M. de Corbière, the Minister of the Interior, has described this massacre as a *salutary rigour*. Dr Lingard would do well to come to France. There he would receive the patronage of M. Frayssinous, the

Bishop of Hermopolis, who is giving places in the University to English Catholic converts.

New Monthly Magazine, October 1826

THE MISFORTUNES OF A NOBLEMAN UNDER THE RESTORATION

It is difficult in England to conceive any idea of the great sensation that has been produced in France by M. de Montlosier's denunciation of the Jesuits. To understand its proper significance you will have to compare the situation of one of your wealthy landowners residing on his country estate and that of a Frenchman of equal means, a peer of France, if you prefer, who spends eight months of the year in his chateau in Burgundy. The Englishman is a Justice of the Peace, and is highly respected by the parson of the parish, who hopes to get a living from him. He is sheriff of the county, or else an intimate friend of the sheriff, who will take good care not to offend him, still less to interfere in his business. The English squire is perhaps unacquainted with the bishop of the diocese in which he resides; but at all events the bishop will do nothing to cause him inconvenience or harm. If the road leading to his house needs making up, he complains to the parish officers, and, if necessary, gives orders for its repair. If he wishes to shoot a partridge, he takes his gun, and far from being interfered with in his sport, will more often be guilty of disturbing his neighbours. The fact is that the English squire is a king on his own estate, while the French landowner, on retiring to his, becomes a slave and feels his slavery in a hundred different ways. You can have no idea of the state of affairs which has prevailed in France over the last three years, ever since the Jesuits, that is, have been given the power of appointing the various officials who tyrannise over the landowners. If our Burgundian gentleman steps out with a gun in his hand, the constable of the district, known as the *garde champêtre*, who has a salary of about two hundred francs a year, comes up and orders him to show his licence for carrying arms. This licence has to be purchased every year from the Prefect. The *garde champêtre* may be a particularly ill-humoured individual, or he may have received a hint from the priest to give the landowner as much trouble as possible. He may therefore insist that the licence is out of order and take him before the Mayor. The Mayor, who is afraid of offending the priest, writes to the Sub-Prefect; the Sub-Prefect, who also has no desire to offend the priest, writes to the Prefect. The Prefect, who knows that the Bishop can get him dismissed, writes to the Minister of the Interior (M. de Corbière), who never replies. Thus it is that, as the entire power is left in the hands of the *garde champêtre*, he can, if the priest so desires, simply confiscate the gentleman's gun. If he resists, the gendarmerie wait on him next morning, and the Court of the First Instance, glad of an opportunity, not just but legal, of fining a man who is no favourite with the Bishop, is not slow in pronouncing judgment against him. Thus it is that the gentleman of property is obliged to pay court to the priest and mayor of the village, to the *garde champêtre*, and the gendarmeries, in fact to all who have it in their power to cause him trouble. But the matter does not end here. He must also take care to keep in good humour all the religious devotees who live under the protection of the priest. Now compare this life with that of a Devonshire squire of five thousand a year, living on his estate. His unfortunate French equivalent, if he wishes to cut down half a dozen trees in his own grounds, must write to the Prefect for permission, and he, in turn, must write to Paris for authority to grant the permission. You will find in Baron Dupin's work on England, and in M. Fiévée's *Lettres Administratives*, a humorous description of the seventeen letters which must be written by the Sub-Prefect, the Prefect and the Minister of the Interior, before our Burgundian gentleman can cut down six trees growing on his own estate. If he wishes to re-inforce the banks, build the smallest bridge or alter the course in the slightest way of a river or stream flowing through his grounds, he is once again obliged to write seven or eight letters to Paris. If the Prefect wishes to be particularly unhelpful, he may allow an interval of three months to elapse between each of these letters.

All this was vexatious enough in 1816; but consider how the tyranny under which the landed proprietors suffer has increased since 1822, ever since the Jesuits, that is, have obtained the right to appoint officials. It is they who appoint the *garde champêtre*, the Justice of the Peace, the officers of the gendarmerie, the Mayor, the priest and the Sub-Prefect, all of whom have an influence which is oppressively felt by an unfortunate gentleman who has left Paris to spend eight months of the year on his estates. Why should the Jesuits take so much trouble to secure the appointment of the six functionaries I have just indicated, unless it is in order to control the activities of the landowner and use him to further their own ends? The result of their influence is that, if he is a member of the Council General of his department, he is obliged to vote additional emoluments to the Bishop, to follow the missionary processions, to support the priests in their persecution of peasants who like to dance on feast days, and submit to many other obligations of a similar nature.

Now, you are certainly aware that all the present French

priests are young peasants, all more or less imbued, unfortunately, with a spirit of fanaticism. They come from seminaries established by the Jesuits, in which they are taught the doctrines of the famous M. de Maistre, a writer who may, at this moment, be regarded as the French St Paul. M. de Maistre declares that all persons in authority, even the King, are subject to the authority of the Pope. Twenty bulls with papal signatures maintain the same pretension. Leo XII protects the *Giornale Ecclesiastico*, which is printed in Rome and which preaches the same doctrine. Everything, therefore, in the Jesuit scheme of things is consistent and well ordered. Our unfortunate Burgundian gentleman is led from one submission to another, until eventually perhaps he becomes a *short-robed Jesuit* like M. de Puiseux, minister under Louis XV and the uncle of Mme de Genlis. (See the *Mémoires de Mme de Genlis*, vol. 2.) His only two means of escape in fact are: 1. To become a short-robed Jesuit; 2. To take refuge in Paris. Paris is, in fact, the only part of France in which there is any liberty at all.

Let us suppose that he has spirit enough to resist becoming a Jesuit. Sooner or later, persecuted by the vexations of the holy fathers, he will leave Burgundy and come to Paris in order to give vent to his impotent rage. What can a single man do, however, even if he is a millionaire and a peer of France, against a society so powerful and with so many adherents? He can do precisely nothing. Imagine his pleasure, nevertheless, if on arriving in Paris, he finds that a man of courage like M. de Montlosier is uttering the very denunciation which he so longs to hear. His pleasure naturally increases when he realises that M. de Montlosier has insisted that the Royal Court of Paris should come to an explanation concerning the privileges and functions of the Order of St Ignatius. Every Royal Court in the kingdom imitates the Royal Court of Paris, while the Courts of the First Instance imitate in their turn the Royal Court of the district. Our landowner therefore begins to cherish the hope of at last obtaining something like justice if he should bring an action against a Court of the First Instance; or if ever he should complain of some vexation caused him by the Mayor or by the young priest of his parish.

To denounce the Jesuits in 1826 is, in France, nothing more or less than to demand a complete change in the internal administration of the country. It is therefore a great mistake on the part of *The Times*, which has so great an influence on public opinion in England, to ridicule the denunciations which are being uttered against the various congregations of Jesuits. In every town there are three congregations, each as well organised as any regiment in the army:

1st, there is the congregation of the gentry. In Paris, M. Ferdinand de Berthier commands the one hundred and eight Jesuits of the short robe, who are members of the Chamber of Deputies. The late Duke Mathieu de Montmorency was colonel-general of all the short-robed Jesuits in France.

2nd, the congregation known as the *Bonnes Etudes*. This society is employed in seducing and crimping students of law and medicine between the ages of seventeen and twenty-two.

3rd, the congregation of the common people, whose business is to seduce servants and employ them as spies upon their masters.

The Times had treated with misplaced derision the denunciation which a man of courage published this month against the *Congrégation des Bonnes Etudes*. I shall therefore bring to your recollection a number of facts to justify my previous assertions. To offer one example of the fanaticism of the young priests formed by the influence of M. de Maistre and the Abbé de La Mennais, you may recall the case of the young priest in the neighbourhood of Lyons, who was acquitted by a Court of the First Instance. It was proved that this priest had climbed up a tree in pursuit of a musician who had been playing to a group of peasants. These peasants had met, after the church service, to dance together before returning home. The priest had finally knocked the unfortunate musician from his seat in the tree. Every day the newspapers relate something of the kind. I have quoted this last example because it rests on judicial proof. Those who find the story hard to believe may find an account of the trial in the *Gazette des Tribunaux*, an excellent newspaper which I recommend to all Englishmen who wish to become acquainted with the true state of French society.

A counsellor of the Royal Court of Grenoble died about two years ago. He was one of the leading figures in the *Congrégation des Bonnes Etudes* and a number of papers found in his desk bearing the signatures of persons of the highest rank were subsequently published. Those who are sceptical of what I am saying will do well to read these truly curious papers. Grenoble is one of the towns most attached to the Charter, and consequently most feared by the Government. The Jesuits have therefore been making every effort to influence the minds of the young law students of the town. What remains to be legally proved is the seduction of servants. Cases of this kind are notoriously public, though no one has yet instituted actions against the offenders. I have read a number of letters on the subject written by English Protestant families residing in France. There is not perhaps a single respectable man in the country who has not, at some time or another, detected attempts to seduce his servants, and to persuade them to report to one of the local priests everything that goes on in their master's house.

There still remains one objection which may naturally occur to the mind of a disinterested foreigner, not thoroughly acquainted with the present state of French society. He may possibly imagine that the liberals themselves wish to exercise a tyrannical authority over those Frenchmen who choose to become Jesuits. This is by no means the case. All we demand is that we should enjoy the same degree of liberty enjoyed by the Jesuits, with the connivance of the Government. Some year ago the Duke de Broglie and several other distinguished men formed a society called the *Society for the Liberty of the Press*. The police suppressed it because it met on certain days and in a number exceeding twenty.

Such meetings were prohibited by a tyrannical law of Bonaparte's, a law which, though abolished by the Charter, still continues to be enforced. At the present moment, the King's ministers apply it to the liberals and not to the Jesuits. All we ask is to be treated in the same way. Let us be permitted to have our congregations, too, and soon there will be no dangerous meetings in France. No meetings are dangerous in England because all are legal.

The Government permits the Jesuits to go about the streets armed, though this is an offence for anyone else. *The Times*, however, seems to have no idea that such things can happen. I am perfectly aware that an English newspaper is written for English readers, but when speaking of a country not more than twenty miles from its own shores, it would be as well if it were to be a little less in the wrong, and if it were not to call black white, and white black.

As to the attacks that have been made on the Jesuits during the past year, you may be sure that what their antagonists desire is a total change in the internal administration of the country. The Jesuits are our masters everywhere except in Paris, and one must either pay them homage or be exposed to their vexations. Do not blame me for making an incursion into the realm of politics. In speaking of the Jesuits, I have merely given you an outline of the conversation of polite society during the months of August and September. It seems that the Government has to some extent deserted them, and we have talked of nothing else.

If you go to the trouble of consulting that excellent work the *Journal de la Librairie*, edited by M. Beuchot, which gives the titles of all the works published in Paris, you will find that the vast majority consists of publications by the disciples of Loyola or by their enemies. During the last six months, the number of purely literary works has been falling off. Take, for instance, number 63 of the *Journal de la Librairie* (August 9th, 1826). There you will find announced: *Nouvelles Etrennes Spirituelles, in-24, La Journée du Chrétien, in-24, Réflections sur la Religion, Lettres d'un Anglican à un Gallican, Les Jésuites Athées, ou la France en danger, Le Catholicisme Primitif* and *La Réfutation de l'opinion de M. l'Abbé de la Mennais sur la Puissance Spirituelle des Papes*. All these works are advertised in a single page of M. Beuchot's journal, and from this you may judge the number of more or less absurd pamphlets to which the disputes concerning the legal status of the Jesuits have given rise.

If the Jesuits were to form a purely religious association, like the various sects of your Methodists, Quakers or Swedenburgians, we should have nothing to say against them. We would merely insist that the Government allow them complete liberty. What they have done, however, is to place under their control *gardes-champêtres*, mayors, parish priests, sub-prefects, prefects and judges, whom they have the power even to appoint in office. These officials render our lives impossible unless we submit to the Jesuits in everything. M. de Villèle's own private secretary is a Jesuit and he has been seeking to get rid of him for the past two years. When a Prime Minister, who is also a man of talent, finds himself as hampered as this, what can the private citizen who has taken refuge in Paris hope to do? He merely spends his time cursing St Ignatius and his disciples and reading all the pamphlets, which are of varying degrees of absurdity, for and against the Congregation. I hope that your readers will now be able to form some idea of the cunning and intricate machinery which at the present moment makes the influence of the Jesuits felt in every corner of France.

New Monthly Magazine, October 1826

CENSORSHIP AND THE DECLINE OF SATIRE

Paris, March 17th, 1828

Sir,

After a long interval, I once more resume my task of keeping you in touch to some extent with French literature and other subjects which occupy the attention of polite society in Paris. For the last two months, it has been generally considered that the King has no confidence in the present ministers whom the last elections obliged him to appoint. He is still secretly guided by M. de Villèle, who is playing the rôle given to Lord Bute at a certain period during the reign of George III.

A government becomes a particular object of public interest when its probable duration and definitive form are matters of uncertainty. An Englishman, if asked what the government of his country will be in ten years time, will confidently reply that the Duke of Clarence or the young princess will be on the throne and that things will go on just as they do now under the powerful influence of an aristocracy which admits all men of outstanding talent into its ranks. This is not the case in France. No one can tell whether, in ten years time, we shall be ruled over by a despot and governed by priests, as we were during the dotage of Louis XIV, or whether our King will merely exert an authority equivalent to that of a President of the United States. This unsettled state of affairs has made the present government extremely suspicious of the influence of literature. Would you ever believe, for example, that in the year 1828 performances of Chénier's tragedy *Tibère* would be prohibited, lest the allusions it contains should be applied to existing circumstances? When people come to Paris from the provinces it is often to perfect their knowledge of spoken and written French. Public opinion throughout the country is formed in the capital; for we have no great provincial towns such as Manchester and Liverpool. It is therefore perfectly natural that the government should keep a watchful eye upon literature.

Every year on the King's birthday, crosses are given to twelve writers whose works are scrupulously innocent of anything that is interesting and of any attempt to ridicule either the miracles with which the priests hoax the public or the Jesuitical tricks by which the ministers seek to turn their private whims into laws. Some time ago, a story was circulated concerning a luminous cross which appeared at Migné in Poitou. Every effort was made to force this miracle down the throats of the public, and finally Leo XII wrote to the Archbishop of Paris saying that he himself believed it to be authentic. None of the King's ministers were as credulous as this; in fact these gentlemen are prudent enough to believe very little. There is not one of them, however, who would have recommended the Legion of Honour to be given to a writer who had ventured to express any scepticism concerning this absurd affair. What is worse, however, is that they have far more substantial gifts than crosses to give away. There are four or five hundred places at the Government's disposal to which men of letters are appointed and to each of which is attached a salary of four or six thousand francs. A favourite of one of the ministers sometimes monopolises five or six of these sinecures, which he continues to occupy all the time that he writes with prudence, and respects old prejudices and new miracles, such as the cross of Migné or a thousand others that I would enumerate if I were not afraid of wearying your patience.

It is principally to the effect on literature of these four hundred places at the government's disposal that the present degenerate state of literature must be attributed. The French are not made to excel in the poetry of passion, poetry such as Lord Byron's *Lara* or *Corsair*. The style of writing most congenial to the national character is that of Montesquieu's *Lettres Persanes*, Voltaire's *Candide* and the comedies of Marivaux and Beaumarchais. A delicate vein of satire runs through all these works. They abound in the caustic and witty. Now this is precisely what the ministers most dread; for they know that an epigram might bring about their downfall.

The Dauphin, the son of Louis XV and the father of Louis XVI, was extremely devout; he was even taken to be a short-robed Jesuit. The Jesuits at the time had under their protection a certain M. Le Franc de Pompignan, an ignorant, conceited fellow, whom they proposed as tutor to the Dauphin's three sons. The Dauphin hated Voltaire more than any man in the world, and he would declare that, if ever he came to the throne, the first act of his reign would be to send the obnoxious writer to the Bastille. Despite this threat, Voltaire wrote a satire on M. de Pompignan in which the following lines occurred:

    César n'a point d'asile où sa cendre repose,
    Et l'ami Pompignan pense être quelque chose![1]

A few days later, the unfortunate M. de Pompignan went to court, and as soon as his name was announced, the Prince involuntarily exclaimed:

---

[1] Caesar has no shelter in which his ashes may rest, and our friend Pompignan has aspirations.

Et l'ami Pompignan pense être quelque chose!

This had so comic an effect that the assembled courtiers burst out laughing. All idea of making M. de Pompignan tutor to the young Princes was now at an end. He could no longer hold up his head in Paris, and shortly afterwards he retired in mortification to the country.

This anecdote is decidedly French, for in no other country would the lash of a blaspheming satirist have deterred a devout Jesuitical prince from entrusting the education of his children to a man strongly recommended by the brothers of the order. Whatever may be the particular bent of a Frenchman's mind, he always retains a keen perception of the ridiculous; the Dauphin's piety, therefore, did not prevent him from feeling the full force of Voltaire's satire.

Today, however, our ministers have little fear of personal ridicule, for they are tolerably indifferent to everything, except the possibility of losing their places. They are always, nevertheless, apprehensive lest ridicule should thwart the measures they introduce. The last law proposed against the liberty of the press, which was given the name of the *Law of Justice and Love*, failed because of the derision it aroused. Its rejection was undoubtedly one of the reasons for the fall of Villèle. From all this it will be readily understood that our ministers, whatever their politics may be, will be always hostile to the drama. This hostility will continue, furthermore, until the rôle which the King of France is to play has been clearly understood. At the moment we have no idea whether the successors of Charles X are to be despots like Louis XIV, constitutional monarchs like the King of England, or Presidents like Washington.

New Monthly Magazine, April 1828

V
OTHER CRITICAL WRITINGS

NOTES ON CORNEILLE: AN ANALYSIS OF CINNA

Act I, scene one: it is unnatural for anyone to talk for so long about her own feelings; it is also ridiculous for her to talk about a conspiracy against the emperor in the emperor's own apartments. It would have been impossible, however, to convince Corneille of its absurdity after he had written, 'The play takes place in Rome.' (See his discourses on dramatic art and particularly the third.)[1]

The main fault of this monologue is that Emilie talks to herself with all the clarity and eloquence of a woman addressing a stranger. We feel that Shakespeare would have made this scene appear altogether more natural by giving Emilie the authentic, simple language of a troubled soul. He would have shown her, for instance, at two o'clock in the morning, leaving her bed and walking agitatedly up and down in her room to the great astonishment of one of her maidservants. What a difference it would make to the interest of the drama if Cinna were to enter her room at two o'clock in order to talk to her of the conspiracy! Otherwise, if the risk were too great, Emilie could have been made to form some decision of which she informed Cinna the following day in the course of a hunt.

The style is not suited to Emilie's character, but if we assume for a moment that it is, we find that it is noble and passionate (or tragic); it is clear, and it has the terseness which is that of a mighty soul. To prove this one has only to imagine the four

[1] See Appendix A.

lines ('Vous prenez sur mon ame', etc.)¹ given to a character like Amenaïde² and the disconcerting effect they would produce.

Imagine that the monologue is a portrait. Imagine, that is, that the poet claimed to be reporting what Emilie herself had said in his hearing. If this were the case, we should blame the poet for everything that strikes us as contrary to nature, just as we blame M. Girodet for the bluish tints in his portrait of M. Redouté. While we notice this defect in the portrait of M. Redouté, the portrait does not fail, nevertheless, to give us some idea of his appearance; in the same way, while we notice the faults indicated above, we are left with some idea of Emilie's character. The problem we wish to raise is this: What would our conception of Emilie be after we had heard this monologue? We would imagine her as a woman of firm character, lacking consequently in grace (in the charms of weakness), a little in love with Cinna and unable to distinguish between her vengeance and her love. It is difficult to imagine (still with reference to this one monologue) one of these two passions, love and vengeance, completely overcoming the other; or in other words, which is the stronger of the two.

Given the stamp of forcefulness and reason that we find in the thought and style of this monologue, I should tend to believe that it is vengeance that would prevail.

Scene 2, page 342:³ 'Toute cette faveur' and the three following lines. If Emilie entertains feelings of tenderness, she should be shocked by the fact that Fulvia seeks to console her for the death of a father by talking of her position and of Auguste's munificence. Instead of this, these four lines seem to reveal a sort of monarchical pride, and on examining the fourth line at all closely we find that it says nothing, has no meaning.

[1] See Appendix B.
[2] Presumably in Voltaire's *Tancrède*.
[3] See Appendix C.

This tirade is full of pride, vengeance and political maxims. A true political talent on Corneille's part would have led him to depict her winning over one leader of the people with the gift of a fine chalice, a second with cash, a third by vanity, and a fourth by coquetterie. To put it briefly, Shakespeare would have made us aware of the internal administration of ambition. An example of what we mean is Macbeth with Banquo's two assassins.

Emilie is far from acting in such a way. Instead of winning over Maxime, she allows herself the luxury of giving vent to her proud and haughty passion.

The tirade on page 343[1] is a perfect model of style, with the exception of 'mon parent'; pride and vengeance are fortified by the maxims of Roman education concerning such qualities as the love of glory and of the fatherland.

Page 344:[2] Emilie describes and does not feel what ought to be her state of mind at the moment ('Je veux et ne veux pas').

Imagine that in a deserted road at night a man comes up and strikes you. You recognise him. He is a ferocious character, who is an excellent pistol shot and swordsman. It depends entirely on you whether the incident is talked about or not. No one will hear about it otherwise, for your swash-buckling aggressor was completely drunk at the time and had no idea what he was doing. However, if you are of an irascible disposition, the thought of this outrage will poison any happiness you might otherwise have felt.

Emilie says, 'Aux mânes paternels je dois ce sacrifice.'[3] Perhaps the Roman ideas of behaviour have imprinted the feeling of this duty on Emilie's heart as deeply as the chivalric code has imprinted on ours the need to insist on an explanation

[1] See Appendix D.
[2] See Appendix E.
[3] 'To the paternal shades I owe this sacrifice.'

and an apology for any affront we receive. This, we feel, is the prime motive for all that she does throughout the tragedy, for she is not to be thought of as a tender-hearted young woman. Such an interpretation is only contradicted by the line 'Et je demeure toujours la fille d'un proscrit', which, as we have observed before, seems to us meaningless.

The entry of Cinna produces no effect and could take place preferably at a moment when nothing else is going on, or else when Emilie is more ready to accept his love. The question with which she opens the third scene is that of a general to a colonel.

It would be best if we were to offer an overall account of *Cinna*; Shakespeare himself could not have offered grander thoughts and the manner in which they are presented (or the style) is that of a mighty soul. There is nothing finer than

'Je les peins dans le meurtre', etc.[1]

and the ten following lines.

This is a perfect model of the tragic style. There is a touch of affectation, but this is in no way cold or vulgar.

'Comme par un effet contraire', etc.[2]

Apart from this, there is no other defect in this speech, nor, we may add, is there any hint that the speaker is a man without character, momentarily exalted.

The ending,

'Demain j'attends la fin', etc.,[3]

announces a mighty character and induces in the reader the quivering of a proud smile: he admires himself and imagines himself to be capable of sentiments as elevated as these.

In Emilie's reply, love occupies only a second place; it is the

[1] See Appendix F.
[2] These words are not to be found in the text of the play. They obviously refer to the passage of Cinna's speech (Act I, scene iii, lines 230-40), in which Cinna imagines Auguste assassinated during the public sacrifices and becoming himself 'by a contrary effect' its victim.
[3] See Appendix G.

love of glory (brought about by the re-establishment of liberty) which predominates. She ought, if she truly existed as a character, to talk of her father and cry, for instance,

'O mon père, tu seras donc enfin vengé.'[1]

The fine things she says concerning Brutus and Cassius should only come in the second line.

In general, in what we have seen of the play, we do not acquire an *intimate knowledge* of the characters. Basing our judgment merely on what they say, we are able to form three or four totally distinct impressions of their character.

Is Emilie moved by the sheer love of liberty, by filial piety, or by the proud desire not to remain unavenged?

After ten lines, we know one of Shakespeare's characters through and through, a talent that Corneille either did not possess or else, seeking to appear noble, was unable to exhibit. It is more probable, however, that he did not possess these gifts, for it was he who reigned over the theatre and established its rules.

After five minutes, we see at once what sort of woman Lady Macbeth is, or Desdemona.

At the end of the first act, Cinna, moved by his own narration, is truly great. The style is as fine as the thought. Its conciseness particularly strikes us as admirable.

Apart from Shakespeare's gift for characterisation, we look in the first act of any play for the fidelity of his brush.

Emilie talks of the tears she sheds for her father, in a single line during the first act. We feel that the tears (fifteen years after his death) are in contradiction with the evident firmness of her character. She must, after all, be a woman accustomed to telling herself that she ought to avenge her father rather than weep for him.

April 2nd, 1811

[1] 'At last then you are to be avenged, my father.'

THE *ARISTARCH* OR UNIVERSAL INDICATOR OF THE BOOKS TO BE READ

The naked truth

What! another literary journal? Allow me to say one thing first of all. This one will be different from all the others; here is the reason. Two citizens were in the service of the state before 1814, occupying two very different posts; one was in France and the other abroad. Since 1814 they have travelled widely, and finally, bored at having nothing to do, they have sought an enterprise in which they can obtain ten per cent profit on anything they invest. They have found that it would be less boring for them to found a literary journal than anything else, one in which every outstanding work published in Europe, America or India can be reviewed with rigorous impartiality.

Jacques and Pierre (these are their names) have considered that the sole qualifications they require are those that they endeavoured to carry into their public duties, that is, intelligence, a considerable integrity, frankness and courage.

They are not what are known as men of letters; they have no such distinction. On the contrary, they know no one and have wedded no literary sect or party. In the extracts of new publications which they intend to present, they will always try to efface the author of the review in order to present all the more clearly the author of the book. They expect to see all the authors whose works they have reviewed become, if not their avowed enemies, at least men who wish them ill in secret. This is very regrettable. However, they prefer this to the tedium of an ordinary commercial enterprise. As for personalities, they intend never to mention them. In order to avoid even the temptation, they will avoid as far as possible knowing, even by sight, the men of letters who honour Europe today.

Their politics are left of centre, that is, more or less those of M. Ternaux.[1]

The two citizens who have undertaken the publication of the *Aristarch* travelled widely between 1814 and 1822. Between them they have a thorough knowledge of German, English and Italian literature. This last phrase is very blunt. It is written in a style, however, which they hope they will be permitted to use on every occasion, calling a spade a spade. What is more, they will be very terse; they consider that a journal such as theirs must look with horror on any sentence of more than four lines. They will carefully avoid any kind of pomposity or rhetoric; their ambition is to be of service to those who wish to buy new books, but only those which stand out a little from the commonplace. Those works which do not fulfil this basic condition will not even be advertised on the cover.

In having the courage to tell the naked truth, they hope that, after two years, they will have realised fifteen per cent profit on their investments. Now the public is fully informed as to their intentions. They will continue to be aristarchs in good faith. In this century of coteries, they rely only on their sincerity to make up for literary talents which they do not possess.

You will ask, however, whether we are really capable of producing a journal of this kind. Our reply to this is a simple one: judge us according to what we write. After you have read

---

[1] Guillaume-Louis Ternaux (1763-1833); an industrialist and member of the Chamber of Deputies. He invented a textile, to produce which he imported goats from Tibet, an enterprise which inspired Stendhal's qualified approval. See *D'un nouveau complot contre les industriels* (*Mélanges de Littérature*, vol. II, page 218. Editions du Divan, Paris 1933).

a few issues, you will know well enough what Jacques and Pierre can do, for there to be no need for us to describe them, and no need to make promises in a style which you would find agreeable enough to read, but which you wouldce rtainly not believe. In this you would be perfectly justified, for we all know what prospectuses are.

On the 15th of every month, there will appear an issue of the *Aristarch*, made up of seven double pages with type facing, paper and layout as in the present editorial prospectus. A subscription will cost twenty-four francs for six months and forty-six francs for a year. If the journal should ever cease publication, two-thirds of the current subscriptions will be paid back.

February 24th, 1822

MEMORIES OF LORD BYRON

I am now free to speak, for every friend that I am about to name is either dead or in irons. Nothing I say can harm those who are in prison, and men of such courage and nobility have little to fear from the truth.

Nor do I fear the reproaches of those who are now dead. They have long since been overwhelmed by the cruel oblivion which follows death, and yet, because they shared a natural human desire not to be forgotten in the world of the living, they would gladly listen to the voice of the friend who is about to name them. In order to be worthy of them, I intend to say nothing which is in the least false or exaggerated.

M. le Marquis de Brême, a wealthy nobleman of Piedmont, who is still perhaps alive, had been Minister of the Interior in

Milan, while Napoleon was King of Italy. After 1814, M. de Brême had found the profession of turn-coat unworthy of his noble birth; he had retired to his estates leaving his palace in Milan to one of his younger sons, Monsignore Ludovic de Brême.

This was a tall, thin young man, already suffering from the disease of the lungs from which he was to die some few years later. He was called *monsignore* because he had been chaplain to the King of Italy, whose Minister of the Interior was his own father. He had refused the bishopric of Mantua, and at a period when his family was more influential than it was ever to be again. M. Ludovic de Brême was remarkable for his high-mindedness, his scholarship and his courtesy. His long melancholy features reminded one of the white marble statues that are to be seen on Italian tombs of the eleventh century. Whenever I think of him, it is to see him climbing the huge staircase of the magnificent, dark old palace which his father had turned over to him for his use.

One day, it occurred to Monsignore de Brême to be brought to see me by M. Guasco, a highly intelligent young liberal. As I had neither a palace of my own nor a title, I had refrained from calling on M. de Brême myself. I found the courteous, genteel tone which his presence inspired among all around him so very delightful, that, in a few days, the friendship became intimate. M. de Brême was a passionate admirer of the works of Mme de Staël and this was to lead to a quarrel between us one evening in his father's box at the Scala. On this occasion, I maintained that Mme de Staël's *Considérations sur la Révolution Française* was chock-full of mistakes. Every evening in this same box, M. de Brême would bring together eight or ten outstanding men. The conversation never ceased to flow and was scarcely even interrupted for the finer passages in the opera.

One evening in the autumn of 1812, after an excursion on

the Lake of Como, I called in at M. de Brême's box at the Scala. I found something solemn and awkward in the atmosphere; no one spoke, and I had begun to listen to the music when M. de Brême said to me indicating my neighbour, 'Monsieur Beyle, this is Lord Byron'. He repeated the same phrase, turning it round for Lord Byron's benefit. I noticed a young man, far from tall, whose eyes were majestic and had something generous about them. At the time I was infatuated with *Lara* and, after a second glance, I saw Lord Byron, no longer as he was, but as the author of *Lara* ought to be. As the conversation was languishing, M. de Brême sought to bring me out and make me talk. This I was unable to do, however. I was overcome by timidity and adoration. If I had dared, I would have kissed Lord Byron's hand and burst into tears. Driven on as I was by M. de Breme's questions, I wanted to say something and succeeded merely in bringing out platitudes which did nothing to break the silence which had descended over the company. At last Lord Byron asked me, as the only person present who spoke English, how to get back to his inn. It was at the other end of the city near the fortress and I could see that he was going to lose his way. In that part of Milan at midnight every shop is closed. He would wander through lonely, badly-lit streets and was unable to speak a word of the language. Out of sheer affection, I had the stupidity to suggest that he took a cab. Immediately a shade of haughtiness appeared on his brow; he gave me to understand, with all the requisite courtesy, that he merely wished to know the way and needed no advice as to how to get there. He left the box and I understood how it was that, when he had come in, he had brought silence with him.

The haughtiness and perfect good breeding of our host had found their match. In Lord Byron's company, no one would have risked the danger which any man incurs, in a group of seven or eight silent men, if he proposes a subject of conversation.

Lord Byron allowed himself to be carried away like a child in a tirade against the English upper classes, that all-powerful aristocracy, inexorable and terrible in its revenge, which turns so many rich fools into eminently respectable men, but which cannot allow itself to be made fun of by one of its own sons, without incurring its own downfall. The fear inspired by that great nation whose leaders were Danton and Carnot has made the English aristocracy what it is today, so powerful, so morose and so full of hypocrisy.

Lord Byron's humour is bitter in *Childe Harold*; it is the anger of youth; it is scarcely more than ironical in *Beppo* and *Don Juan*. But this humour does not bear too close an examination; instead of gaiety and light-heartedness, hatred and unhappiness lie beneath. Lord Byron has only been able to depict one man: himself. Moreover, he considered himself, and was in fact, a nobleman. He wished to appear as such in society, and yet he was also a poet who wished to be admired. These are incompatible pretensions and were to be an immense source of chagrin.

There is no country on earth in which the members of a powerful and rich aristocracy—whose self-esteem is founded on the titles inherited from their ancestors or obtained by themselves—will calmly tolerate the sight of a man who is the centre of public admiration and the object of general regard, merely because he has written two hundred good lines. The aristocracy avenges the acclaim given to the poet by murmuring, 'What lack of tone! What manners!' Neither of these two little exclamations could be uttered, however, when speaking of Lord Byron. They stifled in the heart and bred sheer hatred. This hatred was first evident in a poem written by a certain Mr Southey, who, till then, had been famous only for the odes which he dedicated regularly to the King of England, a man who is the best of Kings, on his birthday. This Southey, protected by the *Quarterly Review*, insulted Lord Byron atrociously and, on one occasion, came near to receiving the honour of a pistol shot for his pains.

In his ordinary, everyday moments, Lord Byron would think of himself as a mighty aristocrat; this was the breastplate by which his delicate and profoundly susceptible nature was protected against the infinite grossness of the vulgar. *Odi profanum vulgus et arceo*. It must be confessed that the vulgar in England, having the spleen for birthright, are more atrocious than anywhere else.

On the days when Byron felt that he could endure to some extent the vulgarity around him, on the days, that is, when he was less susceptible than usual, his affectation of beauty and tone were an asset to him. There were moments, in fact, perhaps two or three times a week, when, for five or six hours at a time, he would be a man of sense and often a great poet.

The excessive study of the Bible gives the English people a tint of Hebraic ferocity; its aristocracy, whose way of life is based on the family gives it an underlying seriousness. Lord Byron was aware of these defects, and, in *Don Juan*, he is gay, witty, sublime and pathetic. He attributed his own transformation to his residence in Venice.

The Venetian aristocracy, which was care-free and noble five or six hundred years before any other in Europe, and which, for this if no other reason, commanded Byron's immediate respect, was led in 1796 by men who were superlatively incompetent in the conduct of public affairs, and, to make up for this, remarkably insolent. They were confronted by a little broken-down army, which they despised, and were too stupid even to fear the genius of its young twenty-eight-year-old commander. The Venetian government either caused or tolerated the assassination of the wounded and sick in Bonaparte's army; this is the true story of the fall of Venice. Never was an aristocracy more doomed to disaster and never was disaster endured with more gaiety.

This is a summary of several long conversations that I had with Lord Byron in 1816.

The gaiety and freedom of Count Bragadin and many other amiable Venetians more noble and more unfortunate than him, made a profound impression on Lord Byron. He was able to enjoy, at the same time, the spectacle of the lively, sincere and continual admiration expressed in polite society for the poetry of M. Buratti. From then on, the light irony of *Don Juan* began to take the place of the bitter sarcasm of *Childe Harold*; the transformation in Byron's character was less marked, but no less real.

Later on, towards 1820, he had the strange idea, among several others equally absurd, of founding a review.[1] He sought the collaboration of a learned man of letters, Mr Hunt, the author subsequently of a very faithful portrait of the poet. Hunt, like Byron, belonged to what is known in England as the liberal party. Another member of the so-called liberal party, however, wrote to Byron in the name of all the liberals of good family, in order to point out to him the harm that would be done to his reputation, if he associated publicly with an author of low birth and with no recognised position in the best society.

Should we wonder that Mr Moore decided to burn the memoirs entrusted to him by his friend?

1829

---

[1] *The Liberal.*

STENDHAL

LORD BYRON IN ITALY
AN EYE-WITNESS ACCOUNT 1816[1]

Was there some murder on Lord Byron's conscience? Today such a question can only damage the man who asks it. What harm could it do to that great figure who, even though he has been in his tomb for six years, continues to strike fear into the hearts of those hypocrites whose cant reigns supreme over their proud country?

For a moment I was afraid of raising such a suspicion. What could be more cruel than to pay court, even if only in appearance, to the wretched and abominable hypocrisy which can describe Lord Byron as the leader of the Satanic school of poetry, or which can attack him even more astutely by seeming to pity him for his grave errors?

This profound hatred is a political hatred. Anyone who reads M. de Custine's account of his travels in England[2] or who goes there himself will soon be convinced that it is a country administered for the sole benefit and glory of between a thousand and twelve hundred families. The younger brothers of the nobility and their tutors find opulence and rich livings in the ecclesiastical establishment. In return they are called upon to mystify a nation of working men who are taught to respect and almost love an aristocracy which shares all the 'dinners' and a good third of the income from the taxes by which the nation is crushed. Some years ago, a pamphleteer was bold enough to publish a curious list showing the number

[1] According to Romain Colomb, the essay itself was written in 1830. 1816 is the year to which it refers. (Editor's note:)
[2] *Mémoires et Voyages ou lettres écrites à diverses époques pendant des courses en Suisse, en Calabre, en Angleterre et en Ecosse.*

of pounds sterling which, on one pretext or another, the family of each peer and the peer himself draw from the public revenue in the form of salaries, pensions, livings, sinecures, etc. Lord Byron's mother and his family are shown in this list as receiving seventeen hundred pounds a year. There is no need to add that the author and printer were both declared at once to be guilty of lying and dishonourable behaviour.[1]

I wish to do justice to the perfect amiability and to the private virtues of several members of the English aristocracy. It gives me pain to have to attack the politics of men whom it is so pleasant to know. This same aristocracy, however, holds Lord Byron in execration, and I am obliged to point out how it is that its opinions can have no claim either to disinterestedness or impartiality. Everything hangs together in the English establishment: the Church teaches the people to venerate the aristocracy and the aristocracy in its turn protects the interests of the Church. A rich man will confess privately that his own views on the truths taught by the latter are the same as those of Hume; a quarter of an hour later, if there are six men around him, he will wither with the most contemptuous epithets the scoundrel who dares to admit the slightest doubt concerning the miracles or the divine mission of Jesus Christ. Hypocrisy has made such rapid strides, particularly since trade has gone out of fashion and the British army come in, that every day brings news of the conversion of yet another thinker who, in his youth, had the courage to poke fun at the egoism, gluttony and infinite servility of the English priests.

The tyrannical view of life adopted by the upper classes owes its origin to the intimate union of peers and priests. It is as savage and cruel as it is because of a terror of what is known in London as *public opinion*, and it oppresses the country far more

[1] *A Peep on the Peers*. Stendhal's marginal notes in a copy of this pamphlet suggest that the public funds paid out to the upper classes, and particularly to members of the Church, were higher than the author had indicated. (Editor's note.)

effectively than M. Metternich's armies oppress Italy. Taking all things into consideration, I would suggest that, of the two countries, there is more liberty to be found in Italy than in England. Out of thirty or forty tiny actions which yesterday went to make up my day or yours, two or three would have been rendered impossible by the myrmidons of Austria. Every one of them, without exception, would have been hindered in England. What is sad and strange is that, in a country which was once so fascinating to know, the eccentric seems to have disappeared.

The opinions of the English upper classes are engendered by their interests. They can never therefore be corrected by reason.

What a strange destiny hangs over human affairs! Must we believe that liberty, that first and most essential of man's needs, is impossible in this world? In the states which groan under the police of the petty despotisms of Turin, Modena or Cassel, men sigh for the liberty of New York. And in New York one is less free to do as one pleases than in Venice or Rome. The press, once freed from any prior censorship, brings about a state of political liberty; straight away, however, in order to satisfy a pharisaical public, it prints an account of all you have been doing the day before; in so doing, it deprives you of all personal freedom in the hundred tiny actions which, for good or ill, go to make up each man's daily life. Perhaps one may say, therefore, that the Paris of 1830 is the city which enjoys the highest degree of liberty in the world.

Opinion among the English upper classes, which had for a long time been irritated by Lord Byron's bluntness and candour, turned against him completely a year after his marriage, when his wife left him. He was in despair, for, though he could talk philosophy as well as Cicero, he was no philosopher in reality. So much the better. If he had been a true philosopher he would not have been a great poet. He was the unique and constant object of his own attention. As a result of this pernicious habit, a habit which is the leprosy of civilisation, he always exaggerated his own misfortunes. In this he was like Jean-Jacques Rousseau, with whom it angered him to be compared.

Deeply injured by the deluge of caricatures, satires, pamphlets and insults of every kind which carried out the sentence pronounced by the aristocracy of his native country, Byron consoled himself with one thought: he hoped for justice after his death, and wrote his own memoirs which he confided to a friend. The friend threw them into the fire. To please whom, and for how much?

After such an act, a similar instance of which cannot be found fortunately among the immoral French, the same friend was bold enough to reproach Lord Byron with a number of youthful follies. These the poet had exaggerated, for, like the regent Duke of Orleans, he enjoyed boasting of the few vices which nature, or rather his Cambridge education, had given him.

In 1817, Monsignore Ludovic de Brême, former first chaplain to Napoleon, the King of Italy, brought together in his box in the Scala of Milan a group of twelve or fifteen young men. Observing an Italian custom, one all too little practised in France, these friends would meet every evening. How can one be affected when talking to a man one meets three hundred times in the course of a year? Affectation, which throws so effective a chill over the French *salon*, is rendered impossible by the social arrangements of Milan.

Today, in 1830, M. de Brême's friends are nearly all, if not dead, condemned to death; I can give every assurance that I have never met men more honest and less seditious.

One evening at the Scala we saw a young man enter our

box. He was fairly short and his eyes were superb; as he made his way towards the far end of the box facing the stage, we noticed that he limped slightly. 'Gentlemen, this is Lord Byron', announced M. de Brême, and then indicated each of us by name to his lordship. The introductions were made with all the gravity that his grandfather, ambassador of the Duke of Savoy to Louis XIV, would have summoned for the occasion.

As we had already acquired some experience of the English character, and knew that its instinct is to fly as soon as it is sought out, we took care not to speak to Lord Byron or even to glance at him. One of M. de Brême's guest, however, was strikingly handsome with a martial bearing, and in talking to him, Lord Byron seemed to lose something of his English aloofness.

We subsequently discovered, or rather imagined we had discovered, that Lord Byron admired Napoleon and, at the same time, was jealous of him. He would say, 'He and I were the only ones to sign our names N.B.' The day of the evening on which he was introduced to M. de Brême's circle of friends he had been told that, among them, he would meet a veteran of the Moscow campaign. In the year 1816 this event still held all the charms of novelty; these charms had not yet been spoilt by the novels which it has since inspired. It so happened that it was the man with moustaches whom Lord Byron assumed to be the survivor of the campaign.

Next day Lord Byron realised his mistake and did me the honour of talking to me about Russia. I adored Napoleon and replied as if to a member of the legislative Chamber which had just condemned that great man to the scaffold of St Helena. Clarity and fidelity to the truth compel the author to introduce himself as an actor in the scenes he describes. It will readily be agreed, however, that it must be modesty rather than pride which can bring him to name himself on the same page as Lord Byron. I had spent the previous night reading the *Corsair*. Despite this, however, I had vowed never to speak with anything but the coldness I owed it to myself to maintain when speaking to a colleague of Lord Bathurst.

It was because I kept my vow that Lord Byron began after a few days to show me such marked kindness. One evening, however, for no apparent reason at all, he spoke to me about the immorality of the French character. I replied with firmness. I spoke of the prison-ships in which French prisoners of war were tortured, of the Russian emperors whose death always happens to be so advantageous to the interests of Great Britain, of the infernal machine, etc., etc. It was thought by those who overheard us that, after what I had so politely and even so respectfully pointed out, Lord Byron would never speak to me again. The day after, however, he took me by the arm and we walked up and down for an hour through the immense, empty ante-rooms and halls of the Scala. He wanted to ask an eye-witness a hundred questions concerning the Moscow campaign; he wished to ascertain the truth by embarrassing me, and what I underwent was in fact a cross-examination, though I did not realise it at the time. The following night I was in ecstasies re-reading *Childe Harold*. I had become enamoured of Lord Byron.

He had had no success, however, among the twelve or fifteen Italians who met every evening in M. de Brême's box. It has to be confessed that one day he gave us to understand in the course of some argument or other—about what I have since forgotten—that he was right and that he was right because he was a peer and a nobleman. This impertinence did not go down at all, and M. de Brême recalled the anecdote of General de Castries, who, shocked by the attention being paid to d'Alembert, cried, 'The man is reasoning and yet he doesn't even have an income of a thousand *écus* a year!'

My Italian friends found Lord Byron haughty, eccentric, and even a little insane.

He was particularly absurd one evening, when he protested against the suggestion that he resembled in any way at all Jean-Jacques Rousseau, with whom a newspaper had recently compared him. His main reason, which he took care to conceal and yet which made him furious, was that Rousseau had been a servant. Furthermore, he was the son of a watch-maker. We laughed heartily when, at the end of the discussion, he asked M. de Brême, who belonged to one of the best families in Turin, for details concerning the household of the Govon family in which Jean-Jacques had been employed.

As it happened, Lord Byron's character had much in common with that of Rousseau. Like Rousseau, he was constantly preoccupied with himself and with the effect he produced on others. Hence his marked hatred for Shakespeare; I believe furthermore that he even despised him for having been able to transform himself into Shylock, a vile Venetian Jew, or Jack Cade, a contemptible demagogue.

One of Lord Byron's principal horrors was that of growing fat. It had become an obsession with him.

M. Polidori, a young doctor who was travelling with him at the time, told us that Lord Byron's mother was small and very dumpy. I must confess that, whenever Byron had just left us, we would spend our time dissecting his character; I had grown to admire the very Italian finesse and perceptiveness of my friends and their ability to see through every appearance. While analysing the character of the great poet who had fallen among us like a bomb, we decided that, for a third of the day, he was simply a dandy, a dandy who was afraid of growing fat, who sought to conceal his right foot which was slightly turned in, and whose ambition was to be attractive to women. His vanity in these matters was so morbid and so excessive, however, that he ended up by sacrificing the end to the means. If love had interfered with his horse-riding, he would have given up the former rather than the latter. In Milan and even more in Venice, some months later, the beauty of his eyes and hair, together with his literary reputation, gave rise to the beginnings of passion among several young ladies who were very young, of very noble birth, and beyond any doubt, very beautiful. One of them travelled more than a hundred miles in order to be present a masked ball which she knew he was to attend. He was told this, and, either through pride or timidity, did not even deign to notice her. 'He is a mere boor!' she was heard to cry as she left him. A failure on his part with a woman of the leading circles of society would have made him die of wounded vanity. As a result of the various pettinesses of English civilisation, he paid court only to the sort of woman for whom the wealth of her lover constitutes his greatest merit.

Not content with being the most handsome man in England, Lord Byron would have liked also to be the most fashionable. When he was being a dandy, he would pronounce the name of Brummel with a quiver of adoration and jealousy. Brummel was the king of fashion in England from 1796 to 1810; his existence was perhaps the most curious that the eighteenth century produced in England, or perhaps in all Europe. This fallen king ended his days in Calais.

When Lord Byron was not thinking of his appearance, it was often because he was thinking of his noble birth. Once, with a simulated and comic good nature, our young Italian friends discussed in his presence whether Henri IV could justly be described as a merciful king after his former comrade-in-arms, the Duc de Biron, had been beheaded on his orders. 'Napoleon would never have done such a thing', replied Lord Byron. What was amusing was to see that he would speak as if he were himself of much nobler birth than the Duc de

Biron and the next moment was obviously envious of the eminence of his family descent. The fact is that very few English families have produced a longer line of courageous warriors than the Birons.

When he was among men and women in whose presence the fatuity of birth and good looks could no longer be to his advantage, Lord Byron would suddenly become a great poet and *a man of sense*. His manner of speaking was never sententious or affected like Mme de Staël's, for instance, whom he had just left at Coppet and who soon afterwards arrived in Milan. If one spoke of literature, he was the opposite of an academician; the thoughts outnumbered the words and there was no striving after elegant phrases. Especially towards midnight, if ever the music of the Opera had moved him, he would speak without thinking of the effect he was producing on others, and would allow himself to be carried away by his emotions like a southern European.

What is so strange is that, in his own prose, he strives to affect wit, wit furthermore of the worst kind, the sort that makes continual allusions to some passage or other in the work of a classical author. I can assure the reader that nothing less resembled his tedious prose, worthy of Archdeacon Trublet, than his charming conversation when he was neither being fatuous nor insane. For I have to admit, and it is more an excuse for, than a condemnation of, this great man, that for a third of the time every week, he seemed to us to be out of his mind. Some claimed that he seemed to be out of his mind through remorse. Could it be, we would say, that in a fit of aristocratic or dandyish pride, he had discovered that a beautiful Greek slave was unfaithful to his bed and had blown out her brains?

Until Parliamentary reform or some other accident breaks down the tyranny imposed by means of the word *improper* on the outlook of ninety-five per cent of the English people, I shall not be in the least surprised to see that the Reviews have declared the 'Satanic' Byron to be capable of murder. These same unfortunate Reviews can only live and prosper if they are bought by the upper classes of society. And it can never be sufficiently imagined on the continent how much more aristocratic the leading circles of society are than those of our most celebrated ultras. An English duke, for instance, can never be ridiculous, whatever he does. This presents a considerable temptation. An academic poet called Southey has had the protection of the English aristocracy on account of the atrocious insults he has directed at Lord Byron. These were such that once at Pisa the latter was on the point of taking a coach and returning to England to fire a pistol at their author. 'Take care', a friend warned him. 'The aristocracy will pay any bad poet it can find and buy his works, as long as it can be sure in return of disturbing the repose of the author of *Don Juan.*'

As far as I can see, the English aristocracy would find it a profitable undertaking to pay out ten million francs and secure the annihilation of this poem. In its insane fury, it even protested against the Lord Chancellor's authorising the bookseller who had printed *Don Juan* to sue the publishers of pirated editions. The result of this folly is that England is now inundated with editions of *Don Juan* which can be bought for two shillings instead of twelve or eighteen shillings. This divine poem provides a cruel antagonist to Paley's theology.

It is entertaining to witness anger which, in the excess of fury and blindness, prejudices its own interests. I see no reason why society should not proclaim Byron to be an assassin. The bill of indictment could be found in his memoirs which Mr Moore has just sold to Murray the bookseller for six thousand pounds.

STENDHAL

In his journal, Lord Byron alludes to an event the memory of which disturbs his sleep and causes him hideous agitation. 'I composed the *Bride of Abydos* in four nights', he writes, 'in order to ward off my dreams of ★★★★. If I had not undertaken this task, I would have gone mad with grief.'[1] Further on, we read: 'I awoke from a dream! —well!—and have not others dreamed?—Such a dream!—but she did not overtake me. I wish the dead would rest, however. Ugh! how my blood chilled—and I could not awake—and—and heigho!

'Shadows to-night
Have struck more terror to the soul of Richard
Than could the substance of ten thousand ★★★s
Arm'd all in proof, and led by shallow ★★★.'

I do not like this dream—I hate its "foregone conclusion". And am I to be shaken by shadows? Ay, when they remind us of —no matter—but if I dream thus again, I will try whether *all* sleep has the like visions.'[2] He adds: 'He [Hobhouse, who is mentioned above] told me an odd report, that *I* am the actual Conrad, the veritable Corsair, and that part of my travels are supposed to have passed in privacy. Um!—people sometimes hit near the truth; but never the whole truth. H. don't know what I was about the year after he left the Levant, nor does any one—nor—nor—nor—however, it is a lie—but "I doubt the equivocation of the fiend that lies like truth!"'[3]

---

[1] This is a translation from Stendhal's French. Everything seems to indicate that it is a misquotation of Byron based on a faulty recollection of the text. It has been suggested to me by Mr D. A. Matthews of the Westminster Central Library that the passage to which Stendhal is referring is the following entry in Lord Byron's diary dated November 14th, 1813 (See *The Works of Lord Byron: with his letters and journals and his life by Thomas Moore, Esq.* 1832-33, volume 2, page 254): 'No more reflections.—Let me see—last night I finished *Zuleika*, my second Turkish Tale. I believe the composition kept me alive—for it was written to drive my thoughts from the recollection of—
"Dear sacred name, rest ever unreveal'd."
At least, even here my hand would tremble to write it.' (Editor's note.)

[2] *The works of Lord Byron: with his letters and journals and his life by Thomas Moore, Esq.*, 17 volumes, 1832-33; volume 2, page 270.

[3] *Ibid*, volume 3, page 12.

Mr Moore offers no explanation of these passages. This astute writer probably failed to realise that these few lines would provide every priest in England and America with a text for his sermons.

What does it matter to Lord Byron, however? Society can stifle a great man; but once he is known, he has an open account with posterity. Greece is about to become a civilised country; it was perhaps in 1811 that Lord Byron played the rôle of Othello. At Athens in 1811 in the Franciscan monastery, he knew moments of insanity, as we can tell from what he said to one of the monks. If there is anything true in such an idea, there are hundreds of witnesses who could be called upon if necessary, and posterity sooner or later will know if his remorse was real, or if it was simply one more affectation.

Is Othello to be despised for having once given in to the atrocious grief of jealousy?

After all, Lord Byron was so easily swayed by emotion when he was not being a dandy that it is very possible that his remorse over a fault committed in his youth had become exaggerated in his mind. The opinion of the twelve jurymen whom fate had brought together in M. de Brême's box was that the crime which sometimes made his handsome eyes seem so wild and haggard had been committed against a woman. On one particular evening, the discussion concerned a beautiful woman, an inhabitant of Milan, who had tried to fight a duel with a lover who had just left her. The conversation turned to a prince who had unceremoniously killed a woman of the lower classes with whom he lived and whom he had discovered to be unfaithful. Lord Byron kept an unbroken silence; he attempted for some time to contain himself, and at last walked out of the box in a rage. If this was fury, it was fury against himself and it absolved him in our eyes. This crime, whatever it was, seems to me of the same kind as the theft of a ribbon committed by Rousseau during his residence as a servant in Turin. Among the men who have some knowledge of the things of this world and who do not confine their experience to what can be talked of in a drawing-room, is there one who, because of this, would declare that Rousseau is less to be esteemed than the immense majority of honest men? It is true that, about the year 1815, a certain modern writer assumed the responsibility of changing the ribbon into a silver service. The assistance rendered by this discovery to the good cause has almost certainly not gone unrewarded; but this is merely one example of the sort of confidence we will be able to place in the merely commonplace historian, as long as a certain party is in power. This party persecutes with its hatred the Emperor Julian, Jean-Jacques Rousseau, Lord Byron and, in fact, all the men who have laughed at hypocrisy with some semblance of success.

Few weeks had gone by before Lord Byron seemed to find society in Milan very much to his taste. Milan is the one town which, since the turn of the century, has not banished good-heartedness from its social relationships. Often, after the evening's performance at the Scala, we would stop in the vestibule and watch the pretty women going by. Few towns have ever possessed an assemblage of beauty to be compared with that which chance had brought together in Milan in the year 1817. Several of them expected Lord Byron to ask to be presented to them. Out of timidity or pride, however, or rather a dandyish desire to do always the opposite of what was expected of him, he always declined this honour. He preferred to spend the evening discussing poetry or philosophy. I remember that we expressed our opinions with such vehemence that the entire pit would sometimes indignantly order us to be quiet.

One evening, at the height of a philosophical discussion on

the principle of *utility*, M. Silvio Pellico, a poet of great charm who has since died in an Austrian prison, came and told Lord Byron that his doctor, M. Polidori, had just been arrested.

We made our way at once to the guard-room. It seemed that M. Polidori, who was very good-looking and very tall, had been scandalised by the bearskin of the officer of the guard which, from where he sat in the pit, had prevented him from seeing the stage and the singers. He had therefore asked the officer to take it off. The fact is that, despite his Italian name, M. Polidori had been born in England and had frequent need, as a result, of someone on whom to vent his spleen.

The great poet Monti had joined us in the guard-room of the theatre and soon there were fifteen or twenty of us round the prisoner. Everyone was talking at once; M. Polidori was beside himself with rage and red as a furnace. As for Lord Byron, he was very pale and keeping his temper with great difficulty. His patrician heart was torn to see how little power or consideration he enjoyed. He was almost certainly regretting for a moment the political opinions which prevented him from being admitted to the dinners and to the intimacy of the Archduke Viceroy of Milan. That is, in any case, how we construed his rage. As for the Austrian officer, however, he very probably saw in us a centre of sedition; perhaps, if he was at all well read, memories of the insurrection of Genoa in 1740 were going through his mind. In any case, Monti saw him run out of the guard-room to call his soldiers, who immediately took up their rifles, which they had placed outside the door. Monti then had an excellent idea: 'Sortiamo tutti; restino solamente i titolati', he said; that is, 'Let us all go out; only those of us who have titles stay inside.'

Monsignor de Brême stayed with the Marquis di Sartirana, his brother, Count Confalonieri and Lord Byron. These gentlemen then wrote down their names. On seeing their titles, the officer of the guard forgot the insult to his bearskin and allowed M. Polidori to leave. Without his headpiece, which was perhaps thirty inches tall, we found that he made a puny figure beside M. Polidori, a fine-looking man of five foot six; he himself was only five feet tall.[1] Vanity alone would have prevented many an officer of the guard in a similar situation from releasing his prisoner.

That very evening at midnight, M. Polidori received an order to leave Milan within twenty-four hours. He was furious and swore that sooner or later he would come back and provoke the governor who had expelled him in this way to a duel. He never carried out his vow and two years afterwards poisoned himself with a full bottle of prussic acid. At least, *sic dicitur*.

The morning after M. Polidori's departure, Lord Byron, with whom I found myself alone in the huge dark foyer of the Scala, complained with all seriousness of the persecution inflicted on him. 'At Coppet', he cried, his teeth clenched with rage and as if talking to himself, 'whenever I came in one door of a drawing-room, all the silly geese from England and Geneva went out through the other.' The last words were pronounced less distinctly, and out of consideration for his grief and rage, his interlocutor withdrew to some distance. On his approaching a second time, Lord Byron complained once more, but this time in more moderate and general terms. His interlocutor had so imperfect a knowledge of *i titolati*, to use Monti's phrase, that he naïvely made the following suggestion: 'Get together four or five hundred thousand francs, and then spread the rumour of your own death; two or three faithful friends will bury a piece of wood in some remote corner of Elba, for instance. The official account

---

[1] The 'feet' are the pre-Revolutionary French measurement. The equivalent English heights would be, roughly, five foot five and five foot eleven inches. (Editor's note.)

of your death will reach England, and during this time, you will assume the name of Smith or Dubois and live in peace and happiness in Lima. Nothing can prevent Mr Smith from coming back to Europe, even when his hair is white, or from buying in any bookshop in Paris or Rome, the thirtieth edition of *Childe Harold* or *Lara*. When he comes to die his real death, he will be able to enjoy an unique and glorious moment: "The Lord Byron who is reported to have been dead for thirty years", he will say, "is in reality myself. English society seemed to me so intolerably stupid, that I decided to have nothing more to do with it." '

'My cousin, who is to inherit my title, would owe you a very sincere letter of thanks', was Lord Byron's rather chilly reply.

The interlocutor, who had perhaps been indiscreet, restrained himself from making a cutting rejoinder of his own. Lord Byron probably suffered from the unhappiness which is not uncommon among those who are used to being treated as the spoilt children of fortune; he nurtured two conflicting desires —and this itself is an immense and inevitable source of unhappiness: did he not long to be accepted in society as an aristocrat, and at the same time be admired as a great poet?

Now society has never really any mercy to spare for those who write. Perhaps it was different in the days of the great Corneille; yet Corneille was nothing more than 'that excellent old man Corneille' (*le bonhomme Corneille*) in the eyes of the noble Dangeau, as we can read in his memoirs. On the evening after our conversation, Lord Byron, who was for the moment in a loyal mood, was extremely grateful to me for speaking highly of the Grand Duke of Tuscany, who, as it happened, deserved what I said.

Elena, an opera by the aged Mayer, was being performed at the time in Milan. The public would put up with the first two acts, which were altogether mediocre, in order to enjoy one sublime sextet, which comes towards the middle. One day, when it was being sung better than usual, I was struck by the look in Lord Byron's eyes; I have never seen anything so fine. If a woman had seen him at that instant, she would have fallen passionately in love with him. I made a vow that I would never again give pain to a man of so beautiful a mind and spirit by using, in his presence, one of those wary, carefully chosen phrases by which we protect our national and individual pride. I have noted somewhere that, on the same evening, we came round to speaking about a curious sonnet by Tasso, where he reveals himself as a sceptic.

> Odi, Filli, che tuona ...
> Ma che cura dobbiam che faccia Giove?
> Godiam noi qui, s'egli è turbato in cielo.
> Tema il volgo i suoi tuoni ...
> Pera il mondo, e rovini! a me non cale
> Se non di quel che più piace e diletta;
> Che, se terra sarò; terra ancor fui.[1]

'These lines are the result of a fit of bad temper and nothing more', said Lord Byron. 'Tasso's tender soul and wild imagination both made him depend on the idea of God. His head was too encumbered with Platonic theories to see the relation between two or three difficult arguments. ... When he wrote this sonnet, Tasso was feeling conscious of his genius, and probably was in need of bread and a mistress.'

With these words, Byron knocked at the door of his inn, and we were forced, to our great regret, to leave him; even the distrustful Italians were under his spell. Lord Byron's inn was half a league from the Scala, on the edge of a deserted quarter

---

[1] Listen, Phyllis, to the thunder. ... But what does it matter to us what Jove does? Let us make merry here if he is troubled in Heaven. Let the vulgar fear his thundering. ... Let the world perish and fall in ruins. I care only for what pleases and delights me; for if I am to become as earth, then earth I always was.

of the city. There were a great many thieves, and to reach it at two o'clock in the morning one had to make one's way alone through a number of highly sinister little streets.

This lent a certain romance to the noble Lord's retreat. I cannot understand how it was that he was never attacked; I feel sure, in any case, that he would have felt extremely humiliated at being relieved of his possessions, if only because of the highly amusing tricks which the thieves were in the habit of playing on the unfortunate pedestrians who were their victims. If ever it was cold and you were going along the street wrapped up in your cloak, the thief would approach softly from behind, pass a metal hoop over your head, imprison your arms and then rob you at his leisure.

M. Polidori told us that often Lord Byron would write a hundred lines in a single morning. In the evening, on returning from the theatre, stirred by the talk or the music, he would go back to his manuscript and, working sometimes until daybreak, reduce his hundred lines to twenty or thirty. As soon as he had four or five hundred, he would send them to Mr Murray, his bookseller in London. When he worked at night, he would drink a sort of grog, made with brandy, juniper and water. It is certainly true that, when his ideas failed him, he would drink more of this grog than usual, but this was yet another vice which he exaggerated out of self-accusation; he was by no means an immoderate drinker in reality. Often, in order not to put on weight, he would miss one of his meals and make do with a single plate of vegetables and a little bread. This frugal dinner cost a franc or two, and so Lord Byron took advantage of what might seem like another vice and boasted of being a miser.

M. Polidori had given us a number of details concerning Lord Byron's marriage. The young heiress who was his bride had all the vanity and much of the stupidity of an only child.

She expected to live the brilliant life of a distinguished lady and found instead nothing but a man of genius who wished neither to command in his own house nor be commanded himself. Lady Byron was irritated by her husband's indifference, and a malicious servant, who was alarmed at her master's eccentric behaviour, spoke to her in a way which embittered her even further; it was at this point that she left him. Society promptly seized on what seemed a favourable pretext for *excommunicating* this great man, and was immediately successful in poisoning his existence.

It was perhaps to this state of perpetual anger and unhappiness that he owed his weakness for music, which would soothe his chagrin by making him shed tears. He was truly sensitive to beautiful music, but with the sensitiveness of a man to whom it is something new. After listening to operas for a year or two, he would have been wildly excited over pieces which, in 1816, gave him no pleasure at all, and that he even condemned as insignificant or distorted.

I have just learned that Lady Byron, or else some priest or other in her name, is about to reply to Mr Moore's recent book. So much the better. If there should be discord among the burners of original testimonies, it will soon be clear to the public what sort of people they were into whose hands Lord Byron had the misfortune to fall.

Byron had all the charm and spontaneous gaiety of a child one day when we went to visit the echo of La Simonetta, two miles out of Milan, which has been made famous by the *Encyclopaedia* and which re-echoes a pistol shot thirty or forty times.

The next day, nevertheless, he was as sombre as Talma in *Britannicus* on his arrival at a large ceremonious dinner given in his honour by Monsignor de Brême. He was the last to arrive, and was obliged to cross an immense drawing-room limping on his twisted foot and watched by every eye. Far from being detached and *blasé*, like a true dandy, he was ceaselessly agitated by some new passion. When the more noble passions left him, an insane vanity, irritated by the slightest pretext, tormented him instead. And yet, if his genius awoke, all was forgotten, the poet was in another world and drew us with him. What divine poetry he gave us one night, when talking of the life of Castruccio Castracani, the Napoleon of the middle ages! We had taken him to see the white marble spires of Milan Cathedral by moonlight.

He suffered from one of the weaknesses of the man of letters: an extreme sensitiveness to praise or blame, especially when they came from fellow-writers. He failed to see that the latter are always dictated by affectation, and that even the best of them can only ever be a *testimonial* of conformity to the truth.

My Italian friends, who were merciless towards him, had noticed that he was as proud as a little boy of the number of languages that he spoke, or rather imagined that he spoke. A genuine scholar of Greek, one who was *not* a charlatan, sometimes joined us in M. de Brême's box. He told us that, in fact, Lord Byron spoke both modern and ancient Greek very badly. The same was true of his knowledge of history, despite his pretensions to the contrary.

I had nearly forgotten to talk of the astonishing effect produced on Lord Byron by a painting in which Daniele Crespi has portrayed a canon lying in his bier in the middle of a church and who, while the office of the dead is being sung around him, suddenly raises the shroud, rises to his feet and cries: 'Justo judicio damnatus sum.' ('I am damned and the judgment of God is just.')

We were unable to tear Byron away from this painting; we saw that he was moved by it to horror; out of the respect due to his genius, we silently remounted our horses and went off to wait for him at a spot which I believe was a mile away from the Charterhouse of Castellazzo, where Crespi has painted frescoes showing the life of St Bruno.[1]

Lord Byron merely laughed at us when we told him, for the first time, that there were ten Italian languages and not one; that two great living poets, Tomasso Grossi and Carline Porta, wrote in the language of Milan; that there was an excellent Italian-Milanese dictionary, and that, out of nineteen million Italians, only those who lived in Rome, Florence or Siena spoke the written language. That charming poet Silvio Pellico said one day to Byron, 'The most delightful of these ten or twelve Italian languages, whose existence is unsuspected north of the Alps, is Venetian. The Venetians are the Frenchman of Italy.'

'Have they any comic poet then who is writing at the moment?' Lord Byron asked.

'Yes', was the reply, 'and an excellent one; only as he finds it impossible to have his comedies performed, he writes them as satires. The name of this enchanting poet is Buratti, and every six months the governor of Venice sends him to prison.'

This conversation with Silvio Pellico was, I feel convinced, a decisive turning point in Lord Byron's poetic career. I have always suspected that inwardly he had a burning desire to see Paris; only he would have liked to be received there in the same way that Hume was in 1765 by the *Société Encyclopédique*.

He enquired enthusiastically for the name of the bookseller who sold the works of Signor Buratti. As he was by now accustomed to the good-humoured lack of ceremony of the

---

[1] In a letter that Lord Byron did me the honour of writing to me in 1823, in order to defend Sir Walter Scott against the charge of excessive servility, he recalls most of the men whom we had known in Milan in 1816 and whom events were to prove as ill-fated as they were loveable. I found a touch of *cant* in Lord Byron's letter, and, in order not to have to say something disagreeable to a man I loved, esteemed and respected, I did not reply. (For Lord Byron's letter, see Appendix H. Editor.)

Milanese, we allowed ourselves to laugh at him outright. He was made to realise that, if Signor Buratti wanted to spend his entire life in prison, there was one infallible means of doing so: that was, to publish. Where too would he find a printer bold enough to assume the responsibility for the publication?[1] Manuscripts, far from complete, cost three or four sequins. The next day the charming Contessina N. was good enough to lend one of us her own collection. Lord Byron, who imagined that he understood the Italian of Dante and Ariosto, at first made nothing of the verses he read. We therefore read over with him some comedies by Goldoni, and at last he set to work on the deliciously comic *Omo, Strofe*, etc. We were even indecent enough to lend him a copy of the *Baffo* sonnets. What a crime in the eyes of Southey! and what a shame that he never heard sooner of this atrocious deed!

It is my own opinion that Lord Byron only wrote *Beppo* and reached the full height of his poetic genius in *Don Juan* as a result of having read Buratti and seen the delicious pleasure which they gave to Venetian society. Venice is a world apart, whose existence is unsuspected by the rest of sad Europe. Signor Buratti's poems kindle a true intoxication in the hearts of its citizens. Never, in my own experience, has *black on white*, as the Venetians say, produced such an effect. But I can no longer see, and I must say nothing more.

Revue de Paris, March 1830

---

[1] Some long time afterwards, a Swiss was bold enough to print Signor Buratti's less spirited poems. (Note in the *Revue de Paris*).

WALTER SCOTT AND LA PRINCESSE DE CLEVES

These two names indicate the two extremes in the novel. Should the novelist describe the dress worn by the various characters, the landscape around them and their physiognomy, or would he do better to depict the passions and sentiments which agitate their souls? My reflections will not be welcome. An immense body of men of letters finds it in its own interest to praise Sir Walter Scott to the skies, together with his method of composition. The doublet and leather collar of a medieval serf are easier to describe than the movements of the human heart. One can either imagine or describe inaccurately medieval costume (we have only a half-knowledge of the customs and the dress worn in Cardinal Richelieu's ante-chamber); whereas we throw the book down in disgust if the author fails to describe the human heart, and ascribes, say, to an illustrious companion-in-arms of the son of Henri IV the ignoble sentiments of a lackey. Everyone recalls Voltaire's famous story. One day he was giving a lesson in tragic diction to a young actress, who recited a lively passage with the utmost coldness. 'But, my dear young lady', cried Voltaire. 'You ought to be acting as though the devil were in you. What would you do if a cruel tyrant had just separated you from your lover?' 'I should take another', was her reply.

I do not wish to suggest that all the makers of historical novels think as reasonably as this prudent young pupil of Voltaire's; but even the most susceptible among them will not suspect me of calumny if I say that it is infinitely easier to describe in picturesque detail a character's dress than to say what he feels and to make him speak. Let us not forget another advantage which is offered by the school of Sir Walter Scott: the description of the costume and posture of a character, however minor he may be, takes at least two pages. The movements of the heart, which, to begin with, are so difficult to discern and so difficult to describe with precision and without either timidity or exaggeration, would scarcely furnish a few lines. Open at random ten pages from one of the volumes of *La Princesse de Clèves*; then compare them with ten pages from *Ivanhoe* or *Quentin Durward*; it will be found that the latter display a *historical merit*.

They teach those who know little or nothing about history a number of minor details concerning the past. Their historical merit has already given great pleasure. I do not wish to deny this, only it is the historical merit which will grow old the soonest. The century will move towards a more true and natural form of expression; and the mannered approximations of Sir Walter Scott will one day seem as distasteful as they at first seemed charming. Perhaps it would be wise if I were to develop these rapid hints and say something more of the future destiny of the fashionable novel.

See what a crowd of men and women have found it in their interest to maintain that Sir Walter Scott is a great man. Despite their numbers, I have no intention of borrowing the mask of hypocrisy which the nineteenth century finds so fashionable. I shall pronounce with all frankness my conviction that, in ten years time, the reputation of the Scottish novelist will have declined by half. Richardson's fame in France was equal to Scott's. Diderot used to say, 'In exile or prison I would ask for only three books: Homer, the Bible, and *Clarissa Harlowe*.' Like Sir Walter Scott, Richardson had a more distinguished reputation in Paris than in England.

Every work of art is a charming lie; anyone who has written knows this well. There is nothing more ridiculous than the advice commonly given to the writer in society: 'Imitate nature.' Confound it, I know that the writer should imitate nature, but to what extent? That is the whole question. Two men of equal genius, Racine and Shakespeare, have depicted, one of them Iphigenia at the moment when her father is about to sacrifice her in Aulis, the other the young Imogen at the moment when a husband she adores is about to have her stabbed somewhere in the mountain country near Milford Haven.

These great poets have both imitated nature; but one wished to amuse country gentlemen who still had the rough stern frankness which was the fruit of the long Wars of the Roses. The other sought the applause of the polite courtiers who, imitating the genteel forms established by Lauzun and the Marquis de Vardes, wished to win favour in the eyes of the king and the general approval of the ladies. 'Imitate nature' is therefore meaningless advice. To what extent must one imitate nature if one is to give pleasure to the reader? This is the main question.

I think that I should insist on one childish detail. If all that had been said at Aulis when Iphigenia was about to be murdered had been taken down on paper and preserved, we would possess five or six volumes, even if we confined ourselves to what was said by the principal characters of Racine's play. It was first necessary to reduce these six volumes to eighty pages. Furthermore, most of what was said by Agamemnon and Calchas would be unintelligible today and, even if we did understand it, would fill us with horror.

Art, then, is nothing more than a charming lie; only Sir Walter Scott has been too much of a liar. He would give greater pleasure to those higher natures who ultimately decide the fate of all literature, if, in his portrayal of the passions, he had admitted a greater number of natural traits. His characters, when they are moved by passion, seem ashamed of themselves, altogether like Mlle Mars when she is playing the part of a stupid, frivolous woman. When she comes on to the stage, this great actress glances meaningfully at the audience with a look that seems to say: 'Now don't go away thinking that I am nothing but a silly goose myself. I've got my wits about me just as much as you have. I merely want you to tell me one thing: in order to give you pleasure and deserve your applause, this being my greatest desire, I have chosen to impersonate this sort of woman. Have I succeeded or not?'

One would say of a painter who displayed this fault, which is to be found in both Scott and Mlle Mars, that his colours lacked freshness and were unnatural.

I will go even further. The more elevated the sentiments which Walter Scott's characters have to express, the less they are bold or confident. I am forced to confess this and it is this which I find most painful in what I have to say about the author and his work. One sees here all the experience and wiliness of an old judge. This is the man who, having been admitted to the table of George IV, when the latter was visiting Edinburgh, enthusiastically asked for the glass in which the King had just drunk the health of his people. Sir Walter Scott was given the precious goblet and placed it in his overcoat pocket. On returning home, however, forgetting this honour for an instant, he threw down his coat and broke the glass, an accident which threw him into despair. Would the elderly Corneille or the excellent Ducis have understood such feelings? In a hundred and forty-six years time, Scott will be less esteemed than Corneille still is a hundred and forty-six years after his death.

Le National, February 19th, 1830

Appendix A

In saying that it is ridiculous for Emilie to talk of a conspiracy against Auguste in Auguste's own imperial apartments, Stendhal is guilty of an injustice to Corneille and a misunderstanding of Corneille's stage directions. In *L'Examen de Cinna*, Corneille takes care to point out that 'La moitié de la pièce se passe chez Emilie, et l'autre dans le cabinet d'Auguste. J'aurois été ridicule si j'avais prétendu que cet empereur délibérât avec Maxime et Cinna s'il quitteroit l'empire ou non, précisément dans la même place où ce dernier vient de se rendre compte à Emilie de la conspiration qu'il a formée contre lui. . . . Emilie ne parle donc pas où parle Auguste, à la réserve du cinquième acte; mais cela n'empêche pas qu'a considérer tout le poëme ensemble, il n'aye son unité de lieu, puisque tout s'y peut passer, non seulement dans Rome ou dans un quartier de Rome, mais dans le seul palais d'Auguste, pourvu que vous y vouliez donner un appartement à Emilie qui soit éloigné du sien.' ('Half of the action of the play takes place in Emilie's apartments, the other half in one of the rooms belonging to Auguste. It would have been ridiculous for me to pretend that Auguste deliberates whether he shall give up the empire or not with Maxime and Cinna, in the very place where the latter has just given an account to Emilie of the conspiracy he has formed against him. . . . Emilie therefore never speaks in the same place as Auguste, except in the fifth act; nevertheless, the poem preserves the unity of place, if one takes it as a whole; for every action can be considered as taking place, not only in Rome or in a single neighbourhood of Rome, but simply in Auguste's palace, provided that you are willing to allow Emilie an apartment at a certain distance from his.') Corneille makes the same justification of this apparent violation of the Unities in the third of his discourses on dramatic art ('Des Unités') to which Stendhal refers.

The point is a very minor one and obviously does nothing to detract from Stendhal's essential criticisms. Even in the passages quoted above, Corneille's ideas of dramatic verisimilitude suggest an extremely limiting conventionality. They seem limiting above all when one contrasts them with the powerful feeling for what is dramatically significant which comes out in Stendhal's analysis of *Cinna* and his references to *Macbeth*. Stendhal is most explicit over what he thinks about the quarrel of the Unities in the *Racine et Shakespeare* (1823-25), where he employs the arguments of Johnson in the *Preface to Shakespeare* and translates, almost word for word, without acknowledging its origin, the following well-known passage:

> The truth is that the spectators are always in their senses and know from the first act to the last, that the stage is only a stage and that the players are only players. They come to hear a certain number of lines recited with just gesture and elegant modulation. The lines relate to some action and an action must be in some place; but the different actions that complete a story may be in places very remote from each other; and where is the absurdity of allowing that space to represent first *Athens* and then *Sicily* which was always known to be neither *Sicily* nor *Athens* but a modern theatre?

Appendix B

> Impatients désirs d'une illustre vengeance
> Dont la mort de mon père a formé la naissance,
> Enfants impétueux de mon ressentiment
> Que ma douleur séduite embrassse aveuglément,
> Vous prenez sur mon âme un trop puissant empire:
> Durant quelques moments souffrez que je respire,
> Et que je considère en l'état où je suis,
> Et ce que je hasarde et ce que je poursuis.
>
> *Cinna*, Act I, scene i, lines 1-8.

(Impatient desires of an illustrious vengeance, engendered by the death of my father, impetuous children of my resentment that my seduced grief blindly embraces, you have come to hold too powerful a sway over my soul: give me a few moments in which to breathe and in which to consider what I am hazarding, while I am in this state of mind and what it is I seek.)

Appendix C

> Toute cette faveur ne me rend pas mon père;
> Et de quelque point de vue que l'on me considère,
> Abondante en richesse, ou puissante en crédit,
> Je demeure toujours la fille d'un proscrit.
>
> *Cinna*, Act I, scene ii, lines 69-72.

(All this favour does not give me back my father; and, however you consider my present situation, whether you consider my abundant wealth or the powerful favour I enjoy, I still remain the daughter of an outlaw.)

Appendix D

Quoi? je le haïrai sans tâcher de lui nuire?
J'attendrai du hasard qu'il ose le détruire?
Et je satisferai des devoirs si pressants
Par une haine obscure et des voeux impuissants?
Sa perte, que je veux, me deviendroit amère,
Si quelqu'un l'immolât à d'autres qu'à mon père;
Et tu verrois mes pleurs couler pour son trépas,
Qui le faisant périr, ne me vengeroit pas.
C'est une lâcheté que de remettre à d'autres
Les intérêts publics qui s'attachent aux nôtres.
Joignons à la douceur de venger nos parents
La gloire qu'on remporte à punir les tyrans,
Et faisons publier par toute l'Italie:
'La Liberté de Rome est l'oeuvre d'Emilie;
On a touché son âme et son coeur s'est épris;
Mais elle n'a donné son amour qu'à ce prix.

Cinna, Act I, scene ii, lines 97-112.

(What? Shall I hate him and yet not seek to do him harm? Shall I merely wait for chance to destroy him? And shall I satisfy such an urgent duty by an obscure hatred and impotent desires? His downfall, which I long for, would overwhelm me with bitterness if he were sacrificed to anyone but my father; and you would see my tears flow for his death, if I knew he had perished without my being avenged. It is cowardice to make others responsible for the public interest when it is at the same time our own. Let us unite with the joy of avenging our parents the glory we win when we punish a tyrant, and let it be known throughout all Italy that Rome's liberty is the work of Emilie; her soul has been stirred and her heart has been moved to love; yet she has given her love only at this price.)

Appendix E

FULVIE

Votre amour à ce prix n'est qu'un présent funeste
Qui porte à votre amant sa perte manifeste,
Pensez mieux, Emilie, a quoi vous l'exposez,
Combien à cet écueil se sont déjà brisés;
Ne vous aveuglez point quand sa mort est visible.

STENDHAL

EMILIE
Ah! tu sais me frapper par où je suis sensible.
Quand je songe aux dangers que je lui fais courir,
La crainte de sa mort me fait déjà mourir;
Mon esprit en désordre à soi-même s'oppose:
Je veux et ne veux pas, je m'emporte et je n'ose;
Et mon devoir confus, languissant, étonné,
Cède aux rebellions de mon coeur mutiné.
Cinna, Act I, scene ii, lines 113-124.

(*Fulvie:* At this price, your love is only a deadly offering which will bring about your lover's evident downfall. Think again, Emilie, to what you are exposing him, how many others have been broken on this reef. Do not blind yourself when his death is visible.
Emilie: Ah! you know the most vulnerable spot at which to strike me. When I think of the dangers he is running for my sake, fear of his death makes me die too; my bewildered mind turns against itself; I wish and yet I do not wish, I am carried away and yet I dare do nothing. And duty, languishing, confused and astounded gives in to the rebellions of my mutinous heart.)

Appendix F

Je les peins dans le meutre à l'envi triomphants,
Rome entière noyée au sang de ses enfants:
Les uns assassinés dans les places publiques,
Les autres dans le sein de leurs dieux domestiques;
Le méchant par le prix au crime encouragé;
Le mari par sa femme en son lit égorgé;
Le fils tout dégouttant du meurtre de son père,
Et sa tête à la main demandant son salaire,
Sans pouvoir exprimer par tant d'horribles traits
Qu'un crayon imparfait de leur sanglante paix.
Cinna, Act I, scene iii, lines 195-204.

(I paint them striving to outdo each other and triumphant in murder, the whole of Rome drowned in its children's blood; some assassinated in the public places, others in the bosom of their household gods; the evil man enticed to crime by gold; the husband's throat cut by his wife as he lies in bed; the son dripping with his father's murder, and asking for his wages as he holds the head in his hand. Yet, despite so many hideous strokes, I am unable to give more than an imperfect sketch of their bloody peace.)

APPENDICES

Appendix G

Voilà, belle Emilie, à quel point nous en sommes.
Demain j'attends la haine ou la faveur des hommes,
Le nom de parricide ou de libérateur,
César celui de prince ou d'un usurpateur.

Cinna, Act I, scene iii, lines 249-53.

(This then, fair Emilie, is where we stand. Tomorrow I am ready for men's hatred or their acclaim, the name of parricide or that of liberator, Caesar the prince or Caesar the usurper.)

Appendix H

Letter from Lord Byron to Stendhal

Genoa, May 29th, 1823

Sir,

At present, that I know to whom I am indebted for a very flattering mention in the *Rome, Naples and Florence*, in 1817, by Mons. Stendhal, it is fit that I should return my thanks (however undesired or undesirable) to Mons. Beyle, with whom I had the honour of being acquainted at Milan in 1816. You only did me too much honour in what you were pleased to say in that work; but it has hardly given me less pleasure than the praise itself, to become at length aware (which I have done by mere accident) that I am indebted for it to one of whose good opinion I was really ambitious. So many changes have taken place since that period in the Milan circle, that I hardly dare recur to it;—some dead, some banished, and some in the Austrian dungeons.—Poor Pellico! I trust that, in his iron solitude, his Muse is consoling him in part—one day to delight us again, when both she and her Poet are restored to freedom.

Of your works I have only seen *Rome*, etc., the lives of Haydn and Mozart, and the *brochure* on Racine and Shakespeare. The *Histoire de la Peinture* I have not yet had the good fortune to possess.

There is one part of your observations in the pamphlet which I shall venture to remark upon;—it regards Walter Scott. You say that 'his character is little worthy of enthusiasm', at the same time that you mention his productions in the manner they deserve. I have known Walter Scott long and well, and in occasional situations which call forth the *real* character —and I can assure you that his character *is* worthy of admiration—that of all men he is the most *open*, the most *honourable*, the most *amiable*. With his politics I have nothing to do: they differ from mine, which renders it difficult for me to speak of them. But he is *perfectly sincere* in them: and Sincerity may be humble, but she cannot be servile. I pray you, therefore, to correct or soften that passage. You may, perhaps, attribute this officiousness of mine to a false affectation of *candour*, as I happen to be a writer also. Attribute it to what motive you please, but *believe the truth*. I say that Walter Scott is as nearly a thorough good man as man can be, because I *know* it by experience to be the case.

If you do me the honour of an answer, may I request a speedy one?—because it is possible (though not yet decided) that circumstances may conduct me once more to Greece. My present address is Genoa, where an answer will reach me in a short time, or be forwarded to me wherever I may be.

I beg you to believe me, with a lively recollection of our brief acquaintance, and the hope of one day renewing it,

Your ever obliged
And obedient humble servant,
NOEL BYRON.

Appendix J

The lines quoted by Stendhal from *L'Orlando Innamorato* are not to be found in most modern editions of the poem. It is almost certain that they are not by Boiardo but by Francesco Berni, whose additions to and alterations of the original text (*Orlando Innamorato* di Matteo M. Boiardo, rifatto da Francesco Berni) are to be found in all but a few of the eighteenth century and early nineteenth century editions.

Appendix K

Lord Norbury's pun on the word 'line' is one of the many for which he was notorious. Chief Justice of the Court of Common Pleas in Ireland from 1800 until 1827, he was known, according to the *Dictionary of National Biography*, for his 'scanty knowledge of law, his gross partiality, his callousness and his buffoonery ... His court was in a constant uproar owing to his noisy merriment. He joked even when the life of a human being was hanging in the balance.'

Index

Abbaye de Belle Chasse, 170
Abelard, Peter, 154
Académie Française, 91, 103, 163, 203, 207-23
Acerbi, Giuseppe, 77
Adelchi (Manzoni), 81
Adolphe (Constant), 29, 70-1
Adrian, Emperor, 219, 220
Aiguillon, Armand Richelieu, Duc de, 229
Albano, Cardinal, 58
D'Alembert, Jean, 305
Alexander I (of Russia), 184, 212, 223
Alfieri, Cesare, 61-2, 80, 87n.
Algarotti, Il Conte Francesco, 57, 62, 65
D'Aligre, Etienne, 228
Amants Chiens, Les (Carmontelle), 121
Ambrogi, Anton, 113
Ancelot, Jacques, 44
Antologia, La (literary review), 76, 81
Antoninus, Emperor, 219, 220
L'Ape (literary review), 79
L'Arcadico (literary review), 79
Ariosto, Luigi, 61, 76, 80, 82, 87n., 100, 105, 321
Aristarch, The, 3n., 292-4
Arlincourt, Charles, Vicomte de, 221
Armida (Rossini), 110, 115, 129
Astros, Paul-Thérèse, Bishop of Bayonne, 144-5
Atala (Chateaubriand), 218, 222
Athenaeum, The (literary review), 1
Attila, 84, 222
L'Auberge des Adrets (Leclercq), 132
Aubernon, Mme Philippe de, 1
Augereau, General Pierre, Duc de Castiglione, 186
Auger, Louis, 208, 210, 214
Augustulus, Emperor, 216, 222
Augustus, Emperor, 219

Baffo (Buratti), 321
Balzac, Honoré de, 4, 13n.
Baour-Lormian, Pierre, 47, 64
Barante, Guillaume, Duc de, 89, 211
Barbaia, Domenico (impresario), 110
Barber of Seville (Rossini), 100, 108-10, 112, 114, 116
Barry, Marie, Comtesse du, 169

Bassano, Hugues Maret, Duc de, 94
Bassville, Hugues de, 58, 63, 64
Bassvilliana (Monti), 10, 56, 58-66, 69, 70
Bathurst, Lord, 305
Baudelaire, Charles, 5, 15
Beauharnais, Prince Eugène de, 103, 190, 240
Beaumarchais, Pierre Augustin Caron de, 283
Bellart, Nicolas, 239
Belloc, Mme (biographer of Byron), 209
Belloc, Mme Pietro, 111
Benda, Julien, 4
Bentham, Jeremy, 164, 231
Beppo (Byron), 10, 297, 321
Béranger, Pierre, 9, 33-42, 47, 211
Berezina, Battle of the, 187, 194
Berio, Il Marchese, 111
Berni, Francesco, 332
Bernadotte, Charles XIV of Sweden, 187
Bernardin de St Pierre, Jacques, 91
Berry, Marie Bourbon, Duchesse de, 173, 236
Berthier, General Alexandre, Prince de Neufchâtel, 186, 191-2, 194-5
Bertin, Louis, 56
Bertolotti, David, 76
Bettinelli, Saverio, 56, 57, 58, 59, 62, 65, 73
Bettoni, Nicolò, 79
Beuchot, Adrien, 233n., 280
Beyle, Henri (Stendhal), 1-20, 43n., 181n., 182, 295-6, 304-5, 314-15, 327-8; *letter to,* 331-2
Bezenval, Pierre, Baron de, 169n.
Bianco e Faliero (Rossini), 112, 115
Biblioteca Italiana, La (literary review), 77
Biron, Charles, Duc de, 307-8
Bioardo, Matteo, 332
Blackwood's Magazine, 9n., 46, 201, 217
Blücher, General Gebhard, Prince of Wahlstatt, 188
Boccaccio, Giovanni, 67, 80
Boileau-Despréaux, Nicolas, 9, 33, 35, 56, 62
Boiste, P. C. V., 156-7
Bologna, 69, 80, 84, 87, 103-4, 114, 115, 127
Bonald, Louis, Vicomte de, 44, 231

INDEX

Bonaparte, Napoleon, 16, 36, 44, 57, 60, 65, 68, 69, 71, 78, 84n., 87, 92-3, 122, 126, 132, 139-45, 151, 158, 161, 162, 163, 169, 170, 172, 176-7, 181-95, 200, 202, 204-7, 210, 213, 214, 217-8, 227, 228, 238, 252, 295, 299, 303, 304, 307
Bordeaux, Henri, Duc de ('Henri V'), 210, 212
Bordogni, Giulio, 130
Boulay-de-la-Meurthe, Antoine, 199
Boulogne, Etienne, Archbishop of Vienne, 179, 200
Bourbons, the, 36-7, 44 and n., 88, 122, 163, 172, 175, 183, 192, 199, 200, 201, 205, 211, 212, 218, 223, 236
Bourget, Paul, 11n.
Braschi, Giovanni, Pope Pius VI, 262
Brême, Lodovico, Marchese di, 294-5
Brême, Lodovico, Monsignore di, 295-6, 303-4, 305, 306, 311, 313, 318, 319
Bride of Abydos, The (Byron), 310
Britannicus (Racine), 145, 318
Brizard, Jean Baptiste, 119
Broglie, Achille, Duc de, 279
Broussais, François, 158, 160, 164
Brummel, George, 307
Buffon, Georges, 92, 152
Buratti, Pietro, 55, 70, 81, 87, 299, 320-1
Burns, Robert, 36
Bute, John Stuart, Lord, 281
Byng, Admiral George, 268
Byron, George Gordon, Lord, 9, 10-11, 14, 24, 30, 36, 38, 41-2, 46, 48, 51-3, 55, 58, 70, 91, 230, 241, 272, 283, 296-321; *quoted:* 242, 244, 245, 248; *letter to Stendhal:* 331-2

Cabanis, Pierre, 158, 164, 195
Caesar, Julius, 185, 216, 219, 222, 263-4
Caligula, Emperor, 219, 220
Cambridge, University of, 137, 303
Cambiale di Matrimonio, La (Rossini), 128
Campan, Jeanne Louise de, 168, 170
Camporesi, Violante, 113
Candide (Voltaire), 283
Canning, George, 92, 93, 94
Canova, Antonio, 126, 145
Cambacérès, Jean-Jacques, Duc de, 195
Carmontelle (Louis Carrogis), 121-2, 123
Carnot, Lazarre, 297
Castries, Charles de la Croix, Marquis de, 305
Castruccio-Castracani, 319

Catinat, General Nicolas, 186
Caulincourt, Louis, Duc de Vicenza, 187
Cayla, Zoé, Comtesse de, 34-5, 71, 172, 209
Cenerentola, La (Rossini), 113
Ce que Dieu garde est bien gardé (Collé), 120
Chambray, Georges, Marquis de, 183
Chansonnier Noir, Le (Béranger), 37
Chant du Sacre, Le (Lamartine), 44, 53
Charles (published anonymously and attributed to Joseph Bernard), 71-2
Charles Edward (The Young Pretender), 183
Charles IX (Joseph Chénier), 136
Charles X, 44, 53-5, 90, 93, 130, 137, 201-2, 205, 215, 224, 225-6, 232n., 237-9, 284
Chartres, Ferdinand, Duc de, 137
Chartreuse de Parme, La (Stendhal), 3, 11, 16
Chateaubriand, François, Vicomte de, 4, 8, 75, 88-92, 158, 163, 167, 203, 206, 208, 210, 216-23, 233
Chazet, André, 43-4, 64
Chénier, André, 271
Chénier, Joseph, 136, 217, 271, 282
Chiabrera, Gabriello, 87n.
Cicero, 67, 222, 302
Cimarosa, Domenico, 81, 99, 102, 112, 113, 118, 128
Cincinnatus, 219
Childe Harold (Byron), 10, 58, 297, 299, 305, 315
Cinna (Corneille), 6, 144, 287-91, 327-8; *quoted:* 328-31
Ciuti, Madame, 130
Clarence, Duke of (became William IV), 281
Clarissa Harlowe (Richardson), 272, 323
Classical Tour (Eustace), 242
Claudius, Emperor, 219, 222
Clement XIV, Pope, 66
Clovis I (of France), 222
Cobbett, William, 272
Cochrane, Alexander, Earl, 235
Code Napoléon, Le, 252
Colburn, Henry, 1-2
De Collardeau, Charles, 56
Collé, Charles, 120-1, 122
Commodus, Emperor, 220-1, 222
Conciliatore, Il (literary review), 77, 78
Condillac, Etienne, 68, 158, 159, 164

INDEX

Condorcet, Antoine, Marquis de, 195
Confalonieri, Federico, Conte di, 313
Conférences sur la religion (Frayssinous), 202-4
Conservateur, Le, 217
Considérations sur la Révolution Française (Mme de Staël), 295
Constant, Benjamin, 15, 29, 70-1, 167-8, 174-80, 196, 197-8, 201, 231
Constitutionnel, Le, 185, 198, 204, 230
Contat, Louise, 139
Conte di Carmagnola, Il (Manzoni), 81
Corbière, Jacques, Comte de, 44 and n., 272, 274
Corinne (Mme de Staël), 168, 266
Correggio, Antonio, 80
Correspondence (Flaubert), 13
Corneille, Pierre, 6, 7, 139-40, 145, 287-91, 315, 325; *quoted:* 327-31
Corsair, The (Byron), 30, 58, 146, 283, 305
Courrier Anglais, Le (Stendhal), 3, 18, 19
Courrier Français, Le, 204
Cousin, Victor, 154, 159-62, 164
Cracas, Giovanni, 75
Cracas, Il (literary review), 75
Crescentini, Girolamo, 236
Crespi, Daniele, 319-20
de Croy, Bishop, 238
de Cubière, Marie, 24, 27
Custine, Astolphe, Marquis de, 300
Cymbeline (Shakespeare), 324

Dalberg, Duchesse de, 234
Dangeau, Philippe, Marquis de, 315
Dante Alighieri, 10, 49, 55, 56-7, 59, 60, 61, 62, 63, 65, 66, 69, 73, 80, 84, 85, 321
Danton, Georges, 297
Daru, Comte Pierre, 94, 187, 193, 205, 210 212-6, 217
David, Giovanni, 125
David, Jacques, 141, 214
Davout, Marshal Louis, Prince d'Eckmühl, 141, 186, 188, 189, 206
Davout, Mme, Princess d'Eckmühl, 143
Delavigne, Casimir, 35-6, 36-7, 37-8, 39-40, 47, 54, 206
Délécluze, Etienne, 1
Delille, L'Abbé Jacques, 27, 40, 48, 56, 61
Delphine (Mme de Staël), 71, 168
Dernier Chant de Childe Harold, Le (Lamartine), 40-2, 44-5, 47-53

Dernier des Abencérages, Le (Chateaubriand), 89-90
Desaix, General Louis, 144, 205
Desaugiers, Marc-Antoine (?), 44
Destouches, Philippe, 170
Diario, Il, 75
Diderot, Louis, 151, 323
Discours sur l'Art Dramatique, Le (Corneille), 287; *quoted:* 327
Dizionario della Crusca, Il, 86
Domitian, Emperor, 219, 220
Don Giovanni (Mozart), 112, 116, 117, 118
Don Juan (Byron), 9, 10, 30, 46, 55, 297, 298, 299, 309, 321
Donna del Lago, La (Rossini), 110, 114
Dorat, Claude de, 56
Dot de Suzette, La (Fiévée), 122
Doudeauville, Louis Sosthène, Duc de, 44, 54, 208, 225-6
Dryden, John, 40
Ducis, Jean, 142, 325
Duel, Le (Leclercq), 123-4
Dumas, General Mathieu, Comte, 193, 205
Dumesnil, Louis, 200
Dupin, Baron Charles, 275
Durante, Francesco, 80
Duras, Claire de Kersaint, Duchesse de, 132
Duroc, Marshal, Duc de Frioul, 193

Eclogues (Virgil), 152n.
Edinburgh Review, The, 27, 28, 157, 217, 271, 272
Education Sentimentale, La (Flaubert), 13
El di d'Incoeu (Grossi), 83-4
Elisa e Claudio (Mercadante), 130
Elena (Mayer), 315
Elizabetta (Rossini), 110
Eloa (Vigny), 29-31
Epinay, Mme de, 168, 169
Esménard, Joseph, 163
De l'Esprit (Helvétius), 155
Etienne, Charles, 211
Etoile, La, 39, 46, 200, 229
Etudes de la Nature (Bernardin de St Pierre), 91
Eufemio da Messina (Pellico), 81
Eugène, Prince de Savoie, 103, 152
Eustace, John Chetwode, 82, 242, 263, 266

INDEX

Fabricius, Gaius Luscinus, 219
Faguet, Emile, 5n.,
Fain, Agathon, 94, 181-2
de la Fare, Anne-Louis, Cardinal, 238
Farina, Monsignore, Bishop of Padua, 66
Fénelon, François de Salignac de la Mothe, 176, 255
Ferdinand VII (of Spain), 52
Feutrier, Jean-François, Bishop of Beauvais, 209
Fiévée, Joseph, 75, 122-3, 216, 275
Fielding, Henry, 35
Fitz-James, Edouard, Duc de, 94
Flaubert, Gustave, 3, 13, 15
Flahaut-Souza, Mme de, 23, 24
Fleurs du Mal, Les (Baudelaire), 5
Florence, 67, 69, 76, 78, 79-80, 82, 84, 85, 86, 87, 127, 320
Forsyth, Joseph, 82
Fortis, Ugo, 67
Foscolo, Ugo, 73, 81, 87n.
Fossombroni, Vittorio, 67
Foy, General Maximilien, 196-7, 201, 217
Francesca da Rimini (Pellico), 81
Francis I (of Austria), 74
François I, 172
Franklin, Benjamin, 177
Frayssinous, Denis, Bishop of Hermopolis, 28, 137, 159, 202-4, 213, 226, 272
Frédéric (Fiévée), 122

Galba, Emperor, 219
Galli, Filippo, 101, 111, 112, 130
Gay, Delphine, 206, 209
Gazza Ladra, La (Rossini), 111, 112, 114
Della Genga, Cardinal (see under Leo XII)
Génie du Christianisme, Le (Chateaubriand), 90, 91, 218, 221, 233
Genlis, Stéphanie, Comtesse de, 120-1, 168, 276
Genoude, L'Abbé Antoine de, 39, 42, 46, 200
George III, 281
George IV, 212, 325
Gerusalemme Liberata, La (Tasso), 70
Giannone, Pietro, 80
Ginguené, Pierre, 57, 61, 81
Gioia, Melchiore, 77
Giornale Blu, Il (see under *Conciliatore*)
Giornale Ecclesiastico, Il, 276
Girardin, Louis, Comte de, 196
Globe, Le, 134, 159, 269, 270, 272

Goldoni, Carlo, 80, 83, 105, 321
Goldsmith, Oliver, 73
Gourgaud, Baron Gaspard, 204-7
Grégoire, Henri, Bishop of Blois, 228
Gouvion St Cyr, Marshal (see under St Cyr)
Grossi, Tomasso, 70, 81, 83, 87, 88, 320
Grotius, Hugo, 155
Guarini, Giovanni, 87n.
Guidi, Carlo, 87n.
Guizot, François, 201
Gunnell, Doris, 2
Guyon, Jeanne de la Motte, de, 176

Hamlet (Shakespeare), 9, 46, 142
Han d'Islande (Hugo), 4
De Hauteville, Nicolas, 204
Helvétius, Claude, 151-3, 155, 203
Henriade, La (Voltaire), 61
Henri IV, 307, 322
Histoire de Guillaume le Conquérant (Thierry), 89
Histoire de l'anarchie de Pologne (Rulhière), 183, 184
Histoire de l'émigration (de Montrol), 199
Histoire de Napoléon et de la Grande Armée en 1812 (Ségur), 181-96, 204-6
Histoire des deux derniers Stuarts (Boulay-de-la-Meurthe), 199
Histoire des deux derniers Stuarts (Sauquaire-Souligné), 199
Histoire des ducs de Bourgogne (Barante), 89, 181
Histoire de Venise (Daru), 213
History of England (Lingard), 272
History of the Reformation (Cobbett), 272
Hobhouse, John Cam, 9, 46, 310
Homer, 323
Horace, 37, 163
Hugo, Victor, 4, 5, 27-8, 206
Hume, David, 301, 320

Idéologie, La (Tracy), 155, 158
Ildegonde (Grossi), 88
L'Inganno Felice (Rossini), 101
Iphigénie (Racine), 324
De l'Irritation et de la Folie (Broussais), 158, 160-2, 164
L'Italiana in Algeri (Rossini), 101, 114
L'Italiano, 78
L'Itinéraire à Jérusalem (Chateaubriand), 88
Ivanhoe (Scott), 13n., 90, 322-3

INDEX

Jacquelin, Jacques, 44
James II, 199, 233
Jansenism, 66, 200, 227
Jeffrey, Fancis, 9
Jesuits, The, 15, 32, 39, 44n., 45-6, 52, 56, 66, 67, 69, 74, 77, 78, 80, 81, 88, 122, 123, 128, 129, 131, 160, 162-3, 174, 175, 184-5, 192, 196, 200, 210, 213, 214 217-8, 223-4, 226-32, 232-4, 237, 245, 255, 261, 272, 273-4, 275-81, 282, 283
John Bull, 201
Johnson, Samuel, 7, 73, 327-8
Joseph II (of Austria), 66
Joséphine de Beauharnais, Empress of France, 170
Journal de la Librairie, Le, 280
Julian, Emperor ('The Apostate'?), 312

Kant, Emmanuel, 151, 153-4
Kean, Edmund, 146, 147
Kemble, Charles, 146
Kinker, Johann, 153
Kinnaird, Douglas, 9, 46
Knowles, James Sheridan, 146

Lablache, Luigi, 125
La Bruyère, Jean, 76, 132
La Chalotais, Louis, 228-30
Lacoste, Robert, 17
Lacretelle, Jean, 210, 214
Ladvocat, 24, 233
Lafayette, Marie-Jean, Marquis de, 202, 231, 237
Lafayette, Marie-Madeleine de, 322-3
Lafontaine, Jean de, 9, 33-4, 35, 42, 47, 51, 127
Lalla Rookh (Thomas Moore), 146
Lally-Tollendal, Trophine, Comte de, 211-2
Lamartine, Alphonse de, 4, 5, 8, 9, 11, 27-8, 33, 35-42, 44-55, 206, 211
Lamb, Charles, 2
Lamennais, Félicité de, 226, 231, 277
Lanjuinais, Jean Denis, Comte de, 228
Lara (Byron), 283, 296, 315
La Reveillère-Lépeaux, Louis-Marie de, 32, 174
Lamothe-Langon, E. L., Baron de, 31n. (see too under *M. le Préfet*)
Las Cases, Emmanuel, Comte de, 187
Latil, Jean-Baptiste, Duc de, Archbishop of Rheims, 53-4, 237, 238
La Tremouille, Charles, Prince de, 224

Lauriston, Jacques Law, Marquis de, 224-5
Lauzun, Antonin de Caumont, Duc de, 324
Lauzun, Armand de Gontaut, Duc de Biron et de, 169
Lebrun, Pierre Antoine, 211
Leclercq, Théodore, 122-4, 131-3, 216
Leigh Hunt, 299
Le Kain, Henri, 136, 138-9, 142, 144
Lemontey, Pierre, 210, 214
Leo, Leonardo, 80
Leo X, 256
Leo XII, 58, 66, 262, 276, 282
Leopold II (of Austria), 255
Letourneur, Pierre, 111
Lettres Administratives (Fiévée), 275
Lettres Persanes (Montesquieu), 283
Lettres Philosophiques (Voltaire), 270
Lettres Provinciales (Pascal), 198
Lettres sur l'Angleterre (Baron de Staël), 271
Liberal, The, 299
Lingard, John, 272
Littérature du midi de l'Europe, La (Sismondi), 81
Locke, John, 158, 159, 164
Lombardi, Fra Baldassari, 65
London, 73, 78, 81, 82, 118, 129, 214
London Magazine, The, 1, 12, 18, 19, 42
Louis XIV, 80, 89, 127, 211, 269 n., 282, 284
Louis XV, 137, 169, 170, 172, 183, 184, 269 and n.
Louis XVI, 23, 64, 137, 138, 162, 169, 173, 229, 237
Louis XVIII, 15, 35, 137, 144, 170-3, 189, 232
Lucan, 60
Lucien Leuwen (Stendhal), 3

Macbeth (Shakespeare), 6, 7, 55, 146, 147, 289, 291, 327
Machiavelli, Nicolô, 92, 105
Macready, William, 136, 146
Maggi, Carlo, 87n.
Maison du Boulevard, La (Carmontelle), 121-2
Maistre, Joseph de, 227, 231, 276, 277
Maistre, Xavier de, 44
Malesherbes, Chrétien de Lamoignon de, 228
Manuscrit de 1813, Le (Fain), 181

INDEX

Manzoni, Alessandro, 81, 87n.
Marchangy, Louis de, 221
Marcolini, Marietta, 101
Marcus Aurelius, Emperor, 219, 220
Mariage de Raison, Le (Scribe), 94
Maria Theresa, Empress of Austria, 62
Marini, Giuseppe, 61
Marivaux, Chamblain de, 29, 283
Marmontel, Jean-François, 151
Mars, Mlle (Anne Boutet), 209, 325
De Martainville, Alphonse, 75
Martignac, Jean-Baptiste, Vicomte de, 198-9
Martineau, Henri, 2, 3, 18, 19
Mascheroniana, La (Monti), 65
Masséna, General André, Prince d'Essling, 141
Matrimonio Segreto, Il (Cimarosa), 113, 116
Mayer, Simon, 315
Mécanique Céleste, La (de la Place), 177
Medici, Lorenzo di, 85
Medici (restoration of), 78
Méditations, Les (Lamartine), 8, 37, 38, 39, 40, 45
Meli, Fr Giovanni, 81
Méneval, Claude, Baron de, 94
Mercadante, Saverio, 125, 130
Merchant of Venice (quoted), 117
Mercure de France, Le, 1
Mérilhou, Joseph, 230
Mérimée, Prosper (Clara Gazull), 44
Merlin, Maria, Comtesse de, 236
Mes Rêveries (Marshal de Saxe), 207
Metastasio, Pietro, 80, 83, 87n.
Metternich, Klemens, Prince von, 77, 302
Meyerbeer, Giacomo, 125, 130, 131
Michelangelo-Buonarotti, 85
Mignet, François, 183, 206
Milan, 1, 62, 69, 74, 76, 77, 79, 80, 81, 83, 84 and n., 85-6, 87, 101-2, 111, 113, 125, 128, 295, 303, 312, 320, 321, 331
Millot, Claude, Abbé de, 184
Mirabeau, Gabriel Riquetti, Comte de, 196-7
Mirbel, Lizinska, 94
Molé, François (actor), 119, 120
Molé, Guillaume, 228
Molé, Louis-Mathieu, Comte de (1781-1855), 94
Molière (Jean Poquelin), 33, 89-90, 91, 105, 113, 132, 230
Mombelli, Ester, 130
Mon coeur mis à nu (Baudelaire), 15

Moniteur, Le, 90, 210n.
M. François ou Chacun sa Manie (based on Leclercq), 131
M. le Préfet (Lamothe-Langon), 12, 13, 14, 31-2
Montesquieu, Charles, Baron de, 72, 76, 92, 216, 219, 283
Montesson, Charlotte, Marquise de (subsequently, by a secret marriage Duchesse d'Orléans), 120-1
Monti, Vincenzo, 10, 56, 57-65, 68-70, 73, 81, 87n., 313
Montlhéry, Battle of, 207
Montlosier, François, Comte de, 226, 228, 229, 273, 276
Montmirail, Battle of, 193
Montmorency, Mathieu, Duc de, 207, 210-6, 223-4, 230, 277
Monvel, Jacques, 119
Moore, Thomas, 299, 303, 309, 311, 318
Morgan, Lady Sydney Owenson, 82
Morning Chronicle, The, 270
Mort de César, La (Voltaire), 140
Mort de Pompée, La (Corneille), 139-40
Moscow, Campaign of, 16, 182-3, 188-95, 204-7, 304-5
Mosè (Rossini), 106, 110, 236
Mozart, Wolfgang Amadeus, 99, 109, 112, 116, 118; Stendhal's life of: 331
Murat, Joachim, King of Naples, 141, 144, 186, 189, 190
Murray, John, 309
Myrrha (ballet by Vigano), 115

Nabucco (Nicolini), 87
Naples, 61, 67, 74, 76, 79, 80, 82, 84, 86, 110, 125, 127
Napoleon (see under Bonaparte)
Nero, Emperor, 219, 220, 222
New Monthly Magazine, The, 1, 2, 18, 19
Ney, Marshal Michel, Prince de la Moskowa, 187, 189-90, 207, 239
Niccolini, Giambattista, 81, 87
Nigel (Scott), 23
Night Thoughts (Young), 28
Norbury, John Toler, First Earl of, 200, 332
Notizie del Giorno, Le, 75
Nouvelles Chansons, Les (Béranger), 9, 33-5
Nouvelle Héloïse, La (Rousseau), 71
Novel in France, The (Turnell), 15n.
Nozze di Figaro, Le (Mozart), 109, 116

INDEX

Odes et Poésies Sacrées (Hugo), 4, 27-8
Old Mortality (Scott), 90
Omo (Buratti), 321
Orlando Innamorato (Boiardo), 332; *quoted:* 257
Orléans, Louis-Philippe, Duc de (1725-85), 120
Orléans, Louis-Philippe, Duc de ('Philippe Egalité'), 239
Orléans, Louis-Philippe, Duc de (became King Louis-Philippe), 54, 239
Otello (Rossini), 110, 112, 113, 116
Oxford, University of, 137

Pacini, Giovanni, 125, 127, 130
Pacini, Luigi, 101, 113
Paisiello, Giovanni, 99, 102, 109, 113, 128
Paley, William, 309
Parini, Giovanni, 67, 87n.
Paris, 24, 54, 56, 73, 78, 80, 82, 101, 107, 110, 113, 117-8, 123, 129, 141, 151, 160, 168, 171, 173-4, 179, 203, 208, 211, 212, 225, 235, 237, 268, 269, 270-1, 302, 320
Paris Monthly Review, The, 1, 18
Pascal, Blaise, 72, 196, 198
Pasta, Mme Giuditta, 101, 130
Pastoret, Amédée, Marquis de, 25, 27, 192
Pellegrini, Felice, 130
Pellico, Silvio, 77, 81, 87n., 313, 320, 331
Père Duchêne, Le, 229
Pergolesi, Giovanni, 80
Petrarch, Francesco, 79, 80, 85
Philip II (of Spain), 57n., 78, 82, 126
Philip III (of Spain), 78
Philosophe marié, Le (Destouches), 170,
Pietra di Paragone, La (Rossini), 101, 102, 114, 128
Pignotti, Lorenzo, 57, 58, 59, 62, 65
Pindemonte, Ippolito, 87n.
Pius VII, 66, 144
La Place, Marquis de, 177
Plato, 79, 154, 159, 164
Plus Beau Jour de ma Vie, Le (Leclercq), 124
Polidori, J. W., 306, 313, 314, 317
Poliziano, Angiolo, 85
Polignac, Yolande, Duchesse de, 169
Pompignan, Le Franc de, 283-4
Pope, Alexander, 56, 57, 62, 65
Porta, Carline, 320

Pradt, Dominique, Abbé de, 27, 228, 229, 270
Précieuses Ridicules, Les (Molière), 89-90
Preface to Shakespeare (Johnson), 7, 327-8
Préjugé à la mode, Le (Destouches), 170
Pretendi Delusi, I (Mosca), 102
Princesse de Clèves, La (Mme de Lafayette), 322-3
Prisonniers du Caucase, Les (Xavier de Maistre), 44
Proposta di Emendazioni al Vocabolario della Crusca (Monti), 68
Proverbes, Les (Leclercq), 122-4, 131-3

Quarterly Review, The, 157, 271, 272, 298
Quelen, Louis, Comte de, Archbishop of Paris, 238
Quentin Durward (Scott), 40, 323

Raccoglitore, Il (literary review), 76
Racine, Jean, 8, 9, 27, 28, 33, 47, 61, 90, 145 and n., 164, 324
Racine et Shakespeare (Stendhal), 1, 5, 7, 327-8, 331
Raphael, Sanzio, 80
Rasori, Giovanni, 79, 158
Ravez, Simon, 198-9
Redgauntlet (Scott), 183
Régnault, Jean-Baptiste, 141
Regulus, Marcus Atilius, 152, 178
Reid, Thomas, 159
Renouard, Augustin, 210
Report on the Constitution of the Jesuits (La Chalotais), 228, 229
Richard III (Shakespeare), 55, 147
Richardson, Samuel, 272, 323
Ricordi, Giovanni, 114
Roger, Jean, 208
Rome, 74, 75, 82, 84, 87, 108-9, 110, 241, 263-4, 320
Romeo and Juliet (quoted), 116
Roscius, Quintus, 138
Roscoe, Arthur, 85
Rossini, Gioacchino, 99-118, 125, 126, 127, 128-30, 234-5
Rouge et le Noir, Le (Stendhal), 2, 11, 12
Rousseau, Jean-Jacques, 71, 72, 152, 196, 203, 226, 303, 306, 312
Rovigo, Anne-Jean, Duc de, 163
Royer-Collard, Pierre, 47, 159, 164, 231
Rulhière, Claude, 183, 184

INDEX

Sacchini, Antonio, 80
Gouvion St Cyr, Marshal Laurent, 192, 224
Sainte-Beuve, Charles, 5-6, 8, 11, 17
St Petersburg, 168, 194, 216
Saxe, Hermann Maurice, Comte de, 207
Schiller, Friedrich, 62
Scienza Nuova, La (Vico), 80
Scipio Nasica, 84
Scipione Ricci (De Potter's life of), 255
Scott, Anne, 93, 94
Scott, Sir Walter, 13n., 23-27, 40, 43, 90, 92-5, 181, 183, 272, 320n., 322-5, 331-2
Scribe, Augustin, 94
Sebastiani, Marshal François, 225
Séguier, Antoine, Baron, 199, 200, 227, 228
Ségur, Louis, Comte de, 184
Ségur, Philippe, Comte de, 16, 181-96, 204-6
Seneca, 184, 185
Sepolcri, I (Foscolo), 73, 81
Shakespeare, William, 6, 7, 10, 49, 55, 56, 66, 111, 122, 142, 164, 245, 287, 289, 290, 291, 306, 324, 327-8; quoted: 116, 117
Sharpe, Sutton, 2
Sheridan, Richard Brinsley, 271
Siéyès, Emmanuel, 208
Sismondi, Jean, 25, 81
Smithson, Harriet, 146-7
Society for the liberty of the press, The, 279
Sografi, Simeone, 107
Somaglia, Cardinal della, 67, 75
Sosthène (see under Doudeauville)
Soult, Nicolas, Duke of Dalmatia, 191-2, 224-5, 226
Soumet, Alexandre, 44
Southey, Robert, 44, 64, 297-8, 309, 321
Souvenirs de Soixante Années (Délécluze), 1
Spectator, The, 244
Spenser, Edmund (quoted), 250
Staël, Germaine Necker, Mme de, 29, 71, 138, 163, 168, 175, 206, 211-2, 243, 266, 295, 308
Staël-Holstein, Auguste, Baron de 236, 271
Stendhal (see under Beyle)
Stendhal et l'Angleterre (Gunnell), 2
Stewart, Dugald, 151
Strofe (Buratti), 321
Suard, Jean-Baptiste, 151

Talleyrand, Charles, Prince de, 47, 187, 199, 237
Talma, François, 101, 134-45, 318
Tambroni, Clotilda, 249
Tamburini, Fr Pietro, 66
Tancredi (Rossini), 101, 114, 115
Tartuffe (Molière), 132
Tasso, Bernardo, 60, 87n.
Tasso, Torquato, 49, 61, 80, 87n., 316
Tassoni, Alessandro, 87n.
Tchaplitz, General, 195
Tchitchakov, Admiral, 195
Terence, 121
Thierry, Jacques, 89
Tibère (Chénier), 282
Tiberius, Emperor, 219
Times, The, 269, 270-1, 277, 279
Tiraboschi, Gerolamo, 81
Titian, 80
Titus, Emperor, 219, 220
Tom Jones (Fielding), 35
Torvaldo e Dorliska (Rossini), 112
Tracy, Claude Destutt, Comte de, 153, 154, 155-6, 164
Trajan, Emperor, 219, 220
Travels in Italy (Galiffe), 267
Trognon, Auguste, 24, 26
Trouvé, Charles, Baron, 32
Trublet, Nicolas, 308
Turco in Italia, Il (Rossini), 113
Turin, 74, 77, 78, 80, 83, 86, 125, 127
Turnell, Martin, 15n.
Tuscany, Leopold II, Grand Duke of, 67, 69, 80, 315
Twelfth Night (Shakespeare), 117

Varano, Alfonso, 63
Vardes, François, Marquis de, 324
Vaublanc, Vincent, Comte de, 211
Venice, 74, 77, 79, 81, 84, 85-6, 87, 100, 128, 298-9, 320
Vera Idea della Santa Fede, La (Tamburini), 66
Vespasian, Emperor, 219, 220
Vestale, La (ballet by Vigano), 115
Viaggio a Rheims (Rossini), 130
Vico, Giambattista, 80
Vienna, Congress of, 74
Vieusseux, Giovanni, 76
Vigano, Salvatore, 112, 115, 126
Vigny, Alfred de, 4, 5, 29-31

INDEX

Villèle, Jean Baptiste, Comte de, 9, 32, 46, 122, 123, 198-9, 200, 216, 225, 232n., 237, 280, 281, 284
Villemain, Abel, 182
Da Vinci, Leonardo, 85
Virgil, 59, 61
Visconti, Il Conte Ermes, 77
Visconti, Lucchino, 85
Vitebsk, Battle of, 192
Vitellius, Emperor, 219
Vitrolles, Eugène, Baron de, 28
Volney, Constantin, Comte de, 202
Voltaire (François Arouet), 24, 35, 47, 56-7, 61, 65, 72, 76, 81, 121, 128, 131, 136, 139, 140, 145n., 152, 180, 184, 196, 201, 203, 215, 217, 226, 230, 268, 270, 271, 288, 322
Voyage à Coblentz, Le (Louis XVIII), 173

Voyage à Rome (Carmontelle), 121
Walpole, Robert, 9, 46
Waterloo, Battle of, 176, 188, 204, 207, 228
Weber, Carl Maria von, 130
Wellington, Duke of, 189
William III, 199
Wilson, Harriet, 42-3
Woodstock (Scott), 92

Young, Edward, 28

Zaïde (Mme de Lafayette), 89
Zelmira (Rossini), 236
Zoraïde (Rossini), 110
Zucchelli, 125, 130
Zuleika (Byron), 310n.

ALMA CLASSICS

ALMA CLASSICS aims to publish mainstream and lesser-known European classics in an innovative and striking way, while employing the highest editorial and production standards. By way of a unique approach the range offers much more, both visually and textually, than readers have come to expect from contemporary classics publishing.

LATEST TITLES PUBLISHED BY ALMA CLASSICS

398 William Makepeace Thackeray, *Vanity Fair*
399 Jules Verne, *A Fantasy of Dr Ox*
400 Anonymous, *Beowulf*
401 Oscar Wilde, *Selected Plays*
402 Alexander Trocchi, *The Holy Man and Other Stories*
403 Charles Dickens, *David Copperfield*
404 Cyrano de Bergerac, *A Voyage to the Moon*
405 Jack London, *White Fang*
406 Antonin Artaud, *Heliogabalus, or The Anarchist Crowned*
407 John Milton, *Paradise Lost*
408 James Fenimore Cooper, *The Last of the Mohicans*
409 Charles Dickens, *Mugby Junction*
410 Robert Louis Stevenson, *Kidnapped*
411 Paul Éluard, *Selected Poems*
412 Alan Burns, *Dreamerika!*
413 Thomas Hardy, *Jude the Obscure*
414 Virginia Woolf, *Flush*
415 Abbé Prevost, *Manon Lescaut*
416 William Blake, *Selected Poems*
417 Alan Riddell, *Eclipse: Concrete Poems*
418 William Wordsworth, *The Prelude and Other Poems*
419 Tobias Smollett, *The Expedition of Humphry Clinker*
420 Pablo Picasso, *The Three Little Girls and Desire Caught by the Tail*
421 Nikolai Gogol, *The Government Inspector*
422 Rudyard Kipling, *Kim*
423 Jean-Paul Sartre, *Politics and Literature*
424 Matthew Lewis, *The Monk*
425 Ambrose Bierce, *The Devil's Dictionary*
426 Frances Hodgson Burnett, *A Little Princess*
427 Walt Whitman, *Leaves of Grass*
428 Daniel Defoe, *Moll Flanders*
429 Mary Wollstonecraft, *The Vindications*
430 Anonymous, *The Song of Roland*
431 Edward Lear, *The Owl and the Pussycat and Other Nonsense Poetry*
432 Anton Chekhov, *Three Years*
433 Fyodor Dostoevsky, *Uncle's Dream*

www.almaclassics.com